DATE DUE

THE KURDISH STRUGGLE, 1920–94

Also by Edgar O'Ballance

ARAB GUERRILLA POWER
CIVIL WAR IN YUGOSLAVIA
NO VICTOR, NO VANQUISHED: The Middle East War 1973
TERRORISM IN IRELAND: The Story of the IRA
TERRORISM IN THE 1980s
THE ARAB–ISRAELI WAR: 1948–9
THE ALGERIAN INSURRECTION: 1954–62
THE CYANIDE WAR
THE ELECTRONIC WAR IN THE MIDDLE EAST: 1968–70
THE FRENCH FOREIGN LEGION
THE GREEK CIVIL WAR: 1944–49
THE GULF WAR
THE INDO–CHINA WAR: 1946–54
THE KURDISH REVOLT: 1961–70
THE LANGUAGE OF VIOLENCE
THE MALAYAN INSURRECTION: 1948–60
THE RED ARMY OF CHINA
THE RED ARMY OF RUSSIA
THE SECOND GULF WAR: The Liberation of Kuwait
THE SECRET WAR IN SUDAN: 1955–72
THE SINAI CAMPAIGN: 1956
THE THIRD ARAB-ISRAELI WAR: 1967
TRACKS OF THE BEAR: US–USSR Relations in the 1970s
WAR IN THE YEMEN: 1962–69
WARS IN AFGHANISTAN: 1839–1992
WARS IN VIETNAM (1954–60)

The Kurdish Struggle 1920–94

Edgar O'Ballance

G21 6XS
and London
Companies and representatives
throughout the world

A catalogue record for this book is available
from the British Library.

ISBN 0-333-64478-6

First published in the United States of America 1996 by
ST. MARTIN'S PRESS, INC.,
Scholarly and Reference Division,
175 Fifth Avenue,
New York, N.Y. 10010

ISBN 0-312-16006-2

Library of Congress Cataloging-in-Publication Data
O'Ballance, Edgar.
The Kurdish struggle, 1920-94 / Edgar O'Ballance.
p. cm.
Includes bibliographical references (p.   ) and index.
ISBN 0-312-16006-2
1. Kurds—History—20th Century.   2. Middle East—Ethnic
relations.   I. Title.
DS59.K86023   1996
305.891'59—dc20   95-26255
                                                  CIP

10   9   8   7   6   5   4   3   2   1
05   04   03   02   01   00   99   98   97   96

Printed and bound in Great Britain by
Antony Rowe Ltd, Chippenham, Wiltshire

Contents

List of Maps

Preface

It is often said that the Kurds have no friends, which unfortunately seems to be true. Having spent days and weeks at a time over the years with Kurds (who today probably number over 23 million), in their mountains and towns, at war, in victory and defeat and in exile, one is constantly surprised how a people, who individually are so delightful, cheerful, helpful and hospitable, can at the same time be so quarrelsome amongst themselves, so vindictive towards each other and so ready to change allegiances.

The plight of the Kurds dawned on Western awareness when Saddam Hussein attacked them with chemical weapons in their villages, and afterwards drove many of them to perish in the snow-clad mountains of northern Iraq, prior to which few in the West knew much about them. Since then Amnesty International has made the Western world aware that a very dirty war between the Turkish army and insurgent Kurds seeking ethnic recognition has been in progress since 1984, in the course of which over 11 000 people have perished. More recently Westerners have become aware that a Kurdish terrorist organisation has been attacking Turkish diplomatic and commercial premises in Western Europe; and in 1994 they began a terrorist campaign to destroy the Turkish tourist industry. Several foreign tourists, including British, have already been killed or injured.

So who are the Kurds, what do they want, and why have they been unable to obtain it? It is hoped that this brief account will give some insight into their background, the milestones in their continuing struggle for a political goal, and something of their many misfortunes.

Upon the break-up of the Ottoman Empire after the First World War the Kurds, an ancient race composed of tribes, tribal confederations and feudal groups with martial traditions, were promised – for the first time in their long history – an independent state in their own mountainous homeland under the Treaty of Sèvres of 1920. The appearance of what became the USSR caused this Kurdish dream to be brushed aside under the Treaty of Lausanne in 1922, whereby Turkey, in which half the Kurdish race resided, was to be made into a bulwark against communism. The contiguous Kurdish homeland was abruptly divided into segments that fell into Turkey, the USSR, Persia (now Iran) and Iraq, separated by new international frontiers. This gave each of these countries a 'Kurdish problem', which they mostly still retain. After the brief appearance of 'Red Kurdistan' (1923–8), the Soviet Union moved most of its troublesome Kurds away from the Kurdish contiguity.

In unifying his new Turkey, Ataturk enlisted the aid of the Kurds to eliminate the Armenians, but when this was accomplished he turned against them, refusing to grant them minority status. Officially there are no Kurds in Turkey, not even to this day, only 'mountain Turks who have forgotten their own language'. Turkish Kurds, who live mainly in the south-eastern provinces, have periodically risen in rebellion and are in open rebellion today.

Iraq was a new country put together from parts of Mesopotamia and Kurdistan by the British. They tried to counterbalance minority groups to ensure that none became too powerful or gained too large a share of the oil fields. However, the Kurds soon became a destabilising factor. Arabs on the Mesopotamian plains feared the mountain Kurds, who in Ottoman times had descended to raid their towns, farms and caravans. The Kurds held the Arabs in contempt, while the Arabs considered that 'Allah sent three plagues – the rat, the locust and the Kurd'. During the interwar years the Arab Iraqi governments never really brought their Kurdish minority under control.

Kurds inhabiting the north-western corner of Iran were a frontier problem to the shahs, who retained their tenuous loyalty by bestowing titles, honours and bribes and used them as frontier mercenary troops. During the Second World War, when northern Iran was occupied by Soviet armed forces, the Kurds were left to their own devices. On Soviet instigation, in January 1946 a collection of Kurdish leaders set up the tiny independent Kurdish Republic of Mahabad, which lasted precisely one year before being extinguished by the shah's army, when the Soviet troops pulled out.

Tribal followers of a prominent Iraqi Kurdish chieftain, Mullah Mustafa Barzani, who had been accorded the rank of general by the Mahabad government, formed the effective part of a tiny Mahabad defence force. After the fall or Mahabad,

Barzani made a fighting withdrawal to the Soviet Union, where he remained for a few years, his fame in Kurdish legend established.

Kurds formed a very small minority in Syria, itself a country of minorities, and as they were in scattered groups – 'colonies' founded by mercenary soldiers or traders over the centuries – they presented little trouble to various Syrian governments.

Returning to Iraq in 1958, Barzani tried to negotiate a form of autonomy for the Iraqi Kurds. When this failed he gathered together certain tribes and fought a 15-year war against the central government. Latterly he was assisted by the shah of Iran, who secretly provided him with weaponry, ammunition and other necessities. As long as Barzani stayed in his mountains and was supported by the shah, he was secure, as the Iraqi army lacked the capability to defeat him.

Under the Algiers Agreement (1975) the shah ceased supplying arms to Barzani in return for concessions on the Shatt al-Arab waterway, part of the Iran–Iraq frontier. Once again Barzani had to make a fighting withdrawal, although he had gained formal recognition for Kurdish autonomy from the Baghdad government. Old and sick, Barzani was taken under the wing of the American CIA, to die in a hospital in America in March 1979.

The Islamic Fundamentalist Revolution in Iran brought Ayatollah Khomeini to power in February 1979, and internal chaos to that country. A strong centralist, Khomeini crushed Kurdish aspirations for autonomy, and upon their formation the revolutionary guards were given the Kurdish problem to deal with.

The next major saga in this region affecting the Kurds was the Iran–Iraq War (1980–8), which soon stalemated along a 600-mile entrenched defensive line that loosely coincided with the mutual border. Both countries subverted and used the other's Kurdish factions. The Baghdad government paid Iranian Kurds to fight against the Tehran government, while the Tehran government paid Iraqi Kurds to fight against that in Baghdad. Kurds were also conscripted into the armies of both sides, and generally gave a good account of themselves in battle.

When the Iran–Iraq War ended through military exhaustion, both governments set about settling accounts with their rebellious Kurdish factions. In Iraq the government launched

punitive military expeditions into its northern Kurdish mountains, but with only partial success. In Iran the revolutionary guards, who were responsible for internal security, strove
to bring rebellious Kurdish factions to heel, while a covert
assassination campaign was mounted against insurrectionary
Kurdish political leaders in exile. In both Iran and Iraq Kurdish
factions fought against each other on their home ground.

During the latter stages of the war Saddam Hussein used
chemical weapons against Iran, but these were deployed with
greater intensity against his own rebellious Kurds, then fighting in the pay of the Tehran government. The main attack was
against the Kurdish town of Halabja in March 1988, when a
probable 5000 Kurds perished from chemical weapon effects.

When Saddam Hussein invaded Kuwait in August 1990 an
Allied coalition was formed under UN authority to oust him,
a task accomplished by March 1991. Kurds played no part in
the Gulf War except as conscripted soldiers.

Anticipating the defeat of Saddam Hussein and his fall, an
impromptu Kurdish uprising occurred in Iraq in March 1991.
This had not been anticipated by Kurdish leaders, who were
carried along with it, and it was probably the first 'popular'
Kurdish uprising in which the people led the way rather than
factional or tribal leaders. As soon as Saddam Hussein had
dealt with a southern Shia revolt, he moved northwards to
wreak vengeance on his Kurds, causing a mass exodus from
cities, towns and villages. Fear that Saddam Hussein might
once again use chemical weapons caused panic among fleeing
Kurds, who sought refuge in remote mountains, and in Turkey
and Iran.

The international media spotlight settled on Kurdish families freezing to death on snow-covered mountainsides, evoking
a swell of sympathy in Western countries. Tardily, the American, British and French governments were pressed by public
opinion to help the Kurds. 'Operation Provide Comfort' (called
'Operation Poised Hammer' by the Americans) was activated to
provide aid and 'safe haven' camps for Kurdish refugees. Iraqi
troops were ordered to remain south of the 36th Parallel, and
Allied combat planes monitored what became a no-fly zone
over Kurdish terrain.

Under Allied and then United Nations encouragement and
help, the Kurds held elections within in the 'safe-haven' zone.

The two main groups – the Patriotic Union of Kurdistan (PUK) and its rival the Kurdistan Democratic Party (KDP) – jointly formed an administration to govern what became known as the Kurdish Autonomous Region (KAR). In May 1994 cordiality broke down, and hostilities re-erupted between the two groups. This continues to rumble on, giving weight to the allegation that the Kurds are forever quarrelling amongst themselves.

Existing precariously under UN military protection, the Kurds fear that the Allies are about to abandon the defenceless KAR at a time when the Iraqi army is mustering just south of the 36th Parallel.

Meanwhile, the faction-ridden Turkey of the 1970s and 1980s was additionally plagued with a discontented Kurdish population that constantly bordered on open insurrection. Several Kurdish resistance groups were active, but one – the Kurdish Worker's Party (PKK), led by Abdullah Ocalan – came to dominate the Kurdish scene. By 1980 its military arm, the People's Liberation Army of Kurdistan (ARGK), claimed a strength of some 12 000 guerrillas, who originally lived within the Kurdish community.

A Turkish military government (1980–3) cracked down on the PKK and its ARGK, killing many, making mass arrests, holding mass trials and (until 1983) carrying out mass executions. Survivors either went deeper underground or sought refuge across borders. Ocalan escaped and was given sanctuary by Syria, then in confrontation with Turkey over the distribution of the Euphrates waters and other matters. He was allowed to operate from Damascus, while remnants of his ARGK were housed in camps in the Lebanese Bekaa Valley, then under Syrian control.

In 1984 Ocalan declared war on the Turkish government and demanded independence. As his ARGK recovered and grew in strength, it seeped back into south-eastern Turkey to resume guerrilla activity, A very dirty war began and atrocities were committed by both sides. Amnesty International reports made horrific reading. The political section of the PKK established front organisations in Western European cities amongst Kurdish exiles, who issued propaganda and organised demonstrations to bring their cause to Western notice and attract support and sympathy.

When Saddam Hussein invaded Kuwait, Prime Minister (later

President) Ozal of Turkey eagerly joined the Allied coalition. The Allies were allowed the use of Turkish bases, for which Ozal expected material reward in due course, his eyes being on the oil fields of Kirkuk. After Saddam Hussein's technical defeat the Allies cooled towards Ozal and they certainly had no intention of rearranging international frontiers for his benefit.

Committed, and hopeful, Ozal assisted the Allies in Operation Provide Comfort, even though he was taking ruthless military action against his own Kurds. The ARGK became bolder, standing up to the Turkish army in the 'dirty war' but coming off second best in set-piece encounters. Eventually the ARGK was forced out of Turkey to seek sanctuary in the mountains of northern Iraq, which brought it into violent conflict with hostile Iraqi Kurds.

The PKK, which was regarded with some toleration by governments in Western Europe who were critical of the Turkish government's record on democratic rule and human rights, found that its policy of largely peaceful demonstrations was proving unsuccesful. In June 1993 attacks were mounted on Turkish diplomatic and commercial premises, followed in Noveber by a fire-bombing blitz on them. Western attitudes hardened and the PKK found itself under intense police scrutiny, whereupon Ocalan switched his attention to attacking Turkey's booming multi-billion dollar tourist industry.

On several occasions Ocalan had sought political contact with the Turkish government, but he had always been ignored. Suddenly, in March 1993 he declared a unilateral cease-fire, by which time he had modified his political demand to that of autonomy. The Turkish army ignored the offer and battled on, but the ARGK remained passive, while the government seemed to sit back and ponder. This lull was abruptly shattered when the ARGK ambushed and massacred Turkish troops. The action was said to have been carried out by a maverick ARGK commander, without Ocalan's authority.

In April 1994 the PKK again appealed for a dialogue, emphasising that it was not speaking from weakness and boasting that it now had over 30 000 armed guerrillas. There was no response from Ankara. The Turkish army knew it was doing well, and thinking it had got the ARGK on the run it had no intention of stopping, overlooking the fact that a military victory over the ARGK would not solve Turkey's Kurdish problem.

Turkey is in a precarious internal position, plagued not only by the PKK but also by the revival of the powerful left-wing Dev Sol movement and a revitalised Islamic Fundamentalist Welfare Party, which seeks to establish Turkey as an Islamic state, similar to that in Iran, and which had unexpected successes in local elections.

As long as adjacent countries continue to give sanctuary to PKK activists the Kurdish insurrection in Turkey will remain almost unquenchable. Like the Kurds, Turkey has no real friends. Sustained by funds gained from controlling a piece of the main Asian–Caucasian–European drug route, the PKK can sustain its present tempo almost indefinitely. The same cannot be said for the Turkish government. A political solution means a form of autonomy within Turkey for its 12–14 million Kurds. An unlikely, but not impossible, future scenario could be one in which the PKK sides with the government against the Dev Sol and the Welfare Party, the PKK's price being autonomy. Much will depend upon whether Ocalan is able to hold the PKK together, and on a steady political and military course.

EDGAR O'BALLANCE

Acknowledgements

A major part of the research for this book has been gained from my visits over the years to Iran, Iraq, Syria and Turkey, where I had a series of briefings, interviews and discussions with VIPs, combatants and others involved with or interested in the Kurds. These included visits to mountain camps, coverage of the Kurdish revolt in Iraq and other Kurdish insurgencies. Where material has been obtained from other sources, and used, due credit is given within the text. All comments, deductions and opinions are my own, and at times these may differ from current, generally perceived wisdom.

Map sources include *The Times Atlas of the World, The Times,* the *Daily Telegraph* and *The Middle East.*

List of Abbreviations

ANAP	Motherland Party (Turkey)
ARGK	People's Liberation Army of Kurdistan
CDKPR	Committee for the Defence of the Kurdish People's Rights
CENTO	Central Treaty Organisation
CHP	Republicans' People's Party (Turkey)
CIA	Central Intelligence Agency (US)
DAWA	Islamic Call
DDKD	Cultural and Democratic Revolutionary Association
DDKO	Organisation of Revolutionary Kurdish Youth
DEP	Democratic Party (Turkey)
DYP	True Path Party (Turkey)
EC	European Community
EEC	European Economic Community
ERNK	National Liberation Front of Kurdistan
GAP	South East Anatolia Project
HEP	People's Labour Party
HEVA	Kurdish Nationalist Party
ICO	Islamic Conference Organisation
ICP	Iraqi Communist Party
IISS	International Institute for Strategic Studies
IKF	Iraqi Kurdistan Front
ILK	Islamic League of Kurdistan
IMIK	Islamic Movement of Iraqi Kurdistan
INC	Iraqi National Congress
IRC	Islamic Revolutoinary Council
KAR	Kurdish Autonomous Region
KCP	Kurdish Communist Party (Turkey)
KDF	Kurdish Democratic Front
KDP	Kurdistan Democratic Party
KDPI	Kurdistan Democratic Party of Iran
KDP (PC)	KDP (Provisional Committee)
KDP (PL)	KDP (Provisional Leadership)
KDP(T)	Kurdistan Democratic Party of Turkey
KDPS	Kurdistan Democratic Party of Syria
KNA	Kurdish National Assembly

KPDP	Kurdistan People's Democratic Party
KSP	Kurdistan Socialist Party
KUK	Partisans of Kurdish National Liberation (Turkey)
KUP	Kurdistan Unity Party
NAP	National Action Party (Turkey)
NDPF	National Democratic and Patriotic Front
NLA (I)	National Liberation Army of Iran
NRC	National Resistance Council
NSP	National Salvation Party (Turkey)
OHRI	Organisation of Human Rights in Iraq
OPEC	Organisation of Petroleum Exporting Countries
PKK	Kurdish Workers' Party (Turkey)
PRF	Popular Resistance Force
PUK	Patriotic Union of Kurdistan
RAF	Royal Air Force (British)
RCC	Revolutionary Command Council (Iraq)
RDF	Rapid deployment force
RP	Welfare Party (Turkey)
SAVAK	Security and Information Organisation (Iran)
SCIRI	Supreme Council of the Islamic Revolution of Iraq
SHP	Social Democratic Popularists (Turkey)
TIKKO	Turkish Workers' and Peasants' Liberation Party
UKDP	United Kurdistan Democratic Party
UN	United Nations
UNHCR	UN High Commissioner for Refugees
USSR	Union of Soviet Socialist Republics

Chronology

1958	(July) Kassem coup in Iraq; (September) Mullah Mustafa Barzani returns to Iraq
1959	(April–May) Kurdish unrest: Iraq; (July) Kirkuk massacre
1960	(January) KDP supercedes the UKDP: Iraq; (April–May) Kurdish unrest in Iraq; (May) Military coup in Turkey, failed Kurdish revolt in Turkey, Fifth Kurdish Congress
1961	(March) Barzani returns to the mountains: Iraq; (September) Kurdish revolt in Iraq begins, Iraqi First Offensive
1962	(March) Barzani's spring offensive; (April) Barzani's manifesto; (July) Turkey creates frontier 'security zone'
1962	(July) Iraqi plane shot down by Turks
1963	(June–October) Iraqi Second Offensive; battle for Ruwanduz Gorge
1964	(February) Cease-fire: Iraq
1965	(April–September) Iraqi Third Offensive
1966	(January) Iraqi commando raid to Panjwin; (February) Talabini plot; (May) Iraqi Fourth Offensive, Mount Handrin ambush; (June) The 12-Point Programme
1969	(January) Iraqi Fifth Offensive; (March) Barzani's counterattack: Iraq; (August–October) Iraqi Sixth Offensive, Komala formed in Iran
1970	(March) 15-Point peace settlement, Iraqi President announces 'War with Kurds is over'
1972	Soviet–Iraqi Friendship Treaty; PKK formed in Turkey
1974	(March) The Autonomy Law: Iraq; (April) Barzani raises insurrection again: Iraq; (April–October) Iraqi Seventh Offensive, DDKD formed in Turkey
1975	(March) The Algiers Agreement, Iraq resumes Seventh Offensive, Kurdish insurgency in Iraq collapses; (June) PUK formed in Iraq
1976	KDP splinters: Iraq
1978	(November) PKK commences operations: Turkey

1979   (February) Islamic revolution in Iran;
            (March) death of Mullah Mustafa Barzani in
            the USA
1979   (March–October) Kurdish uprising in Iran;
            (July) Saddam Hussein becomes President of
            Iraq; (November) Islamic Students seize US
            Embassy in Tehran; (December) Soviets
            begin military occupation of Afghanistan
1980   (April–June) Kurdish uprising in Iran; (Sep-
            tember) another military coup in Turkey,
            Iran–Iraq War begins
1981   (March) Iranian incursion into Turkey;
            (April) KDPI spring offensive: Iran; (June)
            President Bani-Sadr impeached: Iran; (Octo-
            ber) political parties in Turkey dissolved
1982   (April) Gotbzadah plot: Iran; another KDPI
            spring offensive: Iran
1983   (March) Abortive KDPI offensive: Iran, Iraqi–
            Turkish hot-pursuit agreement; (May) Turk-
            ish incursion into Iraq; (July) Iranians seize
            Haj Omran; (October) Iranians attack
            Panjwin; (December) PUK makes agreement
            with Iraqi government, Turkey returns to
            civilian rule
1984   (February) Thrust towards the Dardani Khan
            Dam: Iraq; (June) Pasdaran attack KDPI and
            Komala; (August) Iraqi offensive against
            KDP, PKK declares war on Turkish govern-
            ment, Operation Comfort: Turkey; (October)
            Iraq–Turkey cross-frontier agreement, Opera-
            tion Sun: Turkey, Iraq breaks agreement with
            PUK
1985   (February) Saddam Hussein announces a
            general amnesty: Iraq; (March) Turkish–
            Syrian anti-terrorist agreement
1986   (March) Iranian penetration into Iraqi
            Kurdistan; (May) Iraqi action against liber-
            ated zones; (June) UN Resolution condemns
            Iraq for using chemical weapons; (August)
            Turkish air-strikes into Iraq
1987   (April–September) Iraqi army pressure

	against PUK and KDP; (November) general Election: Ozal returned to power in Turkey
1988	(March) chemical weapons used against Kurds in Halabja: Iraq; (June) PKK offers a cease-fire: Turkey; (August) cease-fire in Iran–Iraq War
1989	(June) Death of Ayatollah Khomeini: Iran; (July) Ghassemlou, leader of KDPI, assassinated; (November) Ozal becomes President: Turkey
1990	(April) Extra security measures; Turkey; (August) Iraq invades Kuwait
1991	(January) Allied air offensive: Kuwait; (February) Allied land offensive: Kuwait; (March) cease-fire in Gulf War, Kurdish Uprising: Iraq, Ocalan admits dissension in the PKK; (April) safe havens established: Iraq
1991	(April) 'Operation Provide Comfort': Iraq; 'Operation Poised Hammer': Iraq
1992	(March) Bloody Nowruz celebrations: Turkey; (May) Kurdish elections: Iraq; (June) Kurdish National Assembly established: Iraq; (October–December) Turkish incursions into northern Iraq
1993	(March) PKK declares a unilateral cease-fire; (April) death of President Ozal: succeeded by Demirel; (May) Bingol ambush – end of cease-fire: Turkey; (June) Ocalan again declares war on Turkish government, Tansu Ciller becomes prime minister of Turkey, PKK mounts demonstrations in Western Europe; (October) Ciller changes policy towards Kurds; (November) PKK fire-bombing in Western Europe; (December) DYP Congress: Turkey
1994	(January) Turkish cross-border raid into Iraq; (February) cease-fire in fighting in the KAR: Iraq; (April) UN helicopter shot down in KAR: Iraq, PKK ask for a dialogue: Turkey, PKK begins terrorist campaign against tourists; (May) PUK–KDP fighting in KAR: Iraq

The Kurds: Approximate Numbers and Locations

Country	Total Population	Kurds
Turkey	59 200 000	12–14 000 000
Iran	58 900 000	6 500 000
Iraq	18 400 000	3 500 000
Syria	13 800 000	800 000
Armenia	3 400 000	300 000
Lebanon	2 700 000	60 000
Germany	79 700 000	330 000
Elsewhere in the diaspora		20 000
Total		23 530 000

Sources: IISS, *Kurdish Life*, *Kurdish Times*, *The Middle East*.

Note that these figures represent a consensus of assessments and claims. Accuracy cannot be guaranteed, but in the absence of anything more reliable they form a rough guide.

Kurds are Muslims, some 85 per cent being of the mainstream Sunni sect, the remainder being Shia or other minority sects, such as Yezedi.

In the UN there are 135 nations whose people number less than the Kurds (*Kurdish Life*).

1 The Kurds

The Kurds are an ancient race who have inhabited the contiguous mountainous regions that now fall mainly into the eastern part of modern Turkey, the north and eastern part of Iraq and the north-east of Iran for some 3000 years (or longer, some historians insist), retaining their own language, customs and culture. A fierce, independent collection of wild mountain tribes, they have ferociously defended their terrain, managing somehow to survive the succession of conquering armies – including Assyrians, Persians and Greeks – that marched and countermarched across Anatolia and Mesopotamia over the centuries. Many Kurds became mercenary soldiers in these armies, their martial qualities being appreciated by commanders.

In the seventh century AD the advancing armies of Islam, the new religion, forcibly converted the Kurds, but they soon departed, leaving only their religion behind, The Arabs were the first to call these people 'Kurds' (from 'Kardu'), a name that stuck. During the eleventh and twelfth centuries most of the Kurdish tribes were either wholly or partly nomadic. In the two following centuries whole populations were eliminated by invading Mongols and Turkomans. The Kurds mainly withdrew into the mountains during such invasions, but as soon as they could they moved into depopulated areas and took possession of tracts of grazing land, especially in Anatolia.

To Western readers the best known Kurd of the Middle Ages is Sala ad-Din al-Ayubi – the Saladin of Crusader fame, born in 1137 at Takrit on the Tigris river (now in Iraq) – who fought against King Richard of England and forced the Crusaders to abandon practically all of the Holy Land (Palestine), except for a few Mediterranean coastal forts. Although born in Takrit, Saladin never lived there, but was a member of a developing military aristocracy. The famous ruins of the Crusader castle, the Krak des Chevaliers in Lebanon, is known in Arabic as the 'Castle of the Kurds' (*Husn al Akrad*) (McDowall, 1985).

When the Mongol hordes withdrew from the region for the last time they were replaced by Ottoman Turks, who soon came into collision with the Persians as both sought to dominate Anatolia and Mesopotamia. After the Battle of Chaldiran

1

in central Anatolia in 1514, in which Kurds helped the Ottomans in their decisive defeat of the Persians, Kurdish commanders were given titles and land so as to encourage their help in driving the Persians further eastwards. A number of 'aghas', were created, some hereditary to a family, which provided a structural link to the Ottoman government.

The Battle of Chaldiran severed Kurdish land contiguity for the first time into two geographical parts, one loosely under the influence of the Ottoman Empire and the other under the Persian Safavid Empire. Since the early thirteenth century the area inhabited by Kurds had been loosely known as 'Kurdistan', but it was not until the sixteenth century – when as allies of the Ottomans the Kurds moved north and west onto the Anatolian Plain in a series of tribal migrations – that the term came into geographical usage, although its precise boundaries were hazy. In the mountains many Kurdish villages were isolated in winter, villagers being nomadic for the rest of the year. Permanently inhabited settlements were in valleys where running water enabled a sparse agricultural economy to be practised.

In 1502 the Safavids conquered Persia, forcibly converting the inhabitants to the Shia persuasion of Islam, which most have retained since. After their defeat at Chaldiran the Safavids made unsuccessful attempts to bring the Kurds in the northwestern region of Persia under their control, but they soon abandoned this and opted for indirect rule by ennobling certain Kurdish leaders. This led to a small number of powerful Kurdish families controlling Kurdish federations, being nominally loyal to Tehran.

The Persians treated their puppet aghas abrasively, never achieving the same degree of cooperation with them as did the Ottomans. In some measure this was due to the fact that the majority of Kurds were Sunnis while their Persian overlords were Shia, and they were therefore less amenable to acting to defend a Shia empire. Ruling Kurdish families in Persia were often divided into pro-Persian and pro-Ottoman factions, while frontier aghas and tribes played one major power off against the other whenever possible. In 1600 the Persians recruited some Kurdish tribes to defend their northern border in Khoristan against Uzbek invaders, and these developed into a permanent colony.

In 1639, under the Treaty of Zohab, the Turks and Persians demarcated the land frontier between them where the Mesopotamian Plain met the Persian plateau to its east. In those days the modern concept of rigid land frontiers was absent from strategic thought in these regions, where instead of a straight line, often an 'area', undefined in exactitude, was a recognisable and acceptable dividing factor. This Ottoman–Persian frontier cut through the middle of Kurdish territory.

During the seventeenth and eighteenth centuries the Turkish and Persian Empires made little serious attempt to pacify their Kurds, or even penetrate into their mountains, apart from the occasional punitive expedition, which usually had a limited objective. The whole of the Kurdish region – on both sides of the frontier – and its fringes became a lawless tribal no man's land, remote and unstable. The sultan of Turkey looked towards Europe, his empire stretching into the troubled Balkans, while the Shah of Persia tried to put his stamp of authority on parts of Afghanistan. Both seemed content to have this convenient void between them, which contained other ethic and religious groups, some intermixed, some mutually hostile, including Arabs, Armenians, Assyrians, Chaldeans and Nestorians as well as Kurds.

The Kurdish economy rested almost exclusively on grazing flocks, but illegal trading across the new Ottoman–Persian frontier provided additional income. For example the large Herki tribe, which had settled near Urmiya but still migrated in winter to the plains near Arbil for fodder, would take Persian salt to Turkey and bring back wheat to Persia, thus avoiding tariff and customs duties. Another large Kurdish tribe that extended on both sides of the frontier was the Shikaki.

Many Kurdish tribes came to be led by a sheikh, being one with some Islamic qualification who combined both spiritual and temporal authority, although often the Islamic cloak was dubious. About 85 per cent of the Kurds were Sunni and some 15 per cent were Shia, the usual overall ratio, the Shias being mainly situated in Persian territory. There were occasional interreligious squabbles and clashes in the Persian Azerbaijan province, but otherwise there was little religious friction amongst Kurds.

Prior to the nineteenth century the Kurds were mainly pastoral and semi-nomadic, inhabiting a probable area of some

250 000 square miles, the core of which was a mountainous mass. The probable population was said to be of between three and five million but no one knew exactly, although some idea of numbers began to surface as both Ottoman and Persian governments began to tax them whenever they could.

The Kurds were a collection of tribes or groups of tribes, with units varying from as few as 500 families to over 3000 (Arfa, 1966). For sheer survival smaller tribes had to ally themselves to larger ones or with each other, or enter federations, which in turn dissolved or changed in composition, dictated by the fortunes of war and circumstances. Tribes were subdivided into clans and groups of families, each always being on the defensive, ever suspicious of the others, intent upon survival. Each man owed complete allegiance to his family and tribe, and to the tribal sheikh, who settled disputes in accordance with Islamic and tribal law and Kurdish customs.

Within a tribe a strict moral code of behaviour existed in their dealings with one another, but this did not always seem to obtain in intertribal matters, which were frequently marred by bad faith and treachery. Lacking national cohesion, tribes at times allied themselves to enemies of other tribes, and fought against them as an alien foe. Mountain tribesmen lived in small villages and hamlets in valleys, in small stone dwellings shielded from the wind by stone walls. Where possible in the valleys, wheat, barley or maize was grown, their staple daily diet being bread.

Apart from their language, of which there were several dialects, the Kurds were distinguishable by their dress, which for men consisted of baggy trousers secured at the ankle, a cummerbund, frequently an embroidered jacket, and a flattish turban, whose fringe or mode of wearing sometimes denoted individual tribes. Men invariably carried a *khanjar* (a curved dagger) in their cummerbunds as a symbol of manhood and warrior status. Many favoured bandoliers, worn across the chest with cartridges exposed – all men carried or owned, a weapon of some sort, even if it was only an ancient firearm. Kurdish women wore their own traditional, sometimes colourful dress. They were not veiled, being contemptuous of lowland ethnic women who were.

Like most mountain races the Kurds were of sturdy physique, and many had lighter skins. Blue eyes were not uncommon, and it was said with some pride that this was a heritage of Alexander's soldiers of centuries ago. Health was a problem for mountain Kurds, especially in severe winters, and they were often plagued with diseases such as cholera because of insanitary conditions.

MARTIAL HERITAGE

The Kurds were proud of their martial heritage and regarded the profession of arms highly. Some writers say that Kurdish family and tribal life is still based on a military pattern as over the centuries they have been compelled to always be on their guard and ready to fight at a moment's notice. In the Middle Ages, in search of plunder the Kurds – mounted on small, sturdy ponies and armed with swords and lances – emerged from their mountains to sweep down on to the plains, their fierce cavalry charges and war cries gaining them a formidable reputation and much loot.

In the latter part of the nineteenth century the Kurds began to acquire modern rifles and their tactics changed. Cavalry shock assaults gave way to dismounted 'fire and movement' infiltration tactics, but to their enemies on the plains the former Kurdish cavalry reputation lived on. When ponies were used to carry them to battle the Kurds dismounted to fight, no longer charging en masse although they did so on occasion to frighten the enemy or to get close to him. In the mountains the horse was maintained just for purposes of war, being expensive to keep. Travel was often quicker by foot in mountainous terrain and the beast of burden was the humble donkey.

The Kurdish method of attacking a village was first to occupy adjacent hills and then to creep closer to take the defenders by surprise if possible. Otherwise attack was by fire-and-movement, ending in a final infantry charge. In defence of a village women too joined in the fighting, and usually gave a good account themselves. Swords and lances were abandoned in favour of the rifle, as in hand-to-hand combat the Kurds preferred their long curved daggers.

In the past, Kurdish offensive military activity – apart from intertribal squabbles and when bribed to fight – had usually been for purposes of plundering cities and caravans and dominating good grazing land. If they ran into opposition and losses became heavy, they stopped, divided any loot and returned home. They were able to do this with some impunity as their mountains were their sanctuary and deterrent, the terrain presenting many obstacles and hazards to an attacker while their warlike reputation engendered caution against punitive reaction.

SETTLED KURDS

Not all Kurds remained in the mountains, and when the opportunity arose some descended to adjacent plains to settle by force, or opportunity, in grazing areas or arable land. However they usually remained semi-nomadic, taking their herds in seasonal search of grazing when necessary. As Kurdish settlements increased in number and size, good free-range grazing became scarcer, which gave rise to tribal quarrels and clashes, As leaders of large tribal federations came to dominate large settled areas a form of feudal servitude developed within them, especially in eastern Anatolia, where wheat was grown for trade and barter, to which tobacco was added later as a ready cash crop.

There were also a number of Kurdish 'colonies' in various other parts of the region, where Kurds and Kurdish mercenaries and their families had settled wherever by chance they had found themselves, joining the myriad other minorities in the patchwork ethnic pattern of that area. Other Kurds left their mountains, tribal restraints or feudal servitude to find employment in cities and towns, where they drew together to form small urban groups.

THE NINETEENTH CENTURY

During the first part of the nineteenth century both Turkey and Persia fought wars with Russia, in which the Persians lost some northern parts of their territory. It was not until the latter part of the century that both governments were able to give more attention to their Kurdish regions, which had become unstable frontier ones that were vulnerable to Russian aggression and subversion. In 1878 the Persians began to raise an irregular 'Cossack Force', similar to that of the Russians, who were successfully using Cossack irregular units to police border regions of their expanding empire, although it is doubtful whether any real Cossacks served in it. The Shah also replaced his agha governors with a direct administration, which caused discontent and disaffection amongst Kurds deprived of authority.

In their wars with Turkey the Russians tried to subvert Kurds to their side, and even raised a few Kurdish units under Russian officers. In 1877, when the Turks and Russians were skirmishing in eastern Anatolia around Erzerum and Van, they were able to raise some of the tribes in brief rebellion against the Ottomans, even though a proportion of their armed forces were conscripted Kurds – sheikhs often sending a quota of men instead of paying taxes.

SHEIKH UBEIDULLAH

The reluctance of Kurdish groups to cooperate with each other brought disorder and rivalry, and the absence of powerful arbitrators enabled religious personalities to fill this void. Two major Islamic orders flourished and spread throughout Kurdistan – the Nakshbandiya and the Qadiriya, members of which became arbiters, as a step towards temporal authority.

One Kurdish leader, Sheikh Ubeidullah of the Nakshbandi order, gained a wide following, calling for an autonomous Kurdish entity. Ubeidullah is usually credited with being one of the first Kurdish nationalists. In 1878 he stated that 'the Kurdish nation is a people apart', claiming that 'the chiefs and rulers of Kurdistan, whether Turkish or Persian subjects, and the inhabitants of Kurdistan, one and all agree that matters cannot be carried on in this way under two opposing governments' (McDowall, 1985). Rather an overoptimistic statement at that time.

Two years later Obeidullah, who lived in what was nominally Turkish territory and who claimed to have a wide influence amongst Kurdish tribes on both sides of the border, mustered his followers and moved eastwards into the Persian sector with

the object of pushing back Persian security forces and bringing about his projected 'Kurdish Autonomous State', which
would owe allegiance to Turkey.

Visualising the acquisition of another slice of Persian territory for his Ottoman Empire at the expense of his old enemies
the Persians, the Sultan initially gave Obeidullah some encouragement. Using revenge for alleged attacks on Kurds by Persian Cossack troops as his excuse, Obeidullah persuaded several
thousand Kurdish tribesmen to join his eastward offensive.
Crossing the border he halted his force in the mountains
overlooking the town of Urmiya just to the west of Lake Urmiya,
on the shore of which lived a small community of Christian
Nestorians, one of the few remaining in the whole region,
which was expecting to be massacred in the traditional
manner.

However that seemed to be the limit of Ubeidullah's eastward advance, as when news came of an approaching Persian
military force his tribal warriors, recruited by the prospect of
loot, began to fade away, forcing him to withdraw to Ottoman territory. Meanwhile the Turkish Sultan had had second
thoughts. Realising that a Kurdish autonomous entity on his
abrasive eastern frontier would not be beneficial to the security of the Ottoman Empire he marched against Ubeidullah.
The unsuccessful Ubeidullah, the first Kurdish nationalist leader
of note in modern history, eventually died in exile in Mecca.

Unlike the Shah, the Sultan did not attempt to impose direct
rule, but in 1891 – with the cooperation of some of his Kurdish
aghas, who were anti-Russian and in principle also hostile to
the Persian Shia state – raised a number of Kurdish cavalry
units, known as the 'Hamidiye Regiments', to police his Kurdish
region and Russian frontier, an area that also contained many
interspersed communities of aggressive Armenians and Assyrians, most having an unfortunate history of committing mini-
massacres against each other whenever the opportunity arose
or revenge insisted.

The manpower of these Hamidiye regiments was provided
by the Aghas. This was largely successful, although partisan,
as local sheikhs commanded their own tribesmen. Many took
action against Armenian communities, which were harshly
suppressed and dispersed, in an interethnic campaign that

reached its climax in 1895–6. As Armenians were ejected, often with some slaughter, Kurdish families were often installed in their depopulated villages and adjoining lands.

THE PERSIAN REVOLUTION 1909

The Anglo–Russian entente of 1907 divided Persia into two separate spheres of influence, the Russians taking the northern part and the British the southern one. The previous year a nationalist organisation had persuaded the Shah to accept a European-type constitution, but the Russians encouraged him to suppress it. A weak central government allowed the northern Kurdish region to run wild, causing Ottoman troops to enter part of it in 1908. In July 1909 revolutionary forces marched into Tehran, deposing the shah in favour of his young son. Internal instability spread. In 1911 the Tehran government organised a gendarmerie to police its unsettled regions, but it was too late to become effective as that year Russian troops entered parts of northern Persia.

THE YOUNG TURKS REVOLUTION OF 1908

In 1908 the Young Turks overthrew the rule of Sultan Abdul Hamid, promising constitutional reform and representative participation of all peoples in the governing of the Ottoman Empire, promises that did not come up to expectations. During the revolution a Kurdish sheikh, with about 1500 irregulars, occupied and held Damascus for the sultan, Syria then being part of the Ottoman Empire.

The new political atmosphere allowed the development of a number of political 'Kurdish clubs' – formed by the tiny contingent of urban Kurdish intelligentsia, army officers and politically inclined – in Baghdad, Bitlis, Diyarbakir, Erzerum, Mosul and Mush (McDowall, 1985). These clubs did not prosper as their attempts to reach the tribesmen were thwarted by the aghas, who saw their authority threatened. A Society for Progress and Mutual Aid was formed in Istanbul by two agha families, but they quarrelled and it was dissolved by the authorities.

THE FIRST WORLD WAR

The First World War began in August 1914, with the Allies (Britain, France and Russia) facing the Central Powers (Germany and Austria). In October Turkey came in on the side of the Central Powers, thus bringing Turkey face to face with its old enemy in the Caucasus and Anatolia. The Kurds accepted conscription against the Christian foe, and many served in the Ottoman armed forces. The Armenians and Assyrians in Turkey, thinking their hour had come, declared war on the Central Powers, anticipating that Russia would rush to their assistance. Initially the Russians did help, and as they moved into Turkish regions they were preceded by Armenian irregulars, who killed and looted as they advanced. It was alleged that 'more than 600 000 Kurds were killed, between 1915 and 1918' (Arfa, 1966). Those Armenians and Assyrians who had taken up arms were soon halted, and were then driven eastwards by Turkish troops into the Persian province of Azerbaijan.

The Assyrians came up against the agha of the powerful Kurdish Shikaki tribe, known as 'Simko' (Ismail Agha) east of Tabriz, whom a weak Tehran government had allowed some jurisdiction. After shaking hands with the Assyrian patriarch, Mar Shimun, Simko treacherously murdered him. An Assyrian force of some 6000 armed men marched against Simko, who with some Turkish help managed to defeat it. Although the Assyrians managed to kill many Shikaki Kurds in revenge, this was virtually the end of the Assyrians as a cohesive body. Later the British allowed the remnants, some 40 000 including families, to move into the newly created Kingdom of Iraq and settle there.

A worse fate was in store for the Armenians, as the Ottoman government mounted a genocide campaign against them in 1915–16. In many instances Kurds were resettled in depopulated Armenian towns, villages and areas.

Persia officially remained neutral in the First World War Parts of its northern regions were already occupied by Russian or Turkish troops, and it had no military capability worth speaking of. Although the Shah remained in Tehran, most of his influential supporters decamped until they could see which side was winning. The only disciplined body in Persia was the

Cossack force, which was far too small to be effective outside Tehran.

When the Russian Revolution occurred in 1917, Russian troops in Kurdistan – in company with many others – shot their officers, threw down their arms and made their way home if possible. Kurds picked up many of the abandoned weapons and ammunition, and Kurdish and other regions of both Persia and Turkey devolved into a chaos of violence.

2 The Kurds Divided

In November 1918 the First World War ended in armistice. The Allies had won and the Central Powers, including Turkey, had been defeated. The victorious Allies – which now included the Americans, strutting onto the world stage for the first time – concerned themselves with dictating the terms of surrender, imposing war reparations, dealing with the defeated, breaking up their empires, creating new states, and granting subject peoples independence. The League of Nations was formed with the intention of it becoming the arbiter of international disputes.

Two new states were carved out of Turkey's Arab and Mesopotamian territory – Iraq, mandated to Britain to prepare it for independence, and Syria, mandated to France. A new iron grid of international frontiers descended on the Kurdish people, who so far had shown little inclination towards modern nationalism, dividing them into contiguous segments.

Shorn of its empire the Turkish government was in a state of dazed confusion, as an internal struggle began between traditionalists and reformers. Kurdish intellectuals and others tried again to form political groups, advocating either independence or autonomy. The principal group was the 'Society for the Recovery of Kurdistan' ('Kurdistan Taali Djiyeti'). This was organised by prominent Kurdish personalities in Istanbul, some of whom were 'autonomists' and wanted to stand by Turkey in its difficulties; others wanted complete independence. However their arguments were soon overtaken by events.

American President Woodrow Wilson produced his 14-Point Programme for World Peace, which stated (Point 12) that 'non-Turkish minorities of the Ottoman Empire should be assured of an absolute, unmolested opportunity for autonomous development'. Wilson, like other European Christian leaders, had a conscience about Armenians and other Christian minorities that had suffered so terribly during the First World War. The Kurds were also an affected minority, but while the Armenians were vocally nationalist in outlook and had powerful advocates working for them, the Kurds lacked both a national approach and international support.

As a body the Kurds were not ready to take advantage of such a unique opportunity to demand an independent state of their own. Tribal loyalty was greater than the urge for Kurdish nationalism. Aghas and sheikhs were more concerned with retaining their own authority and increasing their personal influence at the expense of Kurdish rivals and enemies, than with uniting for a common national purpose. Urban Kurds may have understood what was at stake, but they lacked a popular following and were neither conditioned nor capable of negotiating effectively on an international platform.

The Allies went ahead with planning an independent Armenian state on Turkish territory, which in the event of Kurdish inaction would obviously be to the detriment of the Kurds, as small communities of the two mutually hostile ethnic groups were interspersed. Accordingly a group of Kurds, under General Sharif Pasha, cooperated with the Armenians to present a joint memorandum to the Peace Conference, which had assembled in Paris in 1919. Relevant extracts of that memorandum include – 'prepare for local autonomy in those regions where the Kurdish element is preponderantly lying east of the Euphrates, to the south of the still-to-be established Armenian frontier, and to the north of the frontier between Turkey, Syria and Mesopotamia'; and

> If after one year has elapsed since the formation of the present treaty, the Kurdish population of the areas designated calls on the Council of the League of Nations and demonstrates that a majority of the population in those areas wishes to become independent of Turkey, and if the Council then estimates that the population in question is capable of such independence and recommends that it be granted, then Turkey agrees, as of now, to comply with this recommendation and to renounce all rights and titles to the area. . . . If and when the said renunciation is made, no objection shall be raised by the main Allied powers should the Kurds living in that part of Kurdistan at present included in the vilayet of Mosul seek to become citizens of the newly independent Kurdish state. (McDowall, 1985)

This memorandum was accepted and included in the Treaty of Sèvres, signed by the Allies and the Turkish government on 20 August 1920, being the outcome of the Paris Peace

Conference. It seemed as though autonomous status was about to be bestowed on the Kurds, but it did not work out like that, and was overtaken by momentous events.

The Turkish hero rising from the ashes of the Turkish defeat in the First World War was General Mustafa Kemal, who raised a revolt in Anatolia against the Treaty of Sèvres, appealing for Muslim unity and a Muslim fatherland. Fearful of the appearance of an autonomous Armenia on Turkish soil, the Kurds rallied to Kemal, and Kurdish forces – under Turkish officers – drove the Christian forces from eastern Turkey.

President Wilson's 14-Point Peace Plan was rejected by the Americans. Allied armies were demobilising and there was extreme reluctance to muster an expeditionary military force to bring Kemal to heel. More to the point, the Allies saw a new, major and dangerous enemy rising in the east from the ashes of Czarist Russia – the USSR and the threat of world communism. The Western Allies had a change of heart and began to see Kemal as a possible south-eastern bastion against this new communist threat.

Next Kemal turned his attention to the West and fought a war against the Greeks, defeating them and depriving them of certain territory awarded to them under the Treaty of Sèvres, thus soundly establishing his leadership over Turkey. The Allies were forced to negotiate with Turkey once again, and holes were blown in the Treaty of Sèvres.

Generally the Allies got what they wanted in terms of the map of the Middle East being redrawn to their specifications, an exception being that the French conceded Anatolia to Turkey. None of the Allies were prepared to enforce any of the Treaty of Sèvres conditions that would have involved military force; nor were they prepared to negotiate on behalf of either the Kurds or the Armenians. Despite fine principles, the cause of the Kurds and Armenians was abandoned and they were sold down the river.

Under the Treaty of Lausanne in 1922, in which there was no mention of Kurds or Armenians, Turkey established control over Eastern Thrace and all Anatolia, with only Mosul remaining in dispute.

Working towards turning Turkey into a secular state, Kemal abolished the sultanate in 1922. On 3 March 1924 he abolished the caliphate, thus depriving aghas and sheikhs of their religious authority. He then set about removing all vestiges of a separate Kurdish entity, which had become more than just a general Kurdish talking point. He closed Kurdish schools, teaching foundations and religious fraternities, and banned Kurdish associations and publications. Mustafa Kemal became known as 'Ataturk' ('Great Turk').

THE SHEIKH SAID REVOLT OF 1925

In March 1925 a Kurdish revolt – under the leadership of Sheikh Said, a Nakshbandi agha of Piran whose rallying cry was autonomy – erupted when Said's followers massacred a detachment of Turkish soldiers that had been sent to arrest him. The revolt spread like wildfire to encompass the eastern part of Anatolia, but failed to capture any towns of any size. It was a tribally based uprising and the lively Kurdish nationalist association at Diyarbakir failed to respond to Said's call to join him. Said went on to besiege Diyarbakir, but did not call on the Kurdish urban element within that city to join him because their lowly, non-tribal status deemed them 'unfit to fight' (Arfa, 1966). This demonstrated the very wide gap dividing urban Kurds from their tribal leaders, who held them in contempt.

Ataturk responded swiftly and with a very heavy hand, using the railways to rush troops towards eastern Anatolia, and by mid-April he had completely crushed the insurrection. Retribution was deadly. After a military trial Said and 45 others were executed, many were imprisoned and hundreds of Kurdish villages were destroyed. A large number of Kurds died in the pacification process (although the precise number was not accurately recorded). In addition Ataturk decided to rid eastern Anatolia of its Kurdish population and thousands were driven from their homes.

THE KHOYBUN REVOLT

Almost immediately another Kurdish revolt broke out in the northern area around Mount Ararat. Although this was led by local aghas and sheikhs, it had been largely organised and motivated by a new Kurdish liberation organisation, the 'Khoybun'. Based in Syria and Lebanon, the Khoybun was also given some support by the Shah of Persia, who wanted to destabilise the new Turkey and prevent it from becoming too powerful. This group proved to be more durable than that of the unfortunate Sheikh Said, and developed a Kurdish resistance area between Bitlis, Van and Mount Ararat.

The Shah of Persia continued to lend support to this revolt; Ataturk was unable to reduce it, and a stalemate struggle continued for some four years. It was not until the the Shah was persuaded to stop assisting the insurgent Kurds and allow Turkish troops to move through Persian territory to encircle them that – in the summer of 1930 – the Turkish government was able to launch a successful offensive against them. Again mass depopulation was the reprisal.

THE DERSIM REVOLT

Not all eastern Anatolia was under Turkish central administration, the task being beyond its military capability, and in certain areas there was a live-and-let-live stand-off. One such was the relatively small Dersim area, where a revolt was raised by the aghas and sheikhs without any external Kurdish political motivation or help, being largely a 'religious rising' against Ataturk's secular Turkey. This Kurdish insurrection tied down three Turkish Army corps in guerrilla warfare from about 1930 to the end of 1938 (Arfa, 1966). It was eventually crushed by brutality. After the fall of Dersim the Khoybun went underground in Turkey.

Much of eastern Anatolia became a military zone, ostensibly because of its proximity to the USSR border but in reality to contain insurgent Kurds, who remained under martial law until 1946, a campaign being coincidently launched to repress the Kurdish language, dress, names and folklore. Up to one million Kurds were displaced between 1925 and 1938, but Kurds were conscripted into the army, in order that they might be assimilated (McDowall, 1985). It was the Turkish government's boast that 'Turkey has no Kurds, only mountain Turks who have forgotten their own language'.

THE SIMKO RISING

After the First World War Persia was plunged into turmoil. With British help Reza Khan, commander of the Cossack force, established himself in power in Tehran in 1921, displacing the last of the Qajar shahs in 1923 and proclaiming himself shah in 1925. His overriding concern was to weld his country together and to overcome separatist demands by large minorities, including Kurds.

The largest insurgency, a Kurdish one, erupted in October 1921. This was led by Agha Simko of the Shikaki tribe, who had been accorded government authority in an area west and south of Lake Urmiya at a time when the area was threatened by British, Turkish and Russian armies. At first the Tehran government tried to come to some agreement with him on the basis of limited autonomy, but Simko refused. He was using his position of authority to try to eliminate competing groups of Assyrians and other non-Kurdish minorities.

Simko raised other Kurdish tribes in support of his own, including the Lurs, and occupied the town of Maraghah, east of Lake Urmiya. In 1922 Reza Khan led a military expedition against him, dispersing his followers and driving him into the new, adjacent state of Iraq. Some Kurdish land was confiscated, and sections of the Shikaki and Lurs tribes were deported to other parts of Persia.

THE USSR

As Soviet central government authority became established, the Soviet Red Army launched campaigns into the Caucasus region and elsewhere to regain all former Czarist Russian territories that had ventured to become independent. This resulted in the Socialist Soviet Republics of Georgia and Armenia, which lay against Turkey's north-eastern frontier, a stretch of mountainous border terrain with Kurdish tribes on either side. Amid this chaos the so-called 'Red Kurdistan' entity appeared (1923–8), only to disappear with little trace.

Eventually the Soviets more or less succeeded in sealing off their frontier with Turkey, and to avoid becoming involved in a dispute with that country as a result of Kurdish cross-border activities, in 1937–8 it forcibly deported Kurdish tribes and a few other Kurdish 'colonies' from the border region for provoking frontier incidents.

SYRIA

The new Arab state of Syria, which had been mandated to the French, had a long, common frontier with Turkey to its north, and there was mutual hostility and suspicion between the inhabitants of these two countries. Syria contained a small number of Kurdish colonies, some long established, some semi-nomadic. In the usual colonial manner of divide and rule the French encouraged minorities to establish their own identities, rather than try to assimilate them.

In the 1920s the Turkish campaigns against minorities, especially the Kurds, had caused Kurdish refugees to flood southwards into Syria. Initially there was some cross-border raiding by Kurds against Christian minorities, but as soon as the French organised their occupying military forces and raised local irregular troops this activity was contained. One ethnically mixed force of irregulars, 'Les troupes spéciales du Levant', included Kurds.

The French administration tolerated, perhaps even encouraged, the Kurdish Khoybun. This annoyed the Turks, whose relationship with the French tended to be somewhat strained. Otherwise France tried to maintain a neutral attitude towards the several minorities in Syria. The French also gained the mandate over adjacent Lebanon, which attracted Kurdish refugees.

IRAQ

The new Arab state of Iraq was a British creation, carved mainly out of the Mesopotamian region and including Kurdish territory in the north. An Arab princeling, Amir Feisal Husseini, was brought in to be king and the mandate was awarded to the British. British troops were already on the spot to enforce British decisions, having entered the region during the First World War by way of the Persian Gulf, seizing Baghdad in March 1917 and going on to occupy Mosul in October that year. At first the British toyed with the idea of creating an Arab state, with Kurdish and Christian autonomous provinces loosely attached. The population of Mosul was said to be five-eighths Kurdish (McDowall, 1985). (The later – 1922–24 – Iraqi census showed the Mosul Vilayet to have 494 007 Kurds and 166 941 Arabs.) The Allies soon went off Wilsonian principles under the erroneous illusion that the various minorities would forget their wrongs and prejudices and settle down peacefully together under a mandated government.

Mosul was an initial problem, as under the secret Sykes–Picot Treaty of 1916 between Britain and France, France was to take half of the Vilayet of Mosul to add to its Syrian demands. Oil production and potential was already a strategic factor. Britain wanted both parts of the Mosul Vilayet, which contained Kirkuk. The Sykes–Picot Treaty was pushed aside and Britain got its way. Oil was struck in Kirkuk in 1927, making that area, together with Mosul, the richest known oil-producing region in the world. Oil concessions were dominated by British, French, Dutch and American interests and thereafter no Kurdish separatist movement could expect to gain any Western sympathy or aid for separatism.

Instead of imposing direct rule the British chose to administer through traditional leadership where possible, an old British colonial habit that had been found to have advantages. When the First World War ended the Kurdish region was in turmoil, and at first the Allies were uncertain exactly how to carve it up. In the Suliemaniyeh area they invited the sitting Kurdish governor, Sheikh Mahmoud Barzanji, who had been appointed during the Turkish administration, to continue in office. Mahmoud Barzanji was both an agha and a sheikh, as well as a member of the Nakshbandi order, having considerable spiritual and temporal standing. The British gave him an enlarged area to administer, but this immediately brought him into conflict with other Kurdish aghas and sheikhs. When Barzanji questioned British authority he was removed into exile in India.

British administration of the Kurdish region of Iraq was violently interrupted in 1922 when, after dealing with the revolt in Anatolia, Ataturk moved to try to establish control over the Kurdish mountains in the British sector as far south as Ruwanduz. Barzanji was hastily recalled from exile to stabilise

the situation, which he did in the devious fashion of entering
into negotiations with the new Turkish authorities, and with
their blessing turned against the British in rebellion. When
British RAF aircraft bombed his residence Barzanji retired into
the field to raise Kurdish tribes against the British administration. He attacked and re-entered Suliemaniyeh, but RAF bombing drove him out again, after which an uneasy peace settled
on the Iraqi Kurdish region.

The Anglo–Iraqi Treaty of 1930 gave Iraq sovereign independence, which was implemented in 1932. Under the treaty
Iraq had promised to respect the language and customs of the
Kurds, but little else. This caused Sheikh Mahmoud Barzanji
to raise another revolt in the spring of 1931, this time imprecisely calling for a 'United Kurdistan'. Once again he was
defeated. By now he was an old man and he quietly accepted
house-arrest for himself and his family in southern Iraq. Strikes
and demonstrations in Suliemaniyeh followed, carried out by
urban Kurdish townspeople, traders and workers. These were
not initiated or dominated by tribal Kurds, so this was perhaps
the first real evidence of popular Kurdish separatist aspirations
in Iraq.

The next Kurdish separatist leader of some note was Mullah
Mustafa Barzani. In this case 'Mullah' was a forename and not
a religious title. Mullah was a grandson of Sheikh Mahmoud
Barzanji, whose tribe lived in and around the village of Barzan,
near the headwaters of the Greater Zab, an area of traditional
lawlessness that was seldom touched by external authority. Although the Barzani tribe was comparatively small (precise figures
are almost impossible to ascertain with any accuracy), Mullah
Mustafa Barzani and the Barzani tribe dominated the locality.

Mullah Mustafa Barzani took on his grandfather's secular
leadership mantle, while his elder brother, Sheikh Ahmad
Barzani, took on his spiritual one. The first Barzani clashes
with the central authority were when the Baghdad government
tried to impose taxation on the mountain Kurds, combined
with attempts to resettled (Turkish) Assyrian refugees from the
Hakkari province into Iraqi Kurdish areas. Iraqi troops, supported by RAF aircraft, moved against them, driving the Barzani
brothers over the border into Turkey, where they surrendered.
They were given amnesty and remained there until 1933.

3 The Kurdish Republic of Mahabad: 1946

The ramifications of the Second World War, which began in September 1939, gradually reached out and drew in Iran (the new name for Persia since 1935) and Iraq. Turkey remained neutral until the last days of this conflict and generally succeeded in keeping a tight rein on its restless Kurds, as did Syria, which was successively under French, Vichy French and then Free French military occupation, and which stifled Kurdish thoughts of dissidence. When the Iraqi government hesitated to join the Allies and seemed to be favouring the Axis powers, a British military force landed in Iraq. By May 1941 it was in Baghdad, establishing itself as the protecting power for the remainder of the war.

The Shah of Iran also tried to remain neutral, but when the USSR joined the Allies in June 1941 his territory was required as a supply corridor into southern USSR. Hence in August an Allied joint occupation of Iran was imposed, with the Soviets in the north (which embraced most of the Kurdish territory) and the British in the south. This situation lasted until after the war ended. The British packed off the reluctant Reza Shah Pahlavi into enforced retirement, installing his young son, Mohammed, in his stead. In both Iran and Iraq these military occupations often left Kurdish regions with little or no central government control.

In May 1942 the lawlessness of the Kurds in the Lake Urmiya region of Iran was worrying the Soviets, who were anxious about the security of their vital supply corridor. They therefore authorised the small Iranian army, which had all but disintegrated, to take punitive action against the Kurds but insisted that the Iranian troops remain south of the 'Sardasht–Zanjan Line'. The troops made little impact on the restless Kurds, but did to some degree prevent them from moving any further southwards.

21

THE KOMOLA

The Soviets had the ulterior motive of extending their influence into Iranian and Iraqi border provinces, with the aim of drawing them into their political orbit, perhaps eventually to become Soviet socialist republics within the USSR. The Soviets were as greedy to acquire additional territory and people as any of the other major predators in the region. They set to work on politicising the Iranian Kurds, meeting little success until 16 September 1942, when they sponsored the formation of a Kurdish organisation, on the usual communist pattern, known as the 'Komola' ('Komola Jiwanewey Kurd', which can be translated as the 'Committee for the Life of Kurdistan or the Kurd Resurrection Group'), some 50 miles south of Lake Urmiya in the Kurdish town of Mahabad, which then had a population of about 16 000. There was no Soviet military presence in the Mahabad area, and Iranian authority was less than nominal.

In April 1943 the Komola formed a central committee and secret cells were organised under Soviet guidance. Its underground activities began to spread into other parts of Kurdish Iranian territory under Soviet military occupation, seeping southwards until checked by the presence of Iranian military units. In May a group of Kurds attacked the Mahabad police station, after which all Iranian security forces were withdrawn from the region, leaving the Komola with a free hand.

Meanwhile, in the Kurdish region of Iran many self-appointed sheikhs rose to dominate tribes, valleys, towns and small areas, and often the weak central government in Tehran had no option but to confirm them in the appointments they had assumed. Many spent much of their energy enlarging their fiefdoms, and fighting off rivals. Disliking this outright lawlessness and instability, the Soviets allowed some reorganisation of the small Iranian army, and for it to return to selected towns and areas it had previously vacated, thus regaining some measure of central control. The notable exception was Mahabad, for which the Soviets had a special mission in mind.

One old Kurdish adventurer, Sheikh Hama Rashid, for example, had taken over the town and district of Saqqiz. There he remained 'independent' until Iranian army units moved against him in 1942, driving him into Iraq, where he was detained.

During this period of instability several Kurdish sheikhs unsuccesfully requested to be absorbed into the British sector.

THE TUDEH

When Reza Shah Pahlavi was removed by the British in 1941, political parties were allowed to operate once again. A few were resurrected, but only one became really influential – the Tudeh. This was almost communist in form and practice, being strongly supported by the Soviets in their sector, who saw it as an instrument they could use for their own political ends. The British too courted the Tudeh, seeing it as the only stable thread in the rickety Iranian political structure. The Tudeh published a newspaper, the *Azir*.

THE HEVA

In Iraq in late 1942 a Kurdish political party, founded in Kirkuk, developed into the Kurdish Nationalist Party, the 'Heva', which had branches in Arbil, Baghdad, Mosul and Suliemaniyeh, some of which attracted Iranian Kurdish members. The Heva leadership contained the Iraqi Kurdish intelligentsia such as it was – army officers and government officials – but had a strong left-wing bias. Soon after formation the Heva HQ moved to Baghdad, where it published a newspaper – *Azdai*, or 'Freedom'. The paper expounded a socialist doctrine and communist propaganda, but did not seem to appreciate that these views were contrary to those held by tribal sheikhs and their followers, the grass roots of tribal power, and for that reason alone it never really became a major influence. Also in Iraq, the older Khoybun organisation flickered into life again, but it too was out of touch and sympathy with Kurdish tribal sheikhs and only gained limited influence in some Kurdish towns in the country.

MULLAH MUSTAFA BARZANI

In the meantime Mullah Mustafa Barzani had been allowed to return from exile in Turkey to Iraq, where he remained under house arrest in Suliemaniyeh. He escaped in June 1943, and by way of Iran made his way back to his home town, Barzan, where he began to preach a vague form of Kurdish nationalism. He soon gained widespread support as the unpopular Iraqi government was considered to be anti-Kurdish.

THE SAID BIROKI REVOLT: 1943

Because it was anxious to remain neutral in the Second World War, Turkey, when faced with a Kurdish revolt on its eastern frontier in June 1943, marched swiftly to repress it. The leader of the revolt was Sheikh Said Biroki who, in cooperation with Barzani, had raided a series of Iraqi police and frontier posts on the Iraqi side of the Turkish–Iraqi border. Turkish troops quickly dispersed the Kurdish dissident tribes involved and captured Biroki. Turkey was determined that its frontier would not be compromised by either Iraqi or Iranian Kurdish insurgent activity.

THE DIYANA AMBUSH

Undeterred by the fate of Biroki, Barzani continued his insurrectionary activities in northern Iraq, which in October 1943 resulted in the Baghdad government dispatching a small military column against him. The troops were trapped and defeated near the small town of Diyana, so a detachment of British–Indian occupation troops were rushed northwards to stabilise the embarrassing situation.

Barzani refused to surrender. His victory at Diyana, although a small one, had given him local prestige, which attracted many Kurds to his banner. Indeed a few Kurds deserted from the Iraqi army to join him and by the end of 1943 he had an armed force of several hundred warriors. The British occupying authorities asked Barzani to stop fighting and negotiate with the Baghdad government. Under threat of punitive air strikes against him, Barzani agreed. The Baghdad government offered him the alternative of either crossing into Iran or living in the area of the Pishdari tribe, north-east of Suliemaniyeh, but he rejected both. Further negotiations proved negative.

A GREATER KURDISTAN

The year 1944 was one in which Kurdish nationalism began to develop, mainly in Iraq and Iran but also to some extent in Turkey. In Iraq the Heva and communist factions eyed each other warily, but the communists were divided amongst themselves and one group, although it had no Kurdish members, openly backed the Kurdish cause. Unlike the Kurds in the former Ottoman Empire, who had been vaguely promised independence, which had generated sparks of nationalism, the political aspirations of those in Iran remained tribal and insular, motivated by reluctance to be subjected to central control. Now some Iranian Kurdish leaders were coming into contact with Soviet ideology, and the Soviets were encouraging this interest.

In Iran, relations between the Komola and communist groups were also cold and non-cooperative. A loose coalition of several Kurdish organisations came into being, known as the 'Kurdish Deliverance' ('Razgar i Kurd'). By April the coalition had joined the Komola, whose membership by this time included many Kurdish tribal sheikhs and other personalities, thus producing a fairly robust front.

In May the Komola produced a Kurdish national flag, a tricolour with red, white and green bands (the Iranian flag upside down). It contained a sun symbol flanked by ears of corn, with a mountain and a pen in the background. Inter-Kurdish cooperation and liaison seemed to gather pace, and in August representatives from the main Kurdish organisations in Iran, Iraq and Turkey met near Mount Dalanpur (in Iraq), near where the three countries touched, and agreed to work for a Greater Kurdistan. A map of sorts was produced, showing areas claimed, but it was inaccurate and exaggerated, showing, for example, a Kurdish corridor to the Mediterranean through Aleppo (in Syria).

However the Mount Dalanpur meeting was the exception rather than the rule as the Komola and the Heva found it difficult to get on together. Because neither wanted to be dominated by the other, little real cooperation between them was achieved.

In Mahabad in October, the dominant religious and political personality, Qazi Mohammed, was persuaded to join the

Komola, which had its HQ in that town. Although he was later depicted by several authorities as a comparatively harmless leader unfortunately caught up in events he could not untangle, in effect he was a lively, wily character and a shrewd schemer, his handicap being his limited vision. Qazi Mohammed did not join the central committee of the Komola, remaining a backroom boy, but somehow managed to dominate it, becoming its spokesman and *de facto* leader. From this moment the Komola began to lose much of its secret character and openly discussed Kurdish aspirations and nationalism.

THE FREEDOM PARTY

The only Kurdish leader with any significant military force was Mullah Mustafa Barzani in his homeland mountains. Barzani was not a member of any of the Kurdish organisations although he was in touch with all of them, and with many government officials too. The Heva wanted to bring Barzani into its clutches in order to absorb his army, after which he would be abandoned. This would have made the Heva the most formidable group in Iraq. But Barzani had other ideas. The Heva also tried to use Barzani, but in effect Barzani used the Heva. The Heva leadership wanted to move into the mountains to Barzan to work alongside Barzani and his developing army, but Barzani would not permit this, and blocked off all routes into Barzan to prevent its arrival. He needed the Heva to stay in Baghdad to act as his window on the world and to obtain information and supplies for him.

On 12 February 1945 Barzani formed the 'Freedom Party', which consisted of Kurdish officers, government officials and professional men. The majority were recruited on a non-tribal basis, the object being first to bring about cooperation between all the tribes in the Barzan region and then between all Kurdish tribes. Barzani's Freedom Party, which he soon retitled the Kurdistan Democratic Party (KDP), issued a stream of Kurdish nationalist propaganda. There was both friction and cooperation between Barzani and the Heva.

BARZANI'S REVOLT: AUGUST 1945

An incident at a police post at Margasur, near Barzan, in April 1945 started off a rash of other incidents until the whole Barzan region was in a state of simmering revolt, a condition that continued throughout the summer. Revolt suddenly erupted on 10 August, when Iraqi police attempted to disarm some Barzanis, which caused the Barzanis to attack and occupy several police posts. The Iraqi government immediately dispatched two small military columns, one towards Barzan and the other into the Baradosti tribal area just west of Barzan. Barzani's warriors counterattacked and claimed to have inflicted many casualties.

A third government military column penetrated a short way into the Zibari tribal area, just south of that of the Barzanis, and moving from Akra ran into an ambush organised by Barzani himself. For two days there was hard fighting, and it was only due to the support of the Iraqi air force, assisted by the British RAF, that government forces were able to hold their positions. Iraqi aircraft bombed Barzani villages and the Turkish government assisted by closing its frontier in the north.

During September the Iraqi government enlisted the aid of Kurdish tribes hostile to Barzani. This enabled all three government columns to move slowly forward, until Barzani and his small army were gradually compressed both from the east and the south, and up against the hostile Turkish border.

Realising he was in a trap, Barzani decided to break out before it was too late. His armed groups and their families concentrated just north of Barzan, from where in the last days of the month and the first week in October – in a long silent column, often moving at night – they slipped through the Iraqi military cordon across the border into Iran, making their way to Mahabad. It was generally estimated (although all authorities do not agree) that Barzani's retreating column consisted of about 9000 people, mainly Barzanis but also including a few allies. About 3000 were armed warriors, of whom only about 1200 were personally accountable to Barzani.

This brief Kurdish revolt in Iraq was the first time Kurdish political organisations had actively attempted to cooperate with tribesmen. It failed not so much because of the Iraqi military action against them, but because the Barzanis were disliked by certain tribes that could neither forget old enmities nor miss an opportunity to settle old scores when bribed to do so by government money, arms and promises. Political ideals of unity instantly evaporated. In this revolt the Barzanis were defeated by their old enemies the Baradostis, Surchis and Zibaris.

THE KURDISTAN DEMOCRATIC PARTY OF IRAN

In Mahabad in November 1945 Qazi Mohammed announced that the Komola would become the Kurdistan Democratic Party of Iran (KDPI), and although he held no formal office in this new political party he continued to dominate it. Its aims were autonomy for the Kurds, not complete independence. A Provisional Council of Kurdistan was to be formed. The party's manifesto was a nationalist one, including the use of the Kurdish language. All officials were to be Kurdish, there would be self-government in local affairs and Kurdish revenues would be spent in Kurdish areas. The KDPI was distinct and separate from Barzani's KDP.

A Soviet printing press arrived, and a Kurdish newspaper, *Kurdistan*, was published, which began openly to advocate independence. This was followed by a small consignment of Soviet arms, believed to be about 1200 rifles and pistols, as well as bundles of Soviet military uniforms. The euphoria generated by the Kurds in Mahabad was such that on 11 December 1945 the new Kurdish national flag was hoisted in the town.

On to this scene arrived Mullah Mustafa Barzani and his '9000 followers' in November. At first he was treated with suspicious reserve as he was thought to be in the pay of the British. However Qazi Mohammed, whose defence forces were negligible, cautiously welcomed Barzani and agreed that he and his allies could stay in areas just to the north-east of the town, and that a number could actually live in Mahabad. In view of Barzani's military strength and his own weakness, Qazi Mohammed could do no other.

KURDISH INDEPENDENCE

Contrary to Soviet advice, on 22 January 1946 Qazi Mohammed, wearing a Soviet-type uniform and his religious headdress, proclaimed Kurdish 'independence' to an assembly of Kurds in the 'Chwar Chura' ('Four Lamps'), the open square in the town of Mahabad in the 'Kurdish Republic of Mahabad'. On 11 February Qazi Mohammed was appointed president.

An attempt was made to draw in notables from all over Kurdish territory, especially from Turkey and Iraq, so that the cabinet would have a broad representation. However this did not materialise and the majority of the government, and its administration, were from Mahabad and Kurdish areas under Soviet influence, so although there were a few outsiders the new government could not claim to be truly representative of a Greater Kurdistan. The writ of the new republic only ran about 50 miles or so from Mahabad, stretching merely to Urmiya in the north and unable to incorporate the southern Kurdish areas of Saqqiz, Sanandaj and Kermanshah, which were under joint Anglo–American control.

Many traditional leaders quietly left the area rather than prejudice their own previous relations with the Tehran government. Their land was selectively redistributed, some going to the Barzanis. The three main tribes in the Mahabad area – the Dehbokri, the Mamesh and the Shikaki (Chaliand, 1993) – backed away and avoided involvement with the new republic. Although initially the Soviets persuaded Amir Khan of the Shikaki to join the government, he soon backed out again. While extremely popular in Mahabad, Qazi Mohammed was distrusted by many Kurds because of his seeming friendship with the godless Soviets, and the fact that during the First World War the Russians had sacked the city.

The two tribes nearest to Mahabad, the Mamesh and the Mangur, became openly hostile, and as soon as Barzani's armed followers had worn out their welcome in Mahabad they were sent to quieten them down.

THE MAHABAD ARMY

Qazi Mohammed had two major problems, the first being that the Soviets refused to guarantee the defence of his new republic. The second was that his only means of defence were small groups of armed followers of various sheikhs who had promised allegiance, but these were mercurial, undisciplined and of doubtful reliability. Work was in progress to organise government services and it was also decided to raise a standing army. A Soviet officer was sent to form and train it.

The Mahabad army received two more small consignments of arms in February 1946, believed to consist of about 5000 rifles, a few machine guns, ammunition and some petrol bombs (Eagleton, 1963). At a later date it also received a few Soviet and American military vehicles. These were by no means free gifts as the Soviets took the whole of the republic's tobacco crop in exchange.

At its maximum, in theory at least, the Mahabad army consisted of '70 officers, 40 non-commissioned officers and 1200 soldiers' (Chaliand, 1993). Most of the officers had formerly served in the Iranian or Iraqi armies, or auxiliary services, but many were at once seconded to undertake essential jobs in the administration, so the army was always under-officered.

The Mahabad army remained in or near Mahabad and never achieved any degree of effectiveness, becoming a sort of presidential guard. The real defence of the republic continued to rest in the hands of those tribal sheikhs who were able to muster groups of armed fighting men. Soon the army, as well as members of the government and officials, were clad in Soviet-style uniforms.

On 31 March the Mahabad government appointed four generals, one of whom was Mullah Mustafa Barzani. He proudly retained his rank and used it for the rest of his life. Barzani's personal armed following remained intact and apart, distrusting the Mahabad government. In fact Barzani was secretly lobbying the Soviet authorities to appoint him president in place of Qazi Mohammed, who seemed at times to lose control of events. However the Soviets refused as they did not trust Barzani, and in any case they no longer cared as they were in the process of withdrawing.

On 9 May 1946 the last Soviet troops pulled out from Iran, abandoning the Republic of Mahabad to its fate. The Iranian army, which had mustered about 13 000 troops, had been marching towards Mahabad since early April. Probably about 12 000 armed Kurdish tribesmen were available for defence (Eagleton, 1963), all still under the control of their own sheikhs, and a large proportion of them set off to defend their vague frontiers. For example contingents from the Shikaki and the Herki tribes moved to an area just north of Baneh.

Mustafa Barzani had managed to obtain a share of the Soviet-provided arms, said to be some 1200 rifles, which would bring his armed element up to the 3000 mark (Eagleton, 1963). Barzani marched south towards Saqqiz to counter a small Iranian force that had left that town on 24 April and was moving towards Mahabad. The Iranians were ambushed and the prisoners were send to Mahabad. This boosted the Barzanis' military reputation to such an extent that the government began to plan for a Kurdish, meaning Barzani, advance southwards to occupy as much Kurdish territory as possible.

THE BATTLE FOR THE MAMASHAH HEIGHTS

The Barzanis had taken up positions in mountains overlooking roads leading from Saqqiz to both Baneh and Sardasht (to the south-west), and so were able to block the Iranian advance. On 3 May, under an impromptu agreement between Mullah Mustafa Barzani and Iranian commanders, the Barzanis withdrew a little way to allow the Iranians road access to their beleaguered garrisons. This did not go down very well in Mahabad, where the government was planning to concentrate its forces at Saqqiz, preparatory to an offensive southwards to Sanandaj.

In early June the Barzanis reoccupied their former positions and began to snipe at Iranian military traffic on the roads below. On 13 June an Iranian military force, of probably 2000 men with supporting aircraft and tanks, moved out from Saqqiz to attack a small group of Barzanis who were blocking the Mamashah Heights, a few miles to the north-west. The Barzanis held out all day against aircraft bombing and artillery bombardment, but in the evening the Iranians finally overcame their defences. This was a significant tactical gain for the Iranians, but the Barzanis turned their stubborn defeat into a minor military epic and Barzani fighting stock rose to a new height in Mahabad. After this battle Barzani held local truce talks, and fighting in the area died down.

Increased Iranian military pressure caused differences to arise between Kurds, especially tribal Kurds and urban ones in Mahabad. Sensing a changing atmosphere and seeing little chance of loot, the traditional bait that kept them in the field, several small tribes withdrew their fighting contingents. These gaps in defences, especially on the main southern front, were filled by Barzanis as Barzani, seeing danger ahead, gathered his followers around him.

Probably the last major Mahabad aggressive move was made on 19 July, when cavalry elements of the Shikaki and Herki tribes advanced northwards towards the town of Maku, near the Soviet frontier, and the town of Khei, to the north-east of Lake Urmiya. The adjacent Republic of Azerbaijan (also struggling for expansion and survival) sent troops against them, forcing them to withdraw.

THE COLLAPSE OF THE MAHABAD REPUBLIC

In August, Qazi Mohammed travelled to Tehran to try to negotiate with the central government, which was then involved in a power struggle with the Tudeh Party. His lack of success heralded the writing on the wall. In October a new Iranian government was formed that was determined to restore government control over the whole country, moving first against the 'independent' Azerbaijan Republic. Iranian troops entered Tabriz, its capital, on 13 December 1946, when the self-declared republic collapsed.

As winter approached, tribal support for the Mahabad Republic had fallen rapidly away, and on 19 December its two main supporting tribes, the Shikaki and the Herki, moved off to Tabriz to change their coats. Barzani had withdrawn from his southern front, facing Saqqiz, to Mahabad, with the original intention of defending that town, but recognising that the position was hopeless from a military point of view, in early December he and all his followers moved to the Naqadeh area near the Iraqi border. Thus Mahabad was left with only hopeless remnants of its tiny, indifferent army.

On 16 December Qazi Mohammed went to Miandoab to surrender to the Iranian authorities, and the following day Iranian troops entered Mahabad, accompanied by the sheikhs of the Shikaki, Herki, Mamesh, Mangur and other tribes, who conveniently and timely switched loyalties, some more than once.

This was the humiliating end of the one-year-old Kurdish

Republic and the Iranian government set about destroying all vestiges of it. The printing press was closed, Kurdish books were burned, Kurdish political organisations were banned and townspeople and tribes in the area were disarmed. On 31 March 1947 Qazi Mohammed and two other leaders were hanged in Chwar Chura Square, and eleven tribal sheikhs suffered a similar fate.

It is probable that only 30 per cent of the administration of the short-lived Kurdish Mahabad Republic were Iranian Kurds, the remainder having arrived from Iraq, Turkey and Syria. During the period of Soviet occupation the Iranian Kurds had been left to their own devices, so some claim that the Kurdish Republic in fact endured for about four years.

Soviet radio propaganda failed to stimulate the Iranian Kurds into further resistance and eventually government pressure on them was relaxed, especially with regard to bans on the Kurdish language and dress, for the simple reason that they were unenforceable. The Kurds in Iran had already been badly shaken during the Second World War, when several tribes had been forced from their home areas. In one case 'out of the 10 000 members of the Talali tribe (that had lived near the borders with the USSR and Turkey) deported to central areas in Iran, only a few hundred returned' (Ghassemlou, 1965). Although the Tehran government was able to boast, with a degree of accuracy, that it did not have a Kurdish problem, the sting in the tail was that the illegal KDPI (formerly the Komola) survived underground.

A FIGHTING RETREAT

The well-armed Barzanis remained sullenly in the mountainous Naqadeh area, from where it was thought a major military campaign would be needed to dislodge them. Under safeconduct Barzani went to Tehran to negotiate, but spent a month there without reaching an agreement. The Iranian government offered to resettle the Barzanis around the Mount Alvand area, near Hamadan, if they would hand over their arms. Although Barzani seemed to be in favour, his elder brother, Ahmad Barzani, who had reappeared, was not. Barzani wanted to return home to Barzan (in Iraq), but neither the

British nor the Iraqi government were in favour, and neither would guarantee the safety of the Barzanis.

To Mullah Mustafa Barzani's surprise, in February 1947 the Iranian government mounted a military expedition against the Barzanis, supported by aircraft. The Barzanis were driven further into the mountains and on 22 February Iranian troops entered the small town of Naqadeh. The Iranians also mustered tribal enemies of the Barzanis to fight against them, and throughout March and April the Barzanis were pressed hard on land and harried from the air. Several clashes occurred in which Iranian troops suffered casualties.

In April Barzani led his dispirited people over the border into Iraq, with the intention of submitting to the Iraqi authorities. Almost immediately several Barzani leaders were arrested, others were deprived of property and land, and the whole group was put under close supervision. The following month four Barzani leaders were executed and Mustafa Barzani was condemned to death. The latter managed to evade arrest, although Ahmad Barzani surrendered. Barzani later told me that at the time he had been offered sanctuary in Britain, but had refused it as Britain was too far from Kurdish territory.

The situation became so acute that Barzani decided to fight his way through hostile territory to seek sanctuary in the USSR. Commencing on 27 May 1947, with '496 followers' (Eagleton, 1963) he moved out of Iraq, cut across the north-eastern tip of Turkey and moved west of Mount Dalanpur, on the border, before crossing the mountain ranges back into Iran. He then moved northwards, keeping to the west of Lake Urmiya, through the hostile territory of the Mamesh tribe, to cross the Aras river near Mount Ararat. During his trek, among other allegations 'he murdered eleven aghas' (Adamson, 1964). Barzani entered USSR territory on 15 June 1947, where he stayed for about 14 years.

KURDS IN IRAQ

During the Second World War the Kurds in the northern mountains of Iraq had been comparatively quiet, mainly because the Baghdad government had left them alone. After the war most refused to support the Mahabad Republic, largely out of dislike for the Barzanis. A detachment of Iraqi troops remained in Barzan. However in 1947, old-style traditional hostilities bubbled up again, first between the Barzanis, now led by Mohammed Khalid, son of Ahmad Barzani, and the Jaf tribe, which lived near Suliemaniyeh; and then between the Barzanis and the Pishdaris, who lived near Arbil. It was back to the normal routine again.

The following year there were riots in Baghdad, calling for the release of detained Kurds. Afterwards a period of temporary calm descended on Iraqi Kurdistan, usually accredited to the absence of an effective rabble rouser. The elderly Sheikh Mahmoud Barzanji, who had returned from exile, was infirm (dying in 1956); Sheikh Ahmad Barzani was under house arrest; and Mullah Mustafa Barzani was in the USSR, from where his warlike fame and reputation wafted continually into Kurdish homes.

4 Kurdish Repression: 1950–60

When the Second World War ended and all Allied occupation forces were withdrawn, the governments of Iran and Iraq were free to assert their authority over their Kurdish subjects, although this was somewhat restricted owing to the lack of competent, well-armed defence forces. Often mountain Kurds were left to fight amongst themselves or, if quiescent, left alone for the time being. On the other hand, in the cities detribalised Kurds became active in the Kurdish cause, making strides in political development.

THE UKDP

In Iraq, from the ashes of the Heva and Barzani's Kurdistan Democratic Party (his Freedom Party) arose the United Kurdistan Democratic Party (UKDP), which initially operated underground. In 1952 Ibrahim Ahmad, a communist, was appointed its secretary and the absent Mustafa Barzani was nominated as chairman, apparently without his knowledge or consent. His fame as an active Kurdish leader in the field had made him a star attraction. When the ban on political parties in Iraq was rescinded in 1954, the UKDP was able to operate openly.

COUP IN IRAQ

In Baghdad, on 14 July 1958 a group of free officers, led by Brigadier Abdul Karim Kassem, mounted a successful coup, killed King Feisal and formed a broad-based government that included the UKDP but excluded communists. A new Iraqi constitution was announced, which stated that 'Arabs and Kurds are considered partners in the homeland, and their national rights within Iraqi sovereignty are recognised', but went no further. This principle became known as the 'Partnership of

36

Arabs and Kurds', an expression that was bandied about for a while. Permission to publish a UKDP newspaper was refused, as was the request that the Kurdish Nowruz (New Year) be officially recognised as a public holiday.

Initially Kassem tried to be all things to all men (except communists), and a Kurd (Khalid Nakshbandi) was appointed to the three-man sovereignty council; another (Baba Ali) became a cabinet minister. The Kurds claimed they had played a major part in bringing Kassem to power and some evidence was put forward that Kassem's mother was a Kurd, although Kassem later denied this.

Ibrahim Ahmad led a UKDP delegation to ask Kassem for a degree of Kurdish autonomy. This was refused, but as a gesture of his good faith towards Kurds he released Ahmad Barzani from house arrest, along with many other detained Kurds, but reminded them that the Kurds were part of the Iraqi nation.

THE RETURN OF MULLAH MUSTAFA BARZANI

During his exile in the USSR, Mullah Mustafa Barzani met several senior Soviet officials, who attempted unsuccessfully to convert him to communism. He had been able to travel, visiting Baku and Moscow, and was in Prague when the Kassem coup occurred. Shrewdly he send Kassem a message of congratulations, whilst remaining, as usual, noncommittal. The UKDP wanted him back in order to drawn on his prestige and reputation. In addition, being largely an urban-based organisation, the UKDP wanted support from his tribal areas. The left-leaning UKDP hoped Barzani's stay in the USSR would either have communised him or at least softened his hostility to communist ideas and influences.

On 3 September 1958 Kassem pardoned all Kurds who had been involved in insurrectionary activities prior to his regime, including Mullah Mustafa Barzani. Kassem formally invited Barzani to return to Iraq to take over the leadership of the UKDP. Barzani hesitated for the unusual reason that, although he wanted to return to Iraq, he did not want to be involved with the UKDP. He later stated that 'I was forced to become President (of the UKDP) by Kassem' (Adamson, 1964).

Escorted back to Iraq by a UKDP delegation, Barzani's initial

meeting with Kassem was cordial, but became less so when
Kassem wanted him to forgive his Kurdish enemies. Barzani
would not agree, and so had to remain in Baghdad under
virtual house arrest, with only brief supervised visits to his
mountains. Barzani assumed the chairmanship of the UKDP
and worked uneasily for a while with the communist secretary,
Ibrahim Ahmad, who sought to keep the relationship alive,
knowing how slender the UKDP's urban base was and how
vital it was to obtain massive tribal support.

Traditional enemies of the Barzanis were apprehensive,
especially as some of them had to return confiscated land
and property that had been awarded to them by the government for fighting against the Barzanis. Kurdish sheikhs, landowners and tribesmen were all uneasy, suspecting the ultimate
Baghdad plan was to incorporate them into the Iraqi nation,
when they would be dominated by the Arab majority in all
aspects.

On 16 April 1959 the remainder of Mullah Mustafa Barzani's
followers on his fighting retreat and exile in the USSR, arrived
at Basra by ship and were accorded a heroes' welcome. They
numbered 850, the extra members being Kurdish refugees
who had joined them by force of circumstance, together with
a few 'planted' Sovietised Kurds.

In November 1958 a secret covenant of cooperation between
the UKDP, which was under certain restrictions, and the Iraqi
Communist Party, which was free and powerful, was signed.
This was really a plan to take over the UKDP completely, but
it was thwarted by Barzani and subsequent events.

POPULAR RESISTANCE FORCE

In August 1958 Kassem formed the Popular Resistance Force,
a political militia to defend his revolution. In Kurdish territory
it was dominated by followers of Barzani, some alleged to be
Soviet-trained. After occupying a number of frontier and police posts this section was nominally suspended in January 1959,
although in practice it continued aggressive activities against
Barzani enemies.

As soon as the winter snows began to melt, in April 1959 an

armed group of the Lolani tribe, which inhabited an area to the north-east of Ruwanduz and was led by Sheikh Mohammed Rashid, drove elements of the nominally suspended PRF from the villages of Naba and Kani. Baghdad's retaliation was to send aircraft to bomb Lolani villages. The attack was of such intensity that the whole tribe (estimated to number about 6000) moved across the frontier into Iran (*The Times*).

At the beginning of May Sheikh Abbas Mohammed and an armed element of the Pishdari tribe, which lived to the north-east of Suliemaniyeh, took similar action against the Barzani-led section of the PRF, ousting it from frontier and police posts. The Iraqi government mounted a military operation against the Pishdaris with aircraft support and involving the Barzani-section of the PRF, apparently overlooking its January suspension, but the Barzanis refused to obey orders. Again the ferocity of Iraqi bombing forced the whole of this 'Iraqi part' of the Pishdari tribe (which straddled the frontier and was estimated to number some 20 000) across the border into Iran, where they were housed in refugee camps (*The Times*).

Several other Kurdish tribes, especially those hostile to the Barzanis, showed signs of restlessness and of dislike of the 'Barzani-PRF', but the retaliation meted out to the Lolanis and Pishdaris caused them to exercise restraint. The lesson was not lost on Kassem, who placed the PRF in Kurdish territory under regular army officers, disbanding some subunits and disarming others. In June Kassem granted an amnesty to the Lolanis on condition they returned to Iraq, which they were persuaded to do by Ahmad Barzani, exercising his religious influence (Barzani had remained friendly with Kassem).

Realising how unpopular the Barzanis were, Kassem began playing Kurdish tribes off against each other, first giving arms to the Lolanis, then to the Zibaris, then to the Baradostis, and then to others selectively. This caused intertribal warfare to simmer on throughout the remainder of the year, and well into 1960. The situation became such that a group of tribal sheikhs travelled to Baghdad to lobby President (as he had become) Kassem, asking him to stop making trouble between them, and to remove all Kurdish officials from Kurdish territory and replace them with Arabs. Kassem did not meet these requests.

THE MOSUL MUTINY

In March 1959 a communist-inspired mutiny in Mosul, assisted by Nasserites (who wanted to include Iraq in Nasser's United Arab Republic project), was crushed heavily by Kassem, supported by Kurds. Two other Nasserite risings against Kassem, at Akda and Arbil, were crushed, also with Kurdish support. In April the UKDP was allowed to publish a newspaper. Despite resistance from Ibrahim Ahmad, secretary of the UKDP, Barzani drew the organisation away from the cooperation covenant with the communists and suspended all members who had agreed to it.

THE KIRKUK MASSACRE

On 14 July 1959, the first anniversary of Kassem's successful coup, fighting broke out in the streets of Kirkuk between Kurds and Turkomans, in which communist-influenced sections of the PRF were involved. Army units were called in to restore order, but many soldiers were Kurds who refused to fire on Kurds, and order was not restored until the 18th. Many people were killed and many more injured. Kassem later admitted that '79 had been killed, including 40 buried alive, and 140 injured' (*The Times*). This was the first real instance of urban Kurdish military muscle. It also marked the decline of communist influence in Iraq.

THE KURDISTAN DEMOCRATIC PARTY (KDP)

In January 1960, after a brief interval of suppression, certain political parties were again allowed to function openly, including the UKDP, the title of which Barzani insisted should revert to his original Kurdistan Democratic Party (KDP). Members of the KDP had the right to carry firearms, which was not normally permitted to Kurds outside their mountains. Barzani also concentrated on eliminating communists from the KDP. However Kassem was casting a new eye over Barzani and his KDP – they were growing too powerful.

THE FIFTH KURDISH CONGRESS

Soon after returning to Iraq from the USSR, Mullah Mustafa Barzani tried to organise an international Kurdish Congress, hoping his reputation would attract to his banner important Kurdish leaders from Turkey, Iran, Syria and elsewhere, but this failed. Kurds in Iran and Turkey were reluctant to risk punitive action from their own governments, which positively did not want the Kurds to unite – or even to mix – internationally; while Syria was openly hostile to Iraq at this stage.

President Kassem frowned on Mullah Mustafa Barzani. In an attempt to re-establish his claimed paramount position, Barzani held the 'Fifth Kurdish Congress', which was virtually a KDP one, on 5–10 May 1960 in the mountains, at which he was re-elected chairman and Ibrahim Ahmad, presumably still a communist, was re-elected secretary. To show his disapproval, at the same time Kassem received in Baghdad deputations of sheikhs from the Surchi and Herki tribes, traditional enemies of Barzani, who had deliberately absented themselves from the congress.

In the months that followed relations between Kassem and Barzani deteriorated. Kassem refused to consider any form of autonomy for the Kurds, many KDP members were arrested, provincial branches were closed and previously promised improvement schemes in Kurdish territory were deliberately ignored by the Baghdad government. This hard attitude against the KDP may be partly attributed to the fact that many urban Kurds held pro-communist sympathies. KDP meetings began to be held in secret in private houses.

BARZANI VISITS MOSCOW

Early in November 1960 Barzani left Iraq to visit the USSR, ostensibly to attend the annual Revolution ceremonies, but actually to try to persuade the Soviets to put pressure on the Iraqi government to make concessions to the Kurds, being encouraged by anti-Kassem propaganda that was beamed out from Moscow. In January 1961, Barzani returned to Iraq a bitter and disillusioned man, as he had been unable to elicit any favourable response from the Soviets, nor to obtain anything

from the Baghdad government. He reflected that once again
'The Kurds had no friends', a saying from their old brigand-
age days.

MORE TRIBAL CLASHES

During Barzani's absence fighting had broken out between
the Barzanis and their old enemies, the Zibaris and Baradostis,
who had been given arms by the Baghdad government. The
assumption was that Kassem wanted the Barzanis cut down to
size and their preeminence diminished.

In February 1961 there was a tribal clash between the Barzanis
and the Shaklawa tribe, led by Sheikh Niran Osman, a land-
owning ex-National Assembly, pro-Kassemite Kurd. Osman was
killed, and it was alleged that he had been murdered by Ibrahim
Ahmad, secretary of the KDP. A warrant for Ahmad's arrest
was issued, but later withdrawn. Ahmad went underground in
Baghdad, where he remained. Kassem cancelled a conference
of Kurdish teachers and closed down a Kurdish newspaper,
Khabat, the last one in circulation. General hostility made it
necessary for Barzani to have private bodyguards and for the
KDP building in Baghdad to have its own security guards.

Also in February, the Kurdish Arkou tribe, based in Raniya
and preparing for revolt, asked for KDP assistance, which did
not materialise. The Arkou revolt turned out to be a damp
squib. Recriminations followed – the Arkou insisted that the
KDP had let them down, while the KDP replied that it had
made no promises.

BARZANI RETURNS TO THE MOUNTAINS

In March 1961 Mullah Mustafa Barzani was allowed to leave
Baghdad and return to Barzan, where he was the dominant
Kurdish tribal leader. Technically he also remained chairman
of the KDP, but by this time he had lost much influence within
the organisation, which was now dominated by Ibrahim Ahmad
and the central committee. Publicly they gave the impression
they supported Barzani, but really it was his prestige and influence they wanted, especially as the KDP had little or none in

the mountains. In June Barzani presented a petition to Kassem, asking for the Kurdish language to be used in Kurdish schools and a share for the Kurds of the oil revenues from the Mosul and Kirkuk oil fields. Ahmad sent a similar petition to Kassem, who disregarded both.

The popular mood in Baghdad turned against the Kurds, and Arab workers demonstrated outside the KDP HQ building. There were scuffles, shots were fired and several demonstrators were killed or wounded. Lokman Barzani, a son of Mullah Mustafa Barzani, and several KDP members were arrested; others went underground. Ibrahim Ahmad wanted to join Mullah Mustafa Barzani in the mountains, but Barzani refused, demanding that he stay in Baghdad to procure information and supplies. Ahmad Barzani retained friendly relations with Kassem and was allowed to remain at liberty, becoming a sort of go-between between Barzani and the Baghdad government

KURDS IN IRAN

In Iran after the fall of the Mahabad Republic, activists of the Kurdistan Democratic Party of Iran (KDPI) went underground as the authorities were doing their best to suppress all traces of a Kurdish national identity. The first spark of revolt occurred in 1952, when the KDPI persuaded Kurdish peasants in the Bokan area to rise against their Kurdish landlords. Iranian troops swiftly marched against them, crushing resistance with a very hard hand. In succeeding years KDPI cadres managed to raise a few small rumbles of dissidence here and there, but these were contained by harshly repressive methods.

The KDPI met secretly in Iraq in 1956 and adopted a leftish programme, but it was not until after the Iraqi Revolution of 1958, encouraged by the rehabilitation of Mullah Mustafa Barzani, that it was revitalised and became active. However before it could get into its stride the Tehran government moved against it – members of the central committee were arrested and a campaign of harassment was launched against it.

In 1959 'at least 250 Kurdish activists were arrested' (*The Times*), while others escaped to Baghdad. The KDPI-in-exile in Iraq organised a conference, which produced a more moderate political leadership, under Barzani's urging, and many with

strong left-wing or communist views were forcibly prevented
from attending. By 1960 relations between Iraq and Iran were
deteriorating, mainly over conflicting boundary claims, but the
KDPI seemed reluctant to exploit this for its own benefit.

KURDS IN TURKEY

In May 1950 a general election was held in Turkey, the first
free one for 23 years, in which the People's Party, founded by
Ataturk, was defeated by the Democratic Party, led by Celal
Bayar and founded in 1946. Bayar became president and
Adnam Menderes prime minister. A more liberal regime was
introduced, and among other reforms Menderes promised the
restoration of workers' right to strike, within certain limits,
and freedom for the media. Kurds, with their language forbidden, had had no political standing under Ataturk's rigid integration policy, which continued under the Menderes regime.
If mentioned at all they were referred to simply as 'mountain
Turks'. That year a national census showed the population of
Turkey to be 20.9 million, an increase of 2.1 million over the
1945 figure. In February 1952 Turkey became a member of
NATO, which brought it into the Western camp and in confrontation with the USSR, with which it shared a joint frontier.

The Kurds had voted for the Democratic Party, and in
return for this support their exiled aghas and sheikhs were
allowed to return. Their property was restored to them and
once again they became feudal landlords, loyal to the central
government. Kurds were able to enter political life – a few
even became ministers and were able to help develop their
badly neglected eastern provinces. However there was one
proviso: they had to forget they were Kurds and become Turks.
Despite his initial liberalism, Menderes was an integrationist.

Influenced by Kurdish activism in Iraq and Iran, and exposed in eastern Anatolia to Kurdish broadcasts from across
borders, a number of Kurdish political activists developed a
policy that came to be known as 'Eastism', that is, pertaining
to the eastern provinces, advocating their economic development. However this veil was too transparent to disguise their
real policies, and soon '50 leaders were arrested. There were
limits to the Democratic Party's liberalism' (McDowall, 1985).

During the 1950s, as the economy of Turkey began slowly to improve, rural Turks, including Kurds, migrated towards cities and industrial areas. Thus a Kurdish urban element began to develop across the country. In addition, as Western Europe was short of unskilled labour, a huge westward wave of economic migration from Turkey began, which increased when Turkey was accepted into NATO. Finding themselves freed of domestic integration shackles, expatriate Kurds were able to form their own Kurdish associations and political groups in Western European cities.

During the 1950s the Kurdish population remained comparatively quiet, their main struggle being an underlying one of settled Kurds – shackled by feudal restraints – against their Kurdish aghas, and occasional insurgent protests by tribal mountain Kurds, usually led by a discontented sheikh. These soon came to be overshadowed by rivalry between the governing Democratic Party and the now opposition People's Party erupting into violence.

The Menderes government soon shed its liberal character and in 1952 it introduced stringent measures to curb press criticism of its activities. These measures were stepped up in 1954, when heavy penalties were imposed on those publishing adverse comments, which eventually resulted in much publicised trials and imprisonment of editors. Violent clashes between supporters of the two main political parties escalated, as did rowdy student demonstrations in both Ankara and Istanbul, in which the army on occasion had to open fire.

On 27 May 1960 a military coup was effected, the excuse being that it was essential to prevent civil war from breaking out between the two main rival parties. President Bayar, Prime Minister Menderes and many others were arrested, the Grand National Assembly was dissolved, and General Gursel became head of state. Mass arrests were followed by mass trials. In July, Turkish newspaper owners and editors had to sign a Code of Media Ethics. In September 1961 Menderes and two others were executed, and Bayar and many others were sentenced to long terms of imprisonment.

When the coup occurred many Kurds rose against the military government, momentarily forgetting their own political feuds. Extra army units were quickly drafted into Kurdish terrain, and international borders were blocked off as troops closed in on the dissidents, quickly crushing the revolt. Kurdish leaders were arrested, imprisoned or relocated, and concessions granted under the Menderes regime were rescinded.

Many of the detained leaders held feudal sway in the eastern provinces, especially 'in Van and Hakkari, some of them owning 50 or more villages as their personal property, together with immense flocks of sheep and herds of cattle' (*The Times*), where the writ of the central government hardly ran at all. One of the principal charges against the Menderes government was that it had given full rein to these landowners in exchange for their electoral support, in what were regarded as 'backward regions, where there is almost complete illiteracy, and much religious fanaticism' and where whole communities voted according to the instructions of the local landowner.

Of the some '244 land-owners and Sheikhs from eastern turkey' detained at Sivas, in central Anatolia, since the coup, '189 were released' in November, and under a compulsory resettlement law passed by the National Unity Committee, the remaining 55 were sent to enforced residence in Antalya, Bursa, Izmir and other centres in western Turkey, their estates being sold by the government (*The Times*).

5 The Kurdish Revolt in Iraq: 1961–62

The Kurdish Revolt in Iraq began to gather momentum in March 1961, when Mullah Mustafa Barzani arrived back in Barzan. In September, when government forces bombed Barzani villages, Barzani found himself leader of a full-scale armed movement against President Kassem. When he had ridden into the mountains his main intention had been to pay off a few old scores and he had had no intention of rising in arms against the central government: he was drawn into revolt by circumstances.

Barzani spent the summer successfully fighting against his old enemies, mainly the Lolanis and Zibaris, who had been armed by the central government. With his allies, who included the Arkou tribe and other smaller ones, he attacked all others that would not accept his authority. He concentrated upon dominating strategic passes and bridges, but avoided hostile contact with government troops, which generally remained passive.

Amongst his unlikely allies were small surviving groups of Assyrians, who were resentful at their neglect and poor treatment by the Baghdad government. Barzani mustered a force of some 5000 armed men, comprising Kurds and Assyrians (*New York Times*), who advanced into Zibari terrain, burning crops, destroying villages and forcing large numbers of Zibaris over the border into Turkey.

THE REVOLT BEGINS

The actual revolt began on 11 September when the Arkou detachment, led by Sheikh Abbas Mohammed, who was angered by the government's policy of land reform, attacked a military column near Bazyan on the road between Kirkuk and Suliemaniyeh. Kassem immediately responded by bombing Barzani villages, even though Barzani had not been involved in the incident.

This stung Barzani into activity, and his tribesmen and their allies attacked frontier and police posts, and forced their way into major villages and towns, including Zakho, driving out government personnel. Army and police patrols were ambushed and blocks were put on all mountain roads. By the end of September Barzani dominated a mountain area stretching from Zakho, near the Turkish frontier, southwards almost to Suliemaniyeh.

THE FIRST OFFENSIVE

Kassem reacted quickly and on 16 September 1961 launched what became known as the 'First Offensive', moving troops into Kurdish areas and bribing anti-Barzani tribes to fight on the government's side. Within a few days the main roads were reopened and Zakho reoccupied, but troops failed to regain control of the main mountain areas. Aerial bombing caused many casualties, including women and children, forcing families to take refuge in caves or other sheltered positions and dispersing tribal groups. Sustained bombing on this occasion for the first time really brought home to dissident Kurds the enormity and reality of their 'casualty problem', as Kurdish mountain villages were almost bereft of medical facilities or medical evacuation arrangements.

At a press conference on 24 September, Kassem admitted that a Kurdish revolt had erupted in the north and had spread to one third of Iraq, blaming the British and Americans for allegedly supplying arms and money, which they denied. On coming to power Kassem had withdrawn his country from the Baghdad Pact, a Western anti-Soviet treaty. He said that the 'rebels had burned over 50 villages' (*The Times*), but asserted that Zakho had been reoccupied and that the revolt would be crushed within a few days, admitting that many tribesmen had fled into Turkey.

In his next statement to the media, on 10 October, Kassem announced that the army was once again in control in the north and that all military operations had ceased. This was not completely true, but as winter was approaching the tempo was running down. One authority reported that '270 villages had been destroyed and several towns damaged' (*The Times*).

Kurdish casualties must have been heavy, but official figures were absent and no mention was made of government losses.

THE KDP

During the summer of 1961 the central committee of the KDP had been divided over which course of action to take. The majority, led by Ibrahim Ahmad, the secretary, had been in favour of delaying action as long as possible to enable the KDP to build up its strength, as it possessed few arms, and also because precipitous action might bring disaster. Ahmad had the failure of the Mahabad Republic in mind.

A minority of the KDP central committee, led by Jalal Talabani and Omar Mustafa, had been in favour of action, feeling that Kassem had lost the confidence of his army, which was probably one-third Kurd in composition. It was agreed that Talabani would travel to the mountains to see Barzani, still chairman of the KDP, and ascertain his opinion, but Talabani was overtaken by events.

On 23 September Kassem formally dissolved the KDP on the technicality that it had not held an annual conference, as required under the Iraqi Association Law. On the 26th the whole central committee decided to join Barzani in the mountains, but it seemed reluctant to leave Baghdad and did not move north until the first days of January 1962.

Barzani did not want the KDP central committee in the mountains at all, and he and his allied sheikhs refused to allow it into any of the areas they dominated. Eventually in March it settled in the southern part of Kurdish territory in the region between Raniya and Suliemaniyeh, in a sector just south of the Arkou tribe.

Many Kurds in Iraq, excluding tribal ones, now supported the unity of Iraq, having embraced its nationalism; some were even keen Kassemites. Several Kurds had become ministers or held other positions of authority, and were indifferent to Kurdish aspirations. Kurdish senior army officers, government officials, politicians, professional men, townspeople, oil workers and traders, all well detribalised, had become content to live with Iraqi national unity and were becoming proud of their new state, as well as out of sympathy with their backward, tribal brethren. Some were two, three or more generations removed from their tribal home. Kassem worried about potential disloy-alty among the Kurdish element in his army, and whether they would fight Kurdish rebels in the mountains. He need not have worried on the latter score.

BARZANI'S SPRING OFFENSIVE: 1962

Normally, military activity in the mountains ceased between November and the following spring thaw, as snow blocked most of the passes and made movement almost impossible. However on this occasion Kassem ordered his army to fight on throughout the winter, something the Iraqi army was in-capable of doing and therefore hostilities died down in Octo-ber. Units and small outlying garrisons in many places were withdrawn.

Barzani, on the other hand, urged his troops to carry on fighting using guerrilla warfare tactics, mainly against his tribal enemies, who also wanted a break during mid-winter, but also at a low level against Iraqi army positions and supply routes. These tactics enabled Barzani to regain and reoccupy territory from which he had just been driven, between Zakho and the Iranian border to the east. Barzani also seized and took over the administration of the town of Amadiya, the Assyrian base, despite Assyrian protests that they were his allies and had been helping him. This caused Barzani no qualms.

However by mid-December the weather became too severe for any movement and even the Barzani warriors had to call a halt, remaining passive until the spring. On 31 December 1961 Kassem admitted that 'the rebels had taken advantage of heavy snow falls and the withdrawal of several army units to renew their criminal acts' (*The Times*).

Barzani launched his spring offensive in late March 1962, which had some initial success as government troops were not expecting it quite so soon – snow was still blocking passes and choking roads, while bad weather restricted air activity. Barzani's Kurds attacked both Zakho and Dohuk, and although both towns held out they suffered losses, it being reported that government casualties were '50 killed and 150 wounded' (*New York Times*). Kurdish losses were not known.

Barzani then turned against his tribal enemies, and within a fortnight or so many of them had been forced to take refuge in Iran and Turkey. He claimed he had inflicted over 3000 casualties on them – this was not confirmed, although losses were thought to be heavy.

BARZANI'S MANIFESTO

During March Kassem had offered the Kurds a general amnesty if they would lay down their arms, but Barzani had not responded to this while his brief early spring offensive was in progress. He replied on 20 April, saying he would only cease firing if granted autonomy within an Iraqi constitution that guaranteed Kurdish legitimate political, social and cultural rights, and only then if the Kassem government was replaced by a democratic one.

At the same time Barzani issued a manifesto, emphasising that his aim was Kurdish autonomy, and not Kurdish independence, which attracted some Arab sympathy and avoided alienating Arab general opinion in Iraq and elsewhere. He had hit the right note. A few days later a statement by several prominent Iraqi Arab leaders, in support of Barzani's demand, was published in a Baghdad newspaper.

During the spring of 1962 Iraqi troops in the Kurdish region remained fairly defensive, merely launching a few limited punitive operations with the object of keeping road communications to their garrisons open. No 'scorched-earth' reprisals were carried out, although Iraqi planes continually bombed villages. Barzani's tactics were not to attack government-held towns, but to isolate them by disrupting communications and ambushing convoys. Occasionally supplies had to be dropped by air on besieged towns, some of which fell wide of their mark and were retrieved by tribesmen. Barzani claimed to have inflicted over 1000 casualties on government forces, which may have been so in his two-to-three-month spring campaign.

Barzani was not as restrained in his offensives against hostile tribes. Crops were burned, livestock were killed and villages were destroyed, the inhabitants frequently having to take refuge in either Iran or Turkey, whichever was closest, or to flee south-westwards on to the plains. Barzani was using fear to increase his coalition. Smaller tribes, for sheer expediency, joined him and his strength increased considerably. However he was still firmly resisted by larger tribes, including the Baradostis, the Herkis and the Surchis, which had been amply supplied with arms by the Baghdad government.

IRAN–IRAQ RELATIONS

Kurdish tribesmen who had been pushed over the border into Iran were later allowed to return to Iraq through the mediation of the shah, who made it a condition to Kassem that they should not be enlisted to fight against Barzani, while Barzani was made to promise that he would not use them to fight against the Iraqi government. Relations between Iraq and Iran were poor in the 1960s because of frontier differences, and because the shah secretly meddled in the Iraqi Kurdish problem, sometimes to placate his own border Kurdish tribes, which were hostile to Barzani. Covert contact was maintained between the governments of Baghdad and Tehran, and Barzani in the mountains.

BARZANI AS A LEADER

Although personally disliked, distrusted and feared by many tribal Sheikhs by 1962, Mullah Mustafa Barzani had come to be regarded as the undisputed leader of loosely defined Kurdish nationalism. He seemed to be slowly overcoming, by threats and military intimidation it was true, the reluctance of the Kurds to unite as a race, at least in Iraq. His military image as a general in the Mahabad army and his fighting retreat to the USSR were being polished, although his misdeeds and deviousness were not overlooked, especially by his numerous enemies. His main advantage in achieving this reputation pinnacle as a Kurdish military leader was largely because there seemed to be no other reputable contender for that position at that critical moment in Kurdish history.

There is no doubt that he had a strong and persuasive personality, and on occasions I have seen him haranguing groups of reluctant tribesmen, who within minutes were eating out of his hand. He possessed a certain magnetism, his leadership was a personal one, and he seemed to be forever on the move and always in contact with sheikhs and active tribesmen. Barzani was a master of mountain and tribal warfare. His political philosophy and lack of foresight were another matter, but mountain Kurds were more concerned with the fruits of war than the reasons for it. All factions had supported his April manifesto without question.

Apart from a small, trusted bodyguard of some 50–100 of his own tribe, he had to rely upon tribal militias and irregulars to do the fighting for him. These were either volunteers or had been detailed for service by their own sheikhs. They were undisciplined and unreliable. As Barzani did not hold a conventional front line, or even vaguely delineated sectors, but merely moved between government-held garrisons and posts and road communications, these impromptu 'auxiliaries' were suitable for laying ambushes and hit-and-run assaults. They were of especial value in intertribal fighting, which had for them the added zest of pillage and the destruction of their enemies.

At first these auxiliaries were usually assembled for a particular action or raid, after which they returned home to carry on normal life, often hiding their weapons in caves or burying them in fields to avoid being disarmed in any government searches. Their disadvantages were that they would not move far from home, stay in hostile territory too long or fight a particular enemy continually. They were fickle in that they might decide to stop or start fighting as the mood took them, or even to return home at any moment. As more Kurdish officers deserted from the Iraqi army to join Barzani in the mountains, they were set to work to organise, train and bring some semblance of order and regularity into this partisan movement.

As semi-trained armed volunteers became available, some were 'mobilised' to guard strategic locations, defend territory, be available to counterattack if government forces assaulted, and for opportunity operations. This system of part-time militia service gradually strengthened until Barzani had between 5000 and 8000 mobilised but scattered warriors under his direct influence. Total command was another matter, as local sheikhs were reluctant to relinquish their authority over their own tribesmen, no matter where they were. The concept of a standing army, or even a mobilised one, was foreign to mountain Kurds and one that Barzani did not want at that stage, being content to have a fluid mass of militiamen that government forces were unable to target and pin down with any precision. The KDP central committee wanted Barzani to raise a large standing army, which it could penetrate and hopefully subvert.

Although on the surface the KDP central committee continued to accept Barzani's leadership role and openly supported his manifesto, relations between them deteriorated. For his part, Barzani maintained a stand-offish attitude towards them. The KDP central committee set about organising a standing army in its own area.

THE PESH MERGA

The armed force raised by the KDP central committee was known as the Kurdish Revolutionary Army ('Lashgar-i-Shoreshi-ye-Kurd'), which at first had no formal ranks but followed the communist pattern. The 'leaders' became known as 'Sar Merga' (Leading Death) and the soldiers as 'Pesh Merga' (Facing Death), hence Pesh Merga came to be the collective name for the whole force, later copied by Barzani and then used by the media. It began with a small collection of tribal, urban and professional Kurds, the latter including lawyers and teachers (but no doctors, I was later told). Although the force had many teething troubles, by the end of the summer it was reputed to be almost 3000 strong. The KDP Pesh Mergas became more politically orientated than those of Barzani.

As the Pesh Mergas took shape, the smallest group of fighters became known as a 'dasteh' (section), which could be merged to form a 'pel' (company). In turn a number of these could be grouped into a larger formation for operational purposes, known as a 'sar-pel' (battalion or unit), which usually had some 200–250 men. Larger formations were beyond Kurdish means and comprehension. This process took time to accomplish, and for many months subunits and units were known by the names of their leaders. Barzani had the problem of overcoming sheikhs' resistance to the loss of authority over their Pesh Mergas.

By the end of 1962 the KDP central committee had established a central HQ, with both political and military branches. Barzani's Pesh Merga did not have a formal HQ for some time as he was always on the move, having developed a fear that Iraqi aircraft were seeking him out as a target.

At first the Pesh Mergas did not have uniforms, but early on they adopted special badges to indicate units and affiliations. As government uniforms were captured, they were issued out to the men. Early Pesh Mergas were ill-armed, mainly with rifles such as Mausers and French models, some quite old, but the situation improved as weapons, including automatic ones and mortars, were captured from government forces. Weaponry was also brought over by deserters, or otherwise obtained by theft or bribery from Iraqi army sources. Barzani later told me that his heaviest weapon at that stage was a 60mm mortar, and how he longed for a heavier one with a longer range, with which he could bombard Iraqi army encampments.

Contrary to widespread allegations and rumours, neither the USSR nor the Western powers at that stage provided Kurdish insurgents with aid or arms, but Pesh Mergas did obtain weaponry from arms bazaars in Beirut and elsewhere, money being raised by Kurdish agents in Lebanon, Iran and Syria.

Ammunition supply was a continual worry to the Pesh Mergas, as although most of them had been accustomed to using firearms since boyhood, their sense of fire discipline was nonexistent. They were also apt to fire off bursts into the air when excited, and more to the point consensus opinion seemed to be that their marksmanship left much to be desired, although there were obviously many exceptions to this generalisation. Ammunition was very heavy, so only small quantities at a time could be carried in by man or pack animal. Mortar bombs brought in over mountain passes on the backs of donkeys could be fired off within a few seconds, which meant that such mortars as the Pesh Mergas came to possess were often impotent through lack of ammunition.

As the strength of the Pesh Mergas and the duration of mobilisation increased, problems of provision, supply and distribution of food and other necessities arose. For example food and ammunition had to be carried to mountain outposts and other positions by either man or donkey; primitive methods that considerably restricted tactical mobility. The Pesh Merga captured, or otherwise obtained, a few military field radio communication sets, but as their range was often blocked by mountains they were of limited operational use. However they did occasionally allow them to intercept local Iraqi army messages, often enabling them to ambush military supply convoys.

THE KDP SECTOR

Barzani refused to allow any of the elements of the 'Kurdish Revolutionary Army' into his area, and indeed sent his tribal militias to enforce this decision. Therefore two separate, and separated, Kurdish insurgent sectors appeared, the larger northern one, controlled by Barzani, and a much smaller one to the south, controlled by the KDP central committee. The KDP sector materialised where the Barzani writ did not run, in a rough triangle between Raniya in the north, Suliemaniyeh in the south and Kirkuk in the west. The KDP organised its sector into four areas: one based in Malouma, near the centre of the triangle close to the Iranian border, commanded by Ibrahim Ahmad, secretary of the KDP; one at Chwarta, some 30 miles north-west of Panjwin; one at Chami Razan, just north of the Suliemaniyeh–Kirkuk road, commanded by Jalal Talabani; and the fourth, commanded by Omar Mustafa, at Betwahta, about 20 miles north-west of Raniya, the most northern point of the KDP sector, beyond which lay 'Barzani country'.

IRAQI BOMBING

The Iraqi air force, with some 300 fairly modern combat aircraft at its disposal, had been used extensively since September 1961 to bomb, rocket and machine-gun insurgent Kurdish villages. Instead of lowering the morale of the inhabitants, it had the converse effect of uniting many Kurds behind Barzani and against the Iraqi government. These air raids were usually completely unconnected to ground operations and were selectively targeted against tribes supporting Barzani – anti-Barzani tribes, or those that had accepted government bribes to either fight against him or remain neutral, were spared. Tribes that reneged were punished by aerial retribution.

Occasional statements were issued by Barzani, and in one he alleged that in January 1962 some 500 Kurdish villages had been attacked by Iraqi aircraft, and some 80 000 people made homeless. Another statement alleged that during June 1962 about 50 000 people had been killed or injured in air attacks. A consensus of current reports indicated that in the first half of 1962 a probable 3000 people had been killed and 180 000 made homeless in Kurdish areas, but it was all guesswork at that stage – no one knew precisely, only that the slaughter and destruction were considerable.

In July and August the Iraqi government mounted a major aerial onslaught on Kurdish areas in an effort to demoralise resistance completely, but even though the Pesh Mergas had no anti-aircraft weapons, this did not happen. One anomaly was that Barzan, Barzani's home town, was bombed only once and then left alone by Iraqi planes. This was accredited to the fact that Sheikh Ahmad, Barzani's brother, lived there and was a useful intermediary between Barzani, the KDP and the Baghdad government.

THE JASH

Government auxiliaries, meaning Kurds recruited to fight against insurgent Kurds, came to be known as 'Jash', a derisive expression meaning 'little donkeys'. They mainly belonged to tribes hostile to Barzani, but also included a few Barzanis out of sympathy with Barzani or his policies – Barzanis often squabbled amongst themselves. The Jash were mobilised for short, contracted periods of service and at their maximum probably numbered about 10 000, although their strength declined as it became less popular to fight against Barzani and campaigning became more dangerous and less rewarding.

The Jash remained organised on a tribal basis, under their own leaders, and received only general directions from the Iraqi commanders they were supporting. They did not develop into a disciplined military force with an effective capability. Jash were often employed to take action against minor tribes supporting Barzani, and were prominent in killing livestock, burning crops and demolishing buildings, to take the odium from Iraqi troops. The Jash also operated with some zeal against the few remaining groups of Assyrians, and several instances of atrocity came to light. As the need for the Jash lessened and they were gradually forced onto the defensive as Barzani targeted them, recruiting became a problem and their numbers sank to about 5000.

On the other side of the fence, Barzani had already changed his mind about 'scorched earth' activities, realising it was not to his ultimate benefit to devastate Kurdish territory when he could barely feed his own Pesh Mergas. He therefore gave instructions for this barbaric practice to cease, after which only a few minor examples occurred, chiefly as punitive measures or when tribesmen got out of hand.

SUMMER 1962

By summer 1962 Kurdish insurgents dominated a huge area in the Iraqi northern mountains, extending from the Turkish border in the west to the edge of the Khaniqin oilfields in the south-east – a huge crescent-shaped area of some 300 miles in extent and up to 70 miles in depth. Within this crescent Iraqi government presence had disappeared, especially along the borders with Turkey and Iraq as frontier police and guards had either joined the insurgents or openly collaborated with them while remaining in uniform.

The Iraqi army controlled the main roads during daylight hours, while the Kurds retained the freedom of the valleys and mountainsides, although hostile air activity restricted their daylight movements. The aim of the Pesh Mergas was to block roads in an attempt to starve out government garrisons, and to ambush convoys by day, a form of warfare that suited the Kurdish character. For example the road running north-east from Arbil to Ruwanduz was almost continually blocked as a result of sabotage.

At night government troops stayed defensively in their garrisons and camps, and even by day seldom left their positions unless absolutely necessary. Each morning at dawn Iraqi T-34 tanks would emerge from their defences to break through or clear away any obstructions erected on roads during the night by Kurds. With overhead aerial cover, Iraqi military convoys were able to move along most main roads, any obstruction or ambush being dealt with by heavy bombing and artillery fire. The armed forces were being re-equipped with some Soviet material, as Iraq was now being ostracised in this respect by the Western powers.

Conditioning played a part in this struggle as Kurdish insurgents were at home in the mountains, while the members of the mainly Arab-manned Iraqi army from the plains and cities were not. Even the Kurdish recruits (stoically fighting their Kurdish brethren) were mostly long since detribalised and unfamiliar with mountainous terrain. The Kurds were in their historical defensive position, while the Iraqi army, trained for conventional warfare, hesitated helplessly before them, not yet being conditioned to or trained in mountain warfare.

In early autumn Barzani discussed plans to attack and seize Arbil and then Kirkuk, both of which he claimed to contain by night, under the impression that morale in these two garrisons was low, and then to move on to attack and gain a foothold in Suliemaniyeh. However these plans came to nothing as they were beyond the capability of the poorly armed Pesh Merga. In late October mustered Pesh Merga began to return to their home villages before the winter set in. Both Barzani and the KDP central committee had difficulty in holding together a small cadre, and all sides slowed to a stop at about the same time. Several small army garrisons were withdrawn and others remained isolated, some having to be supplied by air throughout the winter months.

PRISONERS

Prisoners were taken by both sides in this conflict. Non-Kurdish Iraqi military personnel who fell into Kurdish hands were usually released after being disarmed, as feeding and guarding them were unwelcome burdens. A few were retained for menial tasks around the camps. When captured, those who were Kurdish were usually persuaded to turn their coats – if they resisted they were put into labour gangs. For propaganda purposes it was invariably claimed that such men were not 'prisoners', but 'deserters from government forces'. Captured Jash had a rough time, and if they survived they too were drafted into labour gangs.

A Barzani statement in November 1962 claimed that the Kurds were holding about 2000 prisoners, about half of whom were Jash. It also stated that, only '172 Kurdish men had been killed or wounded in battle' that month, and that none had been taken prisoner. These figures were regarded with scepticism, but casualty figures of any sort were scarce, and reliable ones more so. Iraqi government forces also held prisoners, presumably about the same number, on the hostage-insurance principle, although small fry were usually released against a promise not to take up arms again.

SABOTAGE AND TERRORISM

Somewhat surprisingly in this type of warfare, the vital oil pipeline from Kirkuk through to Syria and the Mediterranean terminal at Baniyas suffered remarkably little sabotage. Barzani's view was that it would be foolish to disrupt a source of wealth, of which he soon hoped to obtain a large share. The more far-sighted KDP central committee also agreed with this policy but for a different reason, feeling that such sabotage would alienate Western and world opinion, although a minority dissented.

An attack had been made on some oil installations in the Ain Zallah oilfield near the Syrian border, in which some lives had been lost and buildings destroyed. The attack did not seem to have been authorised by either Barzani or the KDP. This was followed in August 1962 by Kurds blowing up part of the oil pipeline near Kirkuk.

During the winter of 1962–3 small groups of Kurds entered Arbil, Kirkuk and Suliemaniyeh to kidnap individuals considered to be traitors to the Kurdish cause, taking them away and shooting them. It was estimated that at least 50 people disappeared during the winter in this manner in Suliemaniyeh alone. These Kurdish night-time terrorist activities caused some alarm, and did much to curb the anti-insurgency opinions of detribalised Kurds.

On 10 October 1962 a British oil technician was kidnapped by the Kurds and held for some weeks as a 'guest', in an attempt to attract world opinion to their cause. Another British subject was seized and treated as a 'guest' on 26 November. The Iraqi government tried to clamp a veil of secrecy over their Kurdish insurgency, forbidding foreign journalists to visit Kurdish areas or the battle fronts, but by this time a small number of Western journalists had managed to enter Kurdish 'forbidden territory' in secret, including David Adamson of the *Sunday Telegraph* and Dana Adam Schmidt of the *New York Times*, who sent back enlightening dispatches.

IRANIAN SUPPLIES AND CONTACTS

In Iran, where since May 1961 the shah had ruled by decree, having closed down the Majlis, there was some degree of satisfaction at President Kassem's discomfiture over his Kurdish problem. While officially disclaiming any contact with insurgent Kurds in Iraq, the Iranian government began to sent some covert aid across the border, including small quantities of arms and ammunition. Most of the aid was sent to the KDP central committee, which had developed direct cross-frontier underground contacts with Tehran. A KDP radio station began to operate on Iranian territory, broadcasting news of events in northern Iraq and anti-Kassem propaganda.

Being under the impression he had his own Kurds fully under control, the shah had ignored the fact that many of them were strongly anti-Barzani. This was especially the case with the large cross-border Mamesh tribe, which vigorously opposed aid being sent through its territory to Barzani. The shah suddenly realised that he too could soon have a Kurdish problem on his hands, and began to move troops into his Kurdish region.

TURKISH–IRAQI HOSTILITY

In Turkey, in 1961 a new constitution was promulgated, which relaxed some political restrictions and resulted in the appearance of a number of political parties and groups. Most of these were very small and seemed to be divided into right wing and radical left wing. Kurds, in their guise as Turks, both urban and rural, responded well to this new political opportunity and invariably joined radical parties. This seemed to fragment rather than unite them, as new would-be Turkish political leaders pedalled their own pet ideologies and demands. A few parties did however include some 'eastern' interests in their manifestos in order to broaden their membership, but not in any separatist context, and a few Turkish–Kurdish dual-language journals made a timid appearance.

From 1962 onwards relations between Turkey and Iraq began to deteriorate, and a number of border incidents occurred involving arms smuggling. As Turkish Kurds were fairly quiet at that time the Turkish government did not want them to become agitated by the Iraqi Kurdish insurrection, and so it formed a 12-mile-wide strip of territory, extending almost along the whole length of the 210-mile Turkish–Iraqi border. This became a 'forbidden zone' (from which many inhabitants were forcibly evacuated), which was was heavily garrisoned and patrolled by the military. This drastic measure did much to curb the cross-border arms traffic that was developing, but did not stop it altogether.

On 9 July 1962 an Iraqi aircraft bombed a Turkish frontier post, and on the 16th, in a similar incident, two Turkish soldiers were killed. The Iraqi government apologised, claiming the actions had been accidental. However Turkish combat aircraft were detailed to patrol the forbidden zone, and on the 18th shot down an Iraqi plane, killing its pilot. The Iraqi government protested, alleging that the aerial clash had occurred '48 miles inside Iraqi territory' (*Sunday Telegraph*). It went on to accuse Turkey of helping the Kurdish insurrection in Iraq, of collaborating with it and of an inability to control its own frontiers. Turkey denied the allegations and withdrew its ambassador from Baghdad.

There was some liaison between Kurds in Iraq and Kurds in Turkey, but so far it had been spasmodic and ineffectual, having little influence on the course of the Barzani insurrection. Kurds on both sides of the border were shortsighted and excessively insular.

INTERNATIONAL AWARENESS

Meanwhile some Kurdish ethnic and nationalistic groups in Western European cities were becoming active and politically aware, although few had direct contact with Kurdish insurgents back home. One of the most prominent was the 'Committee for the Defence of the Kurdish People's Rights' (CDKPR), based in Lausanne (Switzerland), which set out to represent Kurdish interests internationally, and to collect funds for this purpose. The CDKPR had some contact with Barzani, who was a great letter writer, and openly supported him as leader of the Iraqi Kurds in his struggle, although it did not always see eye to eye with him on policy.

On 12 February 1963 the CDKPR issued a statement, declaring that association between Kurds and Arabs must be based on an autonomous Kurdish government in Iraq; that Iraqi troops must quit Kurdish territory; and that an equitable division of oil revenues must be made between the Kurds and the Arabs. This was followed by another statement, on the 15th, denying that it had anything at all to do with communism, a slur that was frequently hurled at Kurdish left-wing organisations in that period. This dictatorial support was not exactly welcomed by the autocratic Barzani.

6 The Second and Third Offensives in Iraq: 1963–65

On 8 February 1963 the Baathist Party – in league with the Free Officers Movement in Iraq – mounted a coup, in which President Kassem was killed and replaced by a national council. Colonel Abdul Salem Aref soon became president. Kassem had initially been friendly towards Iraqi Kurds but had subsequently adopted a hard line against them, so they now hoped for more sympathetic treatment. They were to be disappointed. Talks between the Kurds and the new Baghdad government began on the 19th, with Jalal Talabani as the Kurdish negotiator. The Kurds asked the government to put its proposals in writing, but at once differences arose over the expression 'decentralisation', focusing on the control of foreign affairs and the armed forces. Barzani and Talabani remained adamant in their demands. The Lausanne-based CDKPR, without consulting Barzani, rejected the Baghdad demands, which did not please him.

Talabani continued to lead the Kurdish delegation and visited Egypt to solicit President Nasser's support, who told him that while he could favour Kurdish autonomy within Iraq, he could not support Kurdish independence, which Talabani was touting for. American contacts gave Talabani a similar reply. At the time Nasser was trying to create a solid Arab coalition front against Israel and did not welcome diversions, while the Americans were mainly concerned with the Cold War. On their return to Kirkuk Talabani and his delegation were arrested and held for a while.

The Central Treaty Organisation (CENTO), which superseded the Baghdad Pact when Iraq dropped out, included Turkey (now a NATO member), Iran and Pakistan and was considered to be the West's south-western bastion against the USSR. Its vague forward defence line included Kurdish regions of Turkey and Iran, while those of Iraq now formed a gap. The Western European governments, most of whom were members of NATO, viewed Iraqi Kurdistan with some anxiety in case it be subverted by the Soviets. In general the Soviets were assumed to be in sympathy with Kurdish aspirations, but official tongues in the West were discretely silent on this issue in case a verbal slip should cause Iraqi Kurds to turn towards the USSR for support.

In Baghdad negotiations faltered as arguments developed over the release of prisoners and other details. The Soviets mounted a hostile propaganda campaign against Iraq in support of the Iraqi Kurds, which caused President Aref to allege that the Soviets were supplying them with arms and money, although there was no evidence of this at the time. The Baghdad government made similar wild allegations about the USA, China and other nations, again without supporting evidence. Aref was more cautious about what he said about the Iranians, who were actually about to supply arms to the KDP central committee region.

THE SECOND OFFENSIVE: JUNE–OCTOBER 1963

During the month of May, additional Iraqi troops were moved northwards to contain the Kurdish region, mountain roads were blocked, fortifications and camps constructed, and extra supply bases established. Progressively, curfews and other restrictions were placed on 'mixed ethnic' areas and towns, while oil installations were declared 'prohibited zones', where trespassers could be fired upon – in short they were almost 'free fire zones'. Barzani urged Kurds living in such mixed towns and areas to return to their traditional homes in the mountains, but few seemed to respond.

The Iraqi government's 'Second Offensive', as it became known, began in the early morning of 10 June 1963. Troops moved forward on three separate fronts, using 'four infantry groups on each one, making a total force of 12 divisions' (*New York Times*). The northern column moved against the Barzani sector; the central column, commanded by Omar Mustafa, against part of the KDP sector; and the eastern column against Chami Razan. During the first week these three columns slowly pushed their way along their axes, supported by aircraft, tanks and artillery, picketing the hills as they leap-frogged forward, securing lines of communications.

When announcing its military offensive the Baghdad government had demanded that the Kurds lay down their arms within 24 hours, and placed a price on Barzani's head – dead or alive. Curfews were imposed in Arbil, Kirkuk and Suliemaniyeh, and all Kurds settled on the outskirts of Kirkuk were ordered to return to their homes. The two Kurdish ministers in the Aref government resigned.

The Kurds had prepared as well as they could to meet this expected Second Offensive, mainly by stocking up with food. Shortage of ammunition remained their main problem. It was estimated that the Kurds could muster about '25,000 men, slightly more than in the First Offensive, of whom some 15,000 were Pesh Mergas', the remainder being tribal militias (*New York Times*). The major part of this force was in the northern Barzani sector, with a smaller contingent in the KDP sector, the latter being the target of the government's central and eastern columns. Barzani still had no formal HQ as he was continually on the move and had been stimulated into increased mobility by the price on his head.

On the northern front, Iraqi troops soon occupied large areas of the foothills, with detachments moving individually along roads to Zakho, Dohuk and Akra. Aircraft provided direct support and tanks bulldozed their way through roadblocks. In the face of this relentless advance, in order to avoid being trapped or surrounded some Kurds abandoned their villages to live in valleys. This caused no particular hardship in the summer months, but it left them defenceless. As government troops reached Akra, and then approached Zibar and Barzan, the Kurds were forced farther back into the mountains, where there was an almost total absence of motorable roads. There they expected to be fairly safe from attack, but on this occasion government troops pushed forward on foot in places, surprising the Kurds by their adaptability and new aggressiveness.

On 1 August Zibar was occupied without opposition. Barzan followed on the 4th, while to the west Zakho was entered on the 10th, as Iraqi troops flooded into northern mountainous areas adjacent to the Turkish frontier. Barzani was pushed right back into remoter mountains, but his Pesh Mergas and tribal militias remained more or less in their groups.

By September government military momentum had run down, and the auxiliaries – the 'Jash', of whom there were about 3000 – were left to contain the Barzani forces in their precarious, rugged refuge areas. This was an unexpected setback for Barzani, and made a big dent in his military reputation.

On the central front government military columns thrust forward in the direction of both Ruwanduz and Raniya, but one column almost immediately ran into deep trouble as it became trapped in the formidable Ruwanduz Gorge by a force of about 400 KDP Pesh Mergas, commanded by Omar Mustafa. Other contingents of the central column had to be diverted from their objectives to rush to its assistance.

Intense fighting continued for possession of the Ruwanduz Gorge. The Pesh Merga continued to hold on to their positions, despite heavy aerial bombing, and it was not until 12 August that the Gorge was at last in the hands of government troops. The central front drive had become bogged down almost before it began.

On the eastern front, facing Suliemaniyeh, the first priority of the government columns was to open and clear the road from Kirkuk to Suliemaniyeh. However, in the face of stiff KDP Pesh Merga resistance, the leading element moved forward so slowly that it had to be constantly reinforced. Kurds had to be driven from each position, one by one, by bombing and shelling. It took some eight weeks to open the road, after which military momentum ran down in this sector.

SABOTAGE AND TERRORISM

Coincident with the Second Offensive, about 200 Pesh Merga in small groups embarked upon a campaign of sabotage and terrorism. On 17 June two oil wells at Jambur (20 miles south of Kirkuk) were blown up, and on the 22nd military installations at Kirkuk were attacked. In the fighting that ensued the Baghdad–Kirkuk railway was blocked for some hours.

Government countermeasures were harsh, and the inhabitants of many Kurdish villages within a 25-mile radius of Kirkuk were driven out and their houses destroyed, while livestock were killed and crops burned. On 30 June Barzani announced that already '167 villages had been wiped out, 1,943 civilians had been killed or wounded, including 137 children under

three years of age' (*New York Times*). President Aref was proving to be just as deadly and ruthless as President Kassem, and
his aircraft bombed and rocketed wide areas.

There had been little deliberate Kurdish sabotage in the
Barzani sector, although the government was anxious about
the Dukan Dam on the Greater Zab river, which was floodlit
by night and well guarded. However there was some activity in
the Baghdad area, where on 2 June an explosion occurred at
the Rashid detention camp. This was attributed to Kurdish
saboteurs, but later the Baghdad regime announced there had
been another explosion at the same camp on 3 July and this
was linked to a failed plot to overthrow the Aref regime. Thus
Kurds were not the only activists in this field.

The Iraqis raised a small unit of irregular troops, known as
the Saladin Force, which was trained and equipped on antiguerilla warfare lines. It was to have been composed of local
Arabs and detribalised Kurds in order to demonstrate unity of
purpose against mountain Kurd insurgents, but few Kurds could
be persuaded to join it. The Saladin Force seems to have been
effective in that KDP Pesh Merga subversive operations tended
to subside.

During the Second Offensive, Sheikh Ahmad Barzani, still
the go-between for the Baghdad government, announced he
would take to arms beside his brother, but nothing came of
this as he could not persuade the KDP central committee to
hand over any weapons to his followers. Ahmad Barzani lapsed
back into neutrality and Aref found him a useful tool.

On 30 July 1963 the government reopened negotiations
with the Kurds, dismayed by the lack of progress in the then
ongoing battle for the Ruwanduz Gorge, but still demanded
that the Kurds lay down their arms and accept 'centralisation'.
Jalal Talabani, who had returned to his KDP sector by way of
Iran, led the Kurdish delegation, asserting that they were at
the behest of the Baghdad government. The talks were inconclusive and collapsed on 11 August.

THE SECOND OFFENSIVE RESUMED

In September government forces resumed their offensive,
putting pressure on all three fronts in an attempt to crush

Kurdish resistance before the winter set in. They made little or no progress on the northern and central fronts, but on the eastern front they had better fortune. In a well-coordinated attack the KDP Pesh Merga was driven from its Chami Razan HQ, which was situated in caves in a large valley. After this the government military situation tended to regress.

During October an internal power struggle erupted in Baghdad and a number of military units were hastily recalled to the capital, severely weakening and even denuding the Kurdish fronts. On 18 November an Iraqi-army-instigated coup was mounted against the Baathist Party and the Baathist National Guard militia was crushed. Abdul Salem Aref remained president. Considerable military infighting was followed by purges of Baathist officers from the armed forces. This severely reduced the strength of the forces and left them in no fit condition to mount the projected winter campaign against the Kurds.

This diversion enabled the Pesh Merga in both sectors to reoccupy, often without opposition, large areas from which they had been ejected earlier in the year, including the Chami Razan Valley. By the end of November Pesh Mergas dominated an area larger than the one they had held prior to the commencement of the Second Offensive, embracing several Kurdish villages not previously under Kurdish control.

In early December government units were hastily mustered and deployed to block Kurdish advances. By this time they had taken Suliemaniyeh and were surging southwards towards Khaniqin. Government forces still held the main towns, but in several, including Arbil and Kirkuk, the garrisons had only restricted movement. Despite lurid, wildly inaccurate communiqués issued by both the government and the Kurds for propaganda purposes and for international consumption – of battles fought and won, and of casualties inflicted on the enemy – there was little serious fighting for the remainder of the winter, apart from a few road ambushes, although Iraqi aircraft continued spasmodic bombing whenever the weather permitted.

A CEASE-FIRE

Following further negotiations with the Kurds, on 12 February 1964 President Aref announced a cease-fire, stating that Kurdish national rights would be recognised in a provisional constitution, to be based on 'decentralisation'. The word 'autonomy' was not mentioned. An amnesty was to be granted to all who had fought against the government, and the Jash was to be disbanded. Barzani, who accepted these terms, ordered his Pesh Mergas and tribal militias to return to their homes, but most of them were already there. Although they too accepted Aref's offer, Jalal Talabani, Omar Mustafa and their the KDP central committee were reluctant and suspicious, feeling that a military initiative was being thrown away.

THE KURDISH NATIONAL MOVEMENT

By this time the expression 'Kurdish National Movement' had come into popular usage to embrace all insurgent Iraqi Kurds and their organisations, which were now claimed to include 'over 70 Iraqi Kurdish regular officers and over 9000 Kurdish soldiers' (Arfa, 1966). At last a determined start was made in the Barzani sector to formalise a command structure and slot the Pesh Mergas and tribal militias into a military framework.

Organisational progress was already well advanced in the KDP sector, where a dual command–political leadership structure on the traditional communist pattern had been formed. A training centre for junior leaders was established at Mahvout to teach mountain warfare tactics, with politics subtly intertwined, but no new strategical or tactical doctrines emerged. It was still mountain men against plains men.

The Kurdish National Movement remained ill-equipped, still lacking artillery although a few infantry weapons such as small mortars and rocket launchers were appearing. Barzani's Pesh Mergas had suddenly come to appreciate the value of their field radio communication sets – which had enabled them to listen in to Iraqi army military radio traffic and thus successfully avoid encirclement in the early stages of the Second Offensive – and were demanding more of them.

TURKISH 'OPERATION TIGER'

The Turkish government had watched the Kurdish insurrection in Iraq with anxiety and were apprehensive of it inciting its own uneasy Kurdish population. When in July 1963, at the height of the battle for the Ruwanduz Gorge, a small Kurdish insurrection erupted just south of Van, it was quickly smothered before it could spread. Twenty-five ringleaders were sentenced to death for 'attempting to form an independent state' (*New York Times*).

More serious for Iraqi insurgent Kurds was an alleged plot by the governments of Turkey, Iran and Iraq to crush the Barzani rebellion once and for all. This secret project, known as 'Operation Tiger', involved Turkish troops entering Iraq in the Mosul area and Iranian ones in the Suliemaniyeh region, while Iraqi troops would form the anvil.

KDP agents in Iran discovered this secret project and passed the information on to the USSR, which openly implicated Turkey. On 10 July 1963 Turkey officially denied any intention of interfering in Iraqi affairs. Exposure led to 'Operation Tiger' being aborted but gave credence to the saying 'Kurds have no friends', as all three tentatively mutually hostile powers, all with a Kurdish problem, were prepared to take such extreme steps to crush it. The Turkish government redoubled its efforts to prevent arms being smuggled across its border into the Barzani zone, but was not completely successful. However Barzani was compensated to some degree as the Iranian government's hostile policy towards him was softening.

INTERNATIONAL INTEREST

The international media was beginning to take some interest in the Kurdish insurrection but still knew little about how it came about, nor how many Kurdish aspirations were being hidden by Iraqi censorship. The Lausanne-based CDKPR, the main international Kurdish organisation with a prominent profile, was out of day-to-day touch with Kurds in the field in Iraq, and so was proving to be of little help in arousing world sympathy. However, impressed by the way the Algerian National Liberation Front (NLF) – which had just gained independence from France – had operated successfully from the safety of European cities, from where it could both direct fighters in the field and, unshackled, marshal favourable international opinion, the KDP Central Committee obtained a radio transmitter, which was in action in Iran by the end of 1963. The

KDP Central Committee certainly had a far wider international vision than Barzani.

CEASE-FIRE CONDITIONS

In Baghdad, in February 1964 Abdul Karim Farham, Minister for National Guidance and a Kurd, announced that – as the cease-fire (of the 12th) was becoming effective – army units were returning to their camps and barracks, both sides were releasing prisoners, the government was approving plans to repair damaged buildings, the embargo against the Kurdish region had been lifted, all Kurdish government officials and employees who had been suspended were being reinstated, and an amnesty was being granted to all Kurds involved in the insurrection. Little of this was true, but it was hoped that Barzani would be lulled into acceptance negotiations.

THE NEW PROVISIONAL IRAQI CONSTITUTION

On 3 May 1964 the new provisional constitution for Iraq was promulgated, but it only guaranteed the Kurdish people 'rights within the Iraqi national unity'. Barzani was dismayed as he had been expecting autonomy, but thought he might still be able to obtain his aim by negotiation. Barzani wanted a cease-fire, although on his own terms, but the KDP politburo wanted to fight on, knowing that the government of Iraq was isolated internationally, weak domestically and uncertain of its Kurdish military element.

In an effort to win over the KDP politburo, Barzani held a press conference to explain that the Kurds would not lay down their arms until all political demands had been met, revealing that he had a secret written agreement with the Baghdad government. Both sides tried to present a united front to the world, especially to small groups of exiled Kurdish organisations in major Western European cities, and to prevent an open rupture on home ground.

Both were busy consolidating their own power bases, each thinking they could outsmart the other. At different times both approached President Nasser of Egypt, then probably the most

powerful leader in the Middle East, for support, but were refused. Talabani led a delegation to Iran in March, to coincide
with a visit to that capital by President de Gaulle of France.
Talabani had some success in Tehran as the Shah did not want
a strong Iraq to develop next door, neither did he want his
own Kurds to be infected by the 'independence bug', and so
was content to see them at each other's throats. It was suspected that the Shah encouraged Talabani to defy Barzani,
and to state openly that his KDP would fight on. Barzani tried
to make friends with his old tribal enemies, while the Baghdad
government prevaricated.

On 5 June talks were held at Raniya between Barzani and
the Iraqi Prime Minister, who proposed that Barzani's demands
be set aside until 1967, when the next general election was
due to be held, but Barzani refused. He also refused to dissolve
the KDP, of which he was still nominally chairman, or to hand
over communist refugees in the KDP sector. It was claimed
that it was agreed that the new constitution should be amended
to recognise the existence of the 'Kurdish people, whose development would be parallel with that of the Arabs in Iraq'; that
army units would be withdrawn from the Kurdish region, the
Jash disbanded and the use of the Kurdish language again
permitted in schools.

On 12 June President Aref stated that Mullah Mustafa Barzani
had assured him of his loyalty, but that the KDP were 'war-
mongers, spies and agents', whom he thought Barzani would
like to suppress if he could (*Le Monde*). Two days later Aref
formed the 'Arab Socialist Union of Iraq' (ASU), into which all
legal and approved existing political parties were to be merged.
The KDP was excluded. On the 18th a new Iraqi government
was formed, consisting mainly of Nationalists and Baathists.

BARZANI MOVES AGAINST THE KDP

Having been somewhat successful in patching up his quarrels
with some major tribal enemies, especially in the area between
the KDP sector and his own, with their assistance Barzani began
to push southwards into the KDP sector, dissolving as they
advanced the 'elected peasant councils', which the KDP had
established to 'socialise' the people in its 'liberated areas'. This

brought support for Barzani from traditional sheikhs, many of whom had been neutral so far but now wanted to be on the winning side, and also indirectly from the now anti-communist Baghdad government, which had agreed to deal only with Barzani in negotiations.

Towards the end of June Ibrahim Ahmad organised a KDP conference in his sector, which condemned Barzani's attitude towards the Iraqi government, the continuing cease-fire and his defence of the Kurdish tribal and feudal order. This provoked Barzani into taking more active measures, and, thinking nothing of it, tribes that had so recently been bitterly fighting against Barzani now marched cheerfully with him against the KDP sector.

Barzani called upon the KDP, which still had about 650 armed Pesh Mergas, to hand over its arms to him, but the politburo refused. The KDP politburo was run on communist-style committee lines, with Ahmad taking the political lead and Talabani emerging as the field commander, although a politically orientated one.

During the first week in July, under the command of Lokman Barzani, a force of about 2000 Pesh Mergas, mostly Barzanis, and some 500 new tribal allies moved towards Mahvout, the KDP HQ near the Iranian frontier on the road to the town of Baneh in Iran. As they advanced the KDP HQ evacuated Mahvout and the whole KDP force moved across the Iranian border towards Sardasht, while Ibrahim Ahmad went to Tehran to negotiate with the Iranian government. The Iranian authorities attempted to disarm the KDP Pesh Merga, but Talabani resisted, asserting he was about to move back into Iraq. Ahmad Barzani came briefly into the picture, trying vainly to mediate between Mustafa Barzani and the KDP.

While in Iran Talabani managed to recruit another 100 Pesh Merga from Iraqi Kurdish exiles, and when Ibrahim Ahmad returned disappointed from Tehran the reinforced KDP army attempted to move to Chwarta, some 20 miles south of Mahvout along the road to Suliemaniyeh. Shortly after crossing the frontier into Iraq it was ambushed by Lokman's Pesh Mergas, with disastrous results. In the fighting some 200 KDP Pesh Mergas deserted to Lokman, while the remainder fled hastily back into Iran, where after a few days they were disarmed and placed under surveillance near Baneh. The Iraqi government protested to Iran, after which the KDP group was moved first to Saqqiz and then to Hamadan, to be well away from the frontier.

KDP CONGRESSES

This internecine tactical victory having been gained, in the last days of July Barzani, as chairman, convened a 'KDP' congress at Raniya which, packed with his supporters, expelled the KDP politburo and several members of the central committee. The month of July 1964 had been a bad one for the KDP politburo, but despite its failure to take over the Kurdish insurgency by force, Kurdish overseas political groups, particularly in Lebanon, Syria and Switzerland, mostly continued to support Talabani, who had been lobbying them for some time. As many virile members of the KDP group were in exile, this left the Iraqi Kurdish scene clear for Barzani to strengthen his grassroots tribal support and dominate Kurdish political activities in Iraq.

Barzani then called another KDP congress, in mid-September in Raniya, which voted him full powers as leader of the Kurdish insurrection, but he was invited to recall ousted senior KDP personnel and to reabsorb their energy and talents in the Kurdish cause. Sheikh Hama Rashid of the Baneh tribe (in Iran) became the mediator and eventually persuaded Talabani to return to meet Barzani – old Sheikh Ahmad Barzani also came into this negotiation equation.

Eventually Barzani agreed to take back most of the expelled KDP members, but not Ibrahim Ahmad, nor Said Aziz, a politburo member, insisting they must all cease political activity and come under his direct command. Barzani stated he was assuming both political and military leadership of the Kurds, and that if autonomy was not obtained in a reasonable time he would resume hostilities. The expelled KDP members had many reservations, and only a few returned to join Barzani, the majority remaining in Iran.

On 11 October Barzani accused the Iraqi government of failing to implement the promised Kurdish programme, and of systematically 'Arabising' the oil-producing regions of Arbil and Kirkuk. He also alleged that 'thousands of Kurdish families' had been expelled from the Kirkuk region, and that '37 villages in the Arbil region' had been forcibly cleared and settled by Arabs (*New York Times*). Barzani also complained that Kurds were not allowed to join the ASU, the single permitted legal political coalition in the country.

On 4 October 1964 Barzani held another KDP congress, also at Raniya, which decided that an autonomous Kurdish administration should be established. By the end of that month a council of revolutionary command, an executive committee, and a Kurdish legislature had appeared. Barzani dominated the scene, placing his own nominees in all key positions and on all major committees. Within a few weeks his sector was divided into five districts, each with its own military governor and financial and judicial administrations. Barzani had in fact set up his own Kurdish autonomy.

The previous month a plot against President Aref had been discovered, but was thwarted by Baathists. Some 3000 suspects were detained, so the Baghdad government had plenty of its own problems to cope with at that time. It was not until 14 November 1964 that a new government was formed, with the platform of implementing Iraq's union with Egypt. The Kurds knew that if this materialised all chance of their autonomy surviving would be lost. Barzani protested, and again pressed his demands.

THE THIRD OFFENSIVE

In February 1965 President Nasser sent a message to Barzani, urging him to surrender. Nasser wanted the Kurdish problem to dissolve quickly, but without the use of force. In early April the Iraqi Prime Minister visited Nasser in Cairo to inform him that the Iraqi government was about to mount an offensive against insurgent Kurds. Nasser expressed disapproval, regarding this as weakening the Arab front he was trying to drum up against Israel.

There had been minor clashes between Iraqi troops and Barzani's men since mid-October 1964, which continued on into November, but this chiefly involved elements over which he had little direct control. Barzani was reluctant to reopen hostilities and kept his Pesh Mergas on a tight rein. He did not want to risk losing what he had achieved so far. However on 3 April 1965 government armoured vehicles entered Suliemaniyeh to deal with Kurdish disturbances, and in the street fighting that developed some '60 people were killed and several hundred wounded' (*Sunday Telegraph*). This was an impromptu preliminary.

The Iraqi government's Third Offensive began on 5 April 1965, being launched on a 250-mile arc from Zakho to Khaniqin, with 'nine brigades, some 40 000 troops' (*New York Times*). Iraqi troops, with air cover and direct air support, occupied with little difficulty a number of towns and villages, including Raniya and Halabja. Barzani's Pesh Mergas withdrew to the shelter of the mountains, while government troops used 'scorched earth' tactics and reputedly dropped napalm bombs. However Iraqi troops ran into hard resistance and were repulsed with heavy losses at Qala Diza (10 miles east of Raniya), Chwarta and Mahvout.

When driven out of Raniya, Barzani established an HQ in the mountains some 40 miles to the north in the village of Galala, just north of the road running between Ruwanduz and the Iranian frontier. Barzani was beginning to realise the value of an HQ in a campaign and did not wander about as much as previously. President Aref maintained an official silence on the Third Offensive, and it was not until 14 June that he admitted it was in progress.

Punitive expeditions were launched against Kurdish populations in the areas of Arbil, Zakho, Kirkuk and Suliemaniyeh. It was reported on 7 July that Kurds were using field guns and rockets purchased in Europe (*The Times*), this being the first occasion that this had happened in the current insurrection. Kurds claimed that large numbers of government troops and Jash, 'including 75 officers' (*New York Times*) had deserted the government and come over to them. This was partially confirmed by periodic government notices promising deserters a pardon if they returned to their units.

The Iraqi army was incapable of maintaining the momentum of such a huge and widespread offensive for long, and by the end of July its intensity slackened, allowing Kurds to retain their positions and even regain a few that had been lost. The hot month of August was one of inertia, and by September all the drive and energy of the Third Offensive had drained away.

The government lost the allegiance of the last major Kurdish tribe on its side, the Lolanis, traditional enemies of the Barzanis. The Lolanis severed contact with the Baghdad government (and forfeited subsidies), but continued to fight against the Barzanis. The Jash manpower had shrunk to the 3000 mark, the KDP was reconciled with Barzani and relations with Iran had further deteriorated. In Baghdad the government was again plagued by political dissension and intrigue.

Coincident with the Third Offensive the Yezidi sect had risen in rebellion against the Baghdad government. The Yezidis, said to be some 100 000 strong (Guest, 1989), an extreme Muslim sect known as 'Devil Worshippers', which also propitiated the Devil to prevent evil befalling them, lived in the Jabal Sinjar area some 50 west of Mosul. 'Several brigades had to be withdrawn' from the Third Offensive to quell the Yezidi revolt (*The Times*).

In May 1965 Talabani had made his peace with Barzani, and the former KDP sector sprang to life again as members returned from Iran. Talabani was sent abroad by Barzani on goodwill missions. In London he held a press conference, alleging that the Iraqi army had used poison gas against Kurds on at least two occasions, and appealed to the British government to suspend arms shipments to Iraq, pointing out that both the USA and the USSR were refusing to supply them while fighting in Kurdistan continued. On his return to Iraq Barzani sent him to a remote village, virtually under surveillance. During December there was some scuffling between Barzani's Pesh Mergas and those of the KDP.

In Baghdad, in September 1965 there had been another attempted coup and fighting in the streets, which brought about the replacement of the National Council of the Revolutionary Command by a civilian government.

THE IRANIAN ATTITUDE

During the first part of the Third Offensive there was a degree of collaboration between the governments of Iran and Iraq on containing the Kurdish insurrection, and even a few disjointed military operations aimed at sealing the border, but they were very half-hearted. In one instance in July, a small group of

Iranian troops who had crossed into Iraq suffered a defeat near Qala Diza. The Shah remained undecided over what to do about the Kurdish problem until the latter part of 1965, when he decided to give military support to Barzani. By the end of that year Iranian arms and military supplies were openly reaching the Kurds, being carried from Iran over mountain trails that led to the main road from Panjwin, near the border, to Suliemaniyeh. Kurdish Pesh Mergas, strongly entrenched around Panjwin, controlled this illegal traffic route. Denials came from Tehran, insisting that only humanitarian aid was been sent to the Kurds in Iraq.

THE TURKISH ATTITUDE

The Turkish attitude towards the Iraqi Third Offensive was to maintain a strict blockade to prevent arms from reaching the Kurds. Frontier posts were increased and minefields made more dense. Relations between Turkey and Iraq remained poor, and were not improved by an incident on 28 July, when an Iraqi aircraft mistakenly attacked a Turkish village, killing one person and injuring eight.

In Turkey the Kurds continued to be 'non-persons'. It was coming to be realised by Kurdish political activists that none of the radical parties were involved with, or had any real interest in, Kurdish problems and would never really take them on board, so a few turned to forming Kurdish groups in secret. The first to materialise, in 1965, was the Kurdistan Democratic Party of Turkey (KDP(T)), which was modelled along the lines of Barzani's KDP, having a largely tribal traditional membership that simply asked for autonomy, as indeed Barzani was doing. As in Barzani's KDP, the radical left-wing element within the KDP(T) was soon speaking of separatism.

Kurdish students and activists called for public demonstrations to draw attention to Kurdish demands, and the first of these occurred on 3 August 1967, when more than 25 000 assembled in Diyarbakir, 10 000 in Silvan and lesser numbers at other cities in the eastern provinces (McDowall, 1985). This manifestation of Kurdishness caused Demirel to crack down hard on Kurdish political activity. Turkish–Kurdish journals and newspapers were shut down and editors imprisoned. In addition special police commando groups were sent to the eastern regions to intimidate, search homes and offices and arrest ringleaders and suspects.

The Organisation of Revolutionary Kurdish Youth (DDKO) appeared in 1969 and established 'Eastern Revolutionary Cultural Centres' in Istanbul and Ankara, while the first legal political party in Turkey openly to recognise the existence of the Kurds was the Turkish Workers' Party in October 1970.

In March 1971 the Demirel government was overthrown and mass arrests of Kurds followed, it being alleged that a Kurdish rising had been about to erupt. The DDKO and the Turkish Workers' Party were banned, and the repression of Kurds increased.

7 More Iraqi Offensives: 1966–75

The Iraqi army launched a commando-type raid on 8 January 1966, when two brigades, supported by special forces, penetrated the Panjwin region, taking the Pesh Merga completely by surprise and having some initial success. Despite severe weather conditions and mountainous terrain, they managed to enter the town of Panjwin, a key position in the developing Kurdish supply line from Iran. Kurds boasted that government troops were surrounded by 'Kurdish suicide squads', while Tehran sources stated that 'since the 8th of January, over 200 Iraqi soldiers have been killed near Panjwin'. On the 18th Iraqi troops withdrew from Panjwin and the surrounding area.

This major commando raid severely jolted complacent Kurds, who had previously felt safe in their mountains in winter. Barzani was disconcerted as many of his Pesh Mergas, who were unprepared or conditioned for winter fighting, had hastily abandoned many positions. The morale of the Pesh Mergas dropped. Barzani again appealed to the United Nations to send a fact-finding mission to Iraq, but again failed to elicit a positive response. On the other hand this offensive had been a morale booster for the Iraqi army, encouraging it to plan for a major spring campaign to push insurgent Kurds back into their northern mountains near the Turkish frontier.

THE TALABANI PLOT

In February Jalal Talabani made contact with the Iraqi military attaché in Tehran, whom it was claimed had led him to believe that the Iraqi government might possibly support him in usurping Barzani. Taking into consideration the fact that Iraqi troops could operate in the mountains in winter, the low morale of the Pesh Merga and the war-weariness of Kurds generally, Talabani – claiming over-optimistically to speak for all Kurds in Iraq – made a direct peace offer to the Baghdad government, which he hoped Barzani would automatically reject. This would enable Talabani to pose as a genuine peace-seeker, and with Iraqi military support he might be strong enough to mount a rebellion against Barzani.

On discovering this plot Barzani sent military units to arrest Talabani. Forewarned, he escaped into Iran, where he remained for some time, trying to stitch together a deal with the Iraqi prime minister through his Iraqi intermediary. Barzani neither disowned nor condemned Talabani, but remained in touch with him: an example of Kurdish deviousness and artifice – an enemy today might be a friend tomorrow.

President Abdul Salem Aref of Iraq was killed in a helicopter crash on 13 April 1966 and was replaced as president by his brother, Abdul Rahman Aref. While the former president had operated a strong policy against dissident Kurds, the new one seemed to be more moderate, openly doubting whether there was a military answer to the Kurdish problem. The Prime Minister also wanted peace, but Iraqi generals wanted war.

When the new Iraqi government was formed Barzani announced he would observe a month's truce to give it a chance to reflect on the Kurdish situation, while at the same time reiterating his former demands. Certain detained Kurdish leaders were released from house arrest to try to persuade Barzani to accept minor concessions, which could be granted immediately, on condition that Barzani would disband his '15 000 Pesh Mergas', a figure the government then seemed to accept. Barzani would not agree.

THE FOURTH OFFENSIVE

On 4 May the Iraqis launched their Fourth Offensive, the objective being to sever donkey-trail mountain supply routes from Iran, using some '40 000 troops in nine brigade formations' and including some 2000 Jash, supported by over 100 combat aircraft (*Sunday Telegraph*). One column penetrated eastwards towards Raniya, where it ground to a halt; another was detailed to clear the road from Suliemaniyeh through to the Iranian frontier and reached Panjwin.

This offensive had originally been planned to start on 5 April, but had been delayed by the death of President Abdul Salem Aref. Had it been launched when planned it may have met with more success, as at that time many Pesh Mergas had not returned from their villages or winter quarters to their spring battle positions.

THE MOUNT HANDRIN AMBUSH

The main thrust was in the northern zone, the objective being to drive a wedge into Kurdish territory and split it along the line of the Greater Zab valley to Ruwanduz, and on to the Iranian frontier. Army columns forced their way through the Ruwanduz Gorge to be confronted by two huge mountain massifs guarding its eastern entrance – Mount Handrin and Mount Zozic. Massed together and crammed into the gorge and the valleys below them, the government troops were vulnerable to ambush.

Seizing the opportunity Barzani massed his Pesh Mergas, and on 11 and 12 May descended upon one of the trapped army columns, inflicting severe casualties and causing a rout of the survivors. When the fighting died down 'nearly 2000 dead remained on the floor of this valley' (Mauries, 1967), where large quantities of arms and equipment had been hastily abandoned. During the battle Iraqi shells had fallen on Iranian territory, causing diplomatic protests.

The Baghdad authorities rushed out false communiqués, alleging the 'rebels had suffered a severe defeat' and that only a few pockets of resistance remained. Barzani was slow off the mark, at first not seeming to realise the publicity value of his tactical victory. It was not until 21 May that he issued a communiqué over his new Radio Kurdistan, claiming that 'two army units had been surrounded on 11 and 12 May, and had lost 1000 killed', and that he had captured '980 rifles, six guns and large quantities of ammunition'. Perhaps this was the only Kurdish battle communiqué that contained understatements.

Iranian sources reported that several Iraqi MiG aircraft had been driven back by Iranian anti-aircraft fire, after violating Iranian air space. Some witnesses claimed to have seen an Iraqi aircraft shot down by the Kurds, but there was no confirmation of this.

The Iraqi army issued an ultimatum on 23 May demanding that Kurdish insurgents either surrender or face annihilation.

It also claimed that it had won great victories over them, that 'over 235 Kurds had been killed, including three of Barzani's sons', and that many Kurds had been captured after being turned back at the Iranian border. The army also claimed that 60 Kurdish rebels had been killed in Barzan, 75 in Khorman, 80 in Koreh, and 20 in Khiti, all being large mountain villages (*The Times*).

The Mount Handrin ambush severely shook Iraqi military morale and confidence, and prematurely brought the Fourth Offensive to an abrupt and humiliating end. It was nearly two years before government forces recovered sufficiently to again mount offensive operations against the Kurds in their mountain strongholds. Barzani's reputation as a military commander shot into the ascendant, overshadowing that of his rival, Talabani.

One report stated that while the offensive had been called off the Kurds were still mobile, retaining their initiative by harassing operations. It went on to say that in the fighting at Mount Handrin several Iraqi army platoons had surrendered with their arms, that there had been large-scale desertions, and that both military and civilian hospitals were filled with military casualties (*Daily Telegraph*). Barzani repeated his allegation that the Baghdad government was committing genocide against the Kurds, again accusing the Iraqis of using gas and napalm.

KURDISH EVENTS: 1966–68

In June, Talabani visited Baghdad, seeing both President Aref and his prime minister, both of whom still assumed that Talabani spoke for all Kurds. On the 29th the government issued its 'Twelve Point Programme', being simply a rehash of old demands and compromises and containing nothing new. To Talabani's surprise Barzani immediately accepted, thus thwarting Talabani, who wanted the Kurds to fight on so that he could continue to negotiate to his own advantage. A tacit cease-fire came into effect and lasted for two years.

Barzani then pushed Talabani aside and the members of the Ahmad–Talabani-KDP, as this faction became known, progressively lost influence and power as Barzani tightened his grip on Kurdish territory, virtually dominating the major part of the main KDP organisation. Ahmad–Talabani-KDP Pesh Mergas had played no part in the battle of Mount Handrin. Ahmad and Talabani kept their distance, and their freedom.

The winter of 1966–67 passed comparatively quietly, and in 1967 the third Arab–Israeli War, in which Iraq was marginally involved, overshadowed events in the Middle East region. By the second part of 1967 hardline Ahmad–Talabani-KDP members were filtering back into some of their former positions, re-establishing themselves in Chwarta, Chami-Razan, Dukan, Mahvout and Suliemaniyeh and clashing on several occasions with Barzani's Pesh Mergas and tribesmen. Talabani retained contact with Barzani, and both the Baghdad and the Iranian government. In December 1967 he survived an assassination attempt. He had many enemies, but the finger of suspicion pointed at Barzani.

During 1967 the government's anti-guerrilla Saladin Force was reactivated, still consisting mainly of Arabs, but still containing a few anti-Barzani Kurds, to whom were now added some Ahmad–Talabani-KDP members. By the end of 1967 it was countering sabotage activities in the Kirkuk area.

In April 1968 some '19 people were killed in an interfactional fighting' near Raniya (*The Times*). The same month, in the Arbil area, '68 outlaw elements attacked a government military patrol, killing four soldiers and injuring six civilians' (*Sunday Telegraph*). It was alleged that the culprits were dissident Ahmad–Talabani-KDP members, as Talabani wanted to upstage Barzani and disrupt his relations with the Baghdad government.

In July 1968 President Aref was overthrown by a coup mounted by General Ahmad Hassan Bakr and involving right-wing Baathists and young officers, who formed a Revolutionary Command Council (RCC). Talabani established good relations with Bakr, who became president. Bakr insisted that Talabani be included in all talks with the Kurds, much to Barzani's chagrin.

During September Ahmad–Talabani-KDP members strengthened their hold on their former KDP zone. The following month Barzani sent his Pesh Mergas south to deal with them, managing to jostle them out of several positions. Talabani appealed to Bakr for help – government troops were sent to

Talabani's assistance and Iraqi aircraft bombed several Kurdish villages. Talabani, now openly fighting Barzani, had succeeded in persuading the Baghdad government to side with him against Barzani.

THE FIFTH OFFENSIVE

On 3 January 1969 the Baghdad government launched its Fifth Offensive, using some 6000 troops in some 12 brigades, the object being to take and retain possession of Kurdish territory from Suliemaniyeh to Ruwanduz. Military planners remembered that two years previously their sortie to Panjwin had been on a narrow front. This time the offensive was to be on a very wide one.

Again, by launching a winter offensive the government troops took the Kurds by surprise, catching them at their weakest as many Pesh Mergas were still in their winter homes. Although the action lasted only three weeks before losing its momentum, due mainly to the harsh winter conditions, many shaken and surprised Pesh Mergas were pushed out from their positions and others hastily abandoned theirs. Iraqi troops succeeded in entering and holding both Panjwin and Qala Diza, close to the Iranian frontier. However Kurdish defenders managed to put up sufficient resistance to prevent government troops from gaining their real objective, which was to occupy that section of the frontier.

During the fighting the Iraqis encouraged Ahmad–Talabani-KDP elements to reoccupy their former positions, which this time included both Chwarta and Mahvout. On 4 February Bakr falsely stated that the Twelve-Point Programme had been implemented in an attempt to calm down the Kurds.

BARZANI'S COUNTERATTACK

Mustafa Barzani launched a counterattack on 1 March 1969, aimed at driving government troops from the areas they had just gained. He began his offensive by shelling oil installations near Kirkuk as a diversion (he now had several guns, captured during the Mount Handrin battle), but the main thrust of his attacks was towards the east. The government replied by using its Saladin Force and aircraft activity. Several Iraqi assaults to recapture Panjwin and Qala Diza were repulsed with heavy losses.

One report put Iraqi casualties in these particular battles at about '1000 killed and wounded, for the loss of 150 Pesh Merga' (*Daily Telegraph*). It was also alleged the Iraqi air force dropped napalm and nitric-acid bombs on '37 villages, killing 730 civilians'. Confused fighting dragged on for several weeks, in which the Iraqi army slowly gave way and then withdrew from mountainous areas, leaving the Kurds in possession of all the ground they had held in 1968.

During this fighting Ahmad and Talabani began a serious recruiting campaign, which brought their Pesh Merga strength up to the 500 mark. On 9 April Barzani's vehicle was ambushed and fired upon, allegedly by Ahmad–Talabani-KDP volunteers in the Saladin Force.

THE IRANIAN THREAT

The abrupt termination of the Iraqi government's Fifth Offensive was due largely to the sudden eruption of bad relations with Iran, this time over conflicting claims over the Shatt al-Arab confluence, which marked part of the southern portion of their joint frontier. Reports that Iranian troops were massing in that region caused the withdrawal of Iraqi army formations from their offensive against the Kurds. Having made little indentation on the Kurdish front, and with a looming Iranian problem on his hands, in June 1969 President Bakr began secretly to negotiate with Barzani, the talks being held in Lebanon.

Iraq was in a tight spot as the Shah of Iran was setting out to dominate the Gulf area, and was already illicitly supplying Barzani with a trickle of arms. Iraq is a small country of some 116 000 square miles, and at that time its population numbered about 8.3 million with armed forces totalling less than 83 000 men (IISS figures). Shaken by its recent war with Israel and fatigued by its long-running Kurdish insurrection, of the army's 16 brigade formations, three were in Syria and one in Jordan.

On the other side of the Shatt al-Arab lies Iran, then a key member of the CENTO, which implied Western support. The country covers some 628 000 square miles, and at the time it had a population of about 25 million people. The strength of its armed forces exceeded 180 000 and they were being rapidly re-equipped with modern weaponry by the USA and other Western nations. Its army was formed into eight divisions, with many additional specialised brigades. Iraq seemed to be very much inferior in this strategic balance.

THE SIXTH OFFENSIVE

As secret negotiations with Barzani were leading nowhere, Bakr decided to launch one more determined, all-out campaign to bring his rebellious Kurds to heel in order to clear the decks before the possible confrontation with his giant neighbour, Iran. Accordingly, in the last week of August 1969 he mustered ten army brigades and launched an offensive on a wide front, the main objectives being to secure Zakho, held by Kurds for many months, and to occupy the Ruwanduz, Raniya, Qala Diza, Mahvout and Panjwin areas: an army column being directed towards each target.

Covered by aircraft and supported by artillery and tanks, Iraqi military columns moved slowly forward. They were opposed by '15 000 Pesh Mergas' (still the government's accepted figure), who were soon reinforced by hundreds of tribal militias of various types who had responded to Barzani's rallying call. Government forces included some 2000 Jash and the Ahmad–Talabani-KDP Pesh Mergas.

In the north, the Zakho column completely failed to reach that town and had to withdraw. Another column suffered a similar setback near Arbil, and yet another near Dukan. At Dukan the Kurds claimed that on the night of 20–21 September its Pesh Mergas had carried out an attack on an army camp, destroying over 30 tanks. On the 24th the Kurds claimed to have beaten back an attack by 'Talabani's mercenaries' in the Panjwin area. They also claimed that the Iraqi air force had made '120 attacks on Kurdish villages, forcing some 200 000 villagers' to take refuge in the mountains (*New York Times*).

Fighting around Ruwanduz, Qala Diza and Panjwin soon

bogged down inconclusively, and this 'flash-in-the-pan' Sixth Offensive subsided in October, having accomplished none of its objectives.

Belatedly the Kurds began to appreciate the propaganda value of atrocity stories, lapped up by the media, in influencing world public opinion. Barzani's Radio Kurdistan was now functioning well from a fortified underground bunker at Chouman on the Ruwanduz to Haj Omran road, close to both Galala and the Iranian frontier. It was claimed that on one occasion two Iraqi warplanes attacking it had been shot down by Iranian anti-aircraft missiles from Iranian territory.

On 16 August, even before the Sixth Offensive began, the Kurds alleged that government troops had found Kurds hiding in a cave near the Dukan Dam, Whereupon they had started a fire at the entrance, with only three out of 70 Kurds escaping death (*Daily Telegraph*). Another Kurdish allegation, on 3 October, was that government troops had massacred the entire population of two villages, killing 91 people in one village and 67 in the other. Iraq denied all these allegations, and others too.

On 3 October Radio Baghdad announced that over 30 Iranian soldiers had been killed, and 14 others captured by Iraqi troops, when trying to recross the border back into Iran in an area controlled by Kurds. Prisoners allegedly confessed they were regular soldiers sent to infiltrate into Iraq. This was denied by Iran, who added that elements of the Iraqi Kurdish population may have been driven over the border into Iran by Iraqi aircraft attacks, without Tehran's knowledge. This seemed to confirm indirectly that Kurds crossed and recrossed the frontier fairly freely, and probably Iranian troops too. No Iranian prisoners were produced for the media to interview, so again confirmation was lacking.

THE PEACE SETTLEMENT

Mullah Mustafa Barzani reorganised his political framework into the 'Revolutionary Command Council of Kurdistan', to replace the old KDP politburo and central committee. He remained in secret contact with President Bakr, who once more offered him the same minor concessions. Again these were refused, and on 21 December 1969 Barzani broke off negotiations. Bakr sent his vice president, Saddam Hussein Takriti, to negotiate directly with Barzani, who found the Kurdish leader's priority demands to be (1) that the government should end its relations with the Ahmad–Talabani-KDP faction, (2) the disbandment of the Jash and (3) that the government should abandon its self-appointed mediation role between the two KDP factions. Barzani wanted freedom to build his own solid power base.

These points and several others resolved, some remaining secret, the Iraqi RCC announced on 24 January 1970 that it would implement the promised Twelve-Point Programme to recognise the binational character of the Iraqi republic, in which 'Kurds were to be free and equal partners' (McDowall, 1985). A Kurdish delegation was invited to Baghdad.

On 11 March 1970 a '15-Point Peace Settlement' was signed by Barzani's two sons, Idris Barzani and Masoud Barzani, on behalf of their father; and on the 12th Bakr announced that 'the war against the Kurds is over'. Bakr had wanted to involve Talabani in the signing ceremony, but Barzani had brushed the proposal aside. The Iraqi government established a committee to oversee and work out the details of this agreement. A new Iraqi constitution was promulgated on 16 July, in which Kurds gained 'cultural autonomy and national equality' – most of their other demands were to be met over a four-year implementation period.

During the remainder of 1970, prospects for lasting partnership and peace seemed to be good. Kurdish governors and officials were appointed in the Kurdish provinces of Arbil, Dohuk and Suliemaniyeh, many Kurdish soldiers and officials who had been dismissed were reinstated, and Barzani's Pesh Mergas, whose strength was now officially agreed to be 21 000, achieved by hastily coopting tribesmen, began to be integrated into a 'frontier guard'. In Kurdish provinces the teaching of the Kurdish language was resumed in schools and official documents were printed in both Arabic and Kurdish. Ibrahim Ahmad went abroad for medical treatment and Jalal Talabani was sidelined by the Iraqi government, their newspapers and printing presses were closed down and the Jash was disbanded. The Iraqi government had originally wanted the Ahmad–Talabani-KDP Pesh Mergas to become an internal security force, but Barzani resisted this.

Barzani had been able to retain his '140 guns' for the simple reason that the government was in no position to take them from him. He retained his radio station, giving him an outlet to the world, although at that time he still did not seem to appreciate its full potential. The general assumption was that the war really was over, both sides claiming victory, with divisive issues remaining clouded in a haze of confusing propaganda. Within a year construction of hospitals and schools had begun, and over '2700 houses had been built, or re-built' (McDowall, 1985). The omens for a successful partnership seemed good.

The hard facts were that the Kurdish insurrection, which had dragged on from 1961 until 1970, had been confined to a comparatively small part of Iraq, had involved only a very small proportion of the some three million Iraqi Kurds, and had not developed any significant international ramifications. Turkey, as far as it was able, had closed its border with Iraq, as had Iran initially. Only latterly had Iran supplied illicit arms to insurgent Iraqi Kurds. Kurds in Syria had little or no contact with Barzani, and neither did those in the USSR.

No new significant strategy or tactics had emerged from this struggle, apart from the appearance of Iraqi air power and armoured vehicles, so the military balance remained as it had been for centuries. Kurds in the mountains had been reasonably secure, bombing excepted, but had been at a disadvantage when they ventured into larger valleys in strength or down on to the plains, while Iraqi troops, competent on the plains, had been at a disadvantage in the mountains. It had really been one long stalemate, punctured only when one or the other tried to buck this rough rule of thumb.

Casualties were an unknown factor, although there had been much inflated guesswork, but they must have been heavy, especially amongst civilians from air attacks. In February 1970 the Kurds admitted they had lost over 100 Pesh Mergas since October 1969, when Barzani also stated that about 13 000 families were receiving assistance after losing their breadwinners since 1960. Perhaps these were two of the most accurate casualty statements issued.

Throughout the Barzani insurgency the Iraqi governments, and there had been several of them, had all tried to treat it as a domestic scandal, to be hushed up and dealt with quietly and discretely, something that was no concern of anyone else. Outsiders and outside interference had not been welcomed.

The Iraqi governments had some success in this conspiracy of silence, as the rest of the world knew remarkably little about this phase of the Kurdish armed struggle. One seldom mentioned aspect was the constant failure of communists to hijack the insurrection, which had been due to Barzani's tribal resistance.

DIFFICULTIES ARISE

Difficulties soon began to arise over Kirkuk, Barzani having been granted control of Kirkuk province but not Kirkuk city, which was a mixed ethnic one containing Kurds, Turkomans and Arabs in varying proportions. He was soon complaining that the government was moving huge numbers of Arabs into Kirkuk and other marginal towns and areas, with the intention of turning them into Arab majority ones. Barzani called for a census, but the government resisted. A group of Faili (Shia) Kurds in the Kirkuk area, without Iraqi citizenship, came into the dispute. There were also arguments over the Kurdish share of Kirkuk oil revenues.

The new Iraqi constitution allowed for a Kurdish Iraqi vice president. Ibrahim Ahmad was nominated by a Kurdish congress, but the Baathist Baghdad government refused to accept him because of his suspected communist affiliations and record. The Kurds failed to agree on a replacement nomination. Another point of major disagreement was the government's suspicion that Barzani's Pesh Merga frontier guard, which was patrolling part of the joint Iraq–Iran border, was collaborating with Iran.

Relations between Barzani and the Baghdad government deteriorated in 1971, with Barzani accusing the government of increasing the number of its troops in Kurdish areas while the government accused him of increased collaboration with Iran and aiding Iranian border infringements, as well as alleging that the Shah was supplying Barzani with arms. Incidents of friction between Barzani's Pesh Mergas and Iraqi government troops became more frequent. On 19 September 1971 another attempt was made on Barzani's life, and the finger of suspicion pointed towards the Iraqi government.

IRANIAN GRANDEUR AND WEALTH

The British had withdrawn from the Gulf area by the end of 1972, leaving a major power vacuum that the Shah of Iran, strongly supported by the USA, intended to fill, becoming the USA's 'policeman in the Gulf'. Accordingly the USA was providing modern arms and equipment for the Iranian armed forces, and other military support. The Shah knew that it would be to his advantage if the Kurdish insurrection in Iraq was revived.

When President Nixon of the USA visited Iran in 1972, the subject of arming the Iraqi Kurds was raised by the Shah, both being concerned by the threat from the USSR, which was already arming the Iraqi Baathist government. Both feared that Soviet influence, and even intervention, would extend to Iraq. Although both the State Department and the CIA advised against such a course, they were overruled by Nixon and the CIA was allocated some $16 million for the purpose (John Stathatos, *Sunday Times*). A Kurdish delegation went to the USA to liaise and arrange matters with the CIA. Soon the trickle of arms from Iran to Barzani was increased by a flow of modern American ones, including mortars, infantry missiles and even 122mm guns. The CIA became a player in this fast-moving scenario, liaising with SAVAK, the Iranian secret service.

The Shah's motive was clear – he wanted a Kurdish 'no win' situation to continue to sap Iraqi military strength, but did not want a Kurdish victory as that would affect his own Kurds. He therefore restricted the level of arms supplies, especially ammunition. Nixon's intention, probably with NATO considerations in mind, had been to try to fragment Iraq as it bordered Turkey and might fall into the Soviet camp. Nixon did not understand the Kurdish problem, but then neither did the CIA, which blundered along under the Shah's shadow, without understanding how his mind was working.

In 1953 the CIA had fomented demonstrations that led to a coup in Tehran against the leftish Prime Minister, Mohammed Mossadegh, thus facilitating the return of the young Shah Mohammed Reza Pahlavi to power after a humiliating exile in Italy. The grateful shah became a good friend of the USA, and in particular of its CIA, which consolidated its position cosily within Iran. The US administration considered the young Shah to be an enlightened ruler who would modernise and bring his country into the twentieth century, conveniently overlooking his dictatorial traits.

When British colonial power disappeared from the Gulf region, the USA decided build up Iran into a strong regional state. Modern sophisticated arms were supplied in quantity, being paid for by the Shah's new-found oil wealth, which he personally controlled. It was a partnership that Washington smiled upon, and the Shah played along with the Americans. Western critics carping on about the lack of democracy in Iran and its social problems, had been slightly bedazzled and bemused by the Shah's extravanza at Persepolis in 1971, celebrating in glorious technicolour and costume the 2500th anniversary of the Persian monarchy. The event was a practical political statement of his grandiose ambitions and vision of himself, which should perhaps have been noted and analysed more carefully.

By the early 1970s it was confirmed that Iran sat on the fourth largest known oil reservoir in the world (after Saudi Arabia, the USSR and Kuwait). After the international oil crisis of 1973 the Shah was described as the 'Emperor of Oil' (*Time* magazine), and by the following year Iran was producing some 6.1 million barrels of oil a day. Iran was rich.

DISCONTENT WITHIN THE KDP

Encouraged by Iran, the USA and a supply of American arms and ammunition, during the summer of 1972 Barzani consolidated his control over much of the Kurdish region, amounting probably to about 10 000 square miles. However he came in for criticism from elements of the KDP for his arbitrary manner and rule, and his demands for greater military and political leverage. An internal tussle developed between Barzani's autocratic rule and the left-wing demand for collective leadership. There was evidence that Barzani was still vigorously pursuing tribal vengeance. The Baghdad government demanded that he seal the frontier with Iran and cease dealing with foreign powers. That year the Iraqi government nationalised the Iraq Petroleum Company, and at once arguments again arose over the Kurdish share of oil revenues. The Iraqi government also accused Barzani of helping the Iranian SAVAK to obtain information about the Iraqi armed forces.

Rising discontent within most elements of the KDP, which in theory was working for a popular franchise, surged over the Barzani's dictatorial, pro-tribal attitude. Early in 1974 some former KDP central committee members broke away, accusing Barzani of 'rejecting democratic practices, of kidnapping and executing a number of Kurdish leaders', and for developing an excessive personality cult (McDowall, 1985). One prominent deserter was Barzani's eldest son, Obeidullah Barzani.

THE AUTONOMY LAW

The Autonomy Declaration (Law) of 11 March 1974 offered the Kurds less than that offered in the peace agreement. Barzani was given 14 days to accept, but reluctantly chose to reject, as it failed to fulfil the terms promised and Barzani had already received secret assurances of support from Iran and the USA. He later said, 'Were it not for American promises we would never have become trapped and involved to such an extent' (McDowall, 1985).

At the end of the option period Barzani raised an insurrection, and within a few days was besieging Zakho and securing the Turkish frontier area in the north-western sector of the Kurdish region, driving some 100 000 anti-Barzani tribesmen over the border into Turkey. He then turned his attention to the Suliemaniyeh area. Barzani was in a strong position, having some 40 000 Pesh Mergas and 60 000 tribal militiamen (McDowall, 1985).

Moreover, for the first time he was encouraged by a somewhat unexpected mass wave of support and sympathy from Kurds in Iraq generally, which included previously disinterested urban and other detribalised ones. Some Kurdish ministers and others in authority resigned, and Barzani was joined in the field by '60 doctors, 4500 teachers, 5000 policemen, 160 engineers and 100 army officers' (McDowall, 1985). Even Barzani himself was surprised by this sudden, widespread, across the board, general Kurdish support, which gave this insurrection a Kurdish national character whereas previous ones had been only narrowly supported, mainly by small tribal groups, with hardly any urban enthusiasm.

THE SEVENTH GOVERNMENT OFFENSIVE

Barzanis's sudden popularity and success also surprised the Baghdad government, which – reluctant though it was – was forced in late April 1974 to launch its Seventh Offensive, said to be the largest so far, consisting of some 110 000 troops in six divisions, with supporting arms and services (*Guardian*). One armoured column moved along a new road that had been constructed from Arbil through the mountains to Ruwanduz and on to the Iranian border, becoming involved in two protracted battles. One was in the Mount Handrin area, the other was around Mount Zozic. The latter was not successfully resolved until 24 October.

A second armoured column moving roughly parallel a few miles south of the first one, marched against Raniya and on to Qala Diza. All the columns opened roads and relieved besieged towns, closely supported by the Iraqi air force, which now possessed over 200 modern Soviet warplanes (IISS figures). It was suspected that some of them were being flown by Soviet pilots.

This time, thanks to the Shah and the CIA, Pesh Mergas were better armed than previously and better organised in the military sense. Accordingly, government troops met heavy resistance, and only with difficulty were the frontier towns of Ruwanduz, Raniya and Qala Diza seized and the Kurds forced back into their mountains. During some of the fighting in this region, Iranians gave Barzani support from their long-range guns, some from Iranian territory, some from inside Iraq.

The Iraqi Seventh Offensive died down in October, but troops remained in all the towns and territory gained, thus preventing the Pesh Mergas from repeating their former tactic of simply walking almost casually into positions vacated when the government troops withdrew for the winter months. However there was more to it than that. Once again a military stalemate had been reached between a conventional army matched against mountain fighters. In addition the Kurds' long-range Iranian guns had been able to out-shoot Iraqi ones, and had shelled several towns, including Arbil.

Astonished and somewhat alarmed by Barzani's failure to defeat the Iraqi troops, or even to retain his battle positions, the CIA sent him more arms. The Shah wanted Barzani to continue his insurrection so as to distract the Baghdad government, as he was fearful that the Iraqi troops in the field might tire and perhaps withdraw from the conflict in order to march on Baghdad and overturn the Baathist government. On the other hand, the Bakr regime wanted to crush the Kurdish insurrection quickly and, if possible, once and for all. The Kurdish war was unpopular in Iraq and the Baathist government was in a weak political position, so special efforts had been made to end it.

THE ALGIERS AGREEMENT

In 1972 Iraq had concluded a friendship treaty with the USSR as a counterbalance to the close Iran–USA relationship that was developing. On the initiative of President Boumedienne of Algeria, resolutions on a number of Iran–Iraq border issues and other matters were accepted, the whole package being referred to as the Algiers Treaty. The treaty was signed in Algiers on 5 March 1975 by the Shah of Iran and Saddam Hussein, the Iraqi Vice President, who were attending an OPEC meeting. Saddam Hussein was already being billed as the 'strong man' of Iraq and the power behind the scenes. A significant point of the treaty was that Iraq would forfeit certain rights over the Shatt al-Arab boundary waterway, in return for which the Shah secretly agreed to cease aiding insurgent Iraqi Kurds. The Shah pulled the rug from under Barzani and gained virtual control of the Shatt al-Arab.

The Algiers Treaty took both Barzani and the Americans by surprise. It was 'so unexpected that even the Kurds' intelligence service was caught unawares' (*Guardian*). The CIA had nothing to boast about on this occasion either, its memos referring to Kurds as simply 'a card to play' (*The Sunday Times*).

BARZANI'S RESISTANCE CRUMBLES

On 7 March 1975 Iraqi troops recommenced their military
Seventh Offensive on all fronts, continuing until the 13th when
the Iraqis declared a cease-fire, demanding that the Kurds lay
down their arms. As the majority of the Pesh Merga were as yet
unaware of the Algiers Treaty perfidy, they fought on. When
the Shah stopped their supply of arms and ammunition, and
the shortage of ammunition became acute, it was finally realised that something was amiss. A full Iranian artillery regiment
– armed with US 155mm long-range guns and positioned in
the Chouman valley, the core of the Kurdish sophisticated
defence – began to pull out. Foreign journalists at Haj Omran
watched its departure, which took five days to complete, one
commenting that he had counted '42 Iranian 155mm guns
being withdrawn' (*Guardian*). Iraqi troops had made some inroads into Kurdish defences.

The Baghdad government again called on Barzani to surrender, but instead he rushed off to visit the Shah in Tehran,
only to find he had indeed been sold down the river. In a later
interview Barzani said the Shah 'told me the agreement was
made because it was vital to Iran. I asked what our future was
to be, and the Shah said he would undertake to protect those
Kurds who sought refuge in Iran' (John Stathatos, *The Sunday
Times*). Brief, stark and to the point. Barzani returned to his
HQ at Galala, where he dithered for some days.

By the 13th the true situation was dawning on the Kurdish
insurgents and their families. The Baghdad government gave
them until the end of the month to lay down their arms and
accept an amnesty, failing which it would resume its campaign
against them. A panic exodus into Iran began. The USSR,
Turkey and Syria closed their frontiers to Iraqi Kurdish refugees, and some from the northern Badinan region had to trek
for many miles over mountain tracks to reach Haj Omran and
Iran. Many Pesh Mergas wanted to fight on, and there was
hesitation until Barzani ordered them all to leave for Iraq.
Even then not all obeyed this unpopular order.

On 21 March Barzani ordered Kurdish resistance to end,
and on the 23rd a new Kurdish Revolutionary Command
Council was formed, which immediately declared its faith in
collective leadership. The council included Jalal Talabani,

Ibrahim Ahmad, Ali Askari (a prominent military commander) and others of the younger radical generation. It renounced Barzani's decision to end the armed struggle, but ordered all its officials and Pesh Mergas to withdraw into Iran to save them from the vengeance of the Baghdad government.

On the 24th Barzani's Radio Kurdistan went off the air. On the night of 27–8 March Barzani and his entourage decamped from Galala, and by way of Haj Omran entered Iran, to reach Nagadeh some 20 miles from the frontier, where a large refugee camp was being established. Here he remained virtually under house arrest, surviving another assassination attempt on 27 May. Iranian helicopters had been busily collecting the families of Barzani and other prominent Kurdish leaders from the remote reaches of the Badinan region, including Barzani's 'three wives, ten sons, seven or eight daughters, and about 500 relatives' (*Guardian*).

On 1 April Iraqi troops resumed their advance into Kurdish territory, even though the deadline for the amnesty had been extended to the end of that month. Meeting hardly any opposition at all, they managed to penetrate into Kurdish heartland areas for the first time in about ten years. The Iraqi government accused discontented KDP members of executing relatives of Barzani, and a number of bodies, some with 'chained ankles', were put on show at Galala for the media. In the midst of the confusion that reigned during the mass refugee exodus to Iran, Kurdish vengeance was active against 'traitors'.

The total number of casualties of the 14-year Kurdish insurrection remains a subject of speculation. Iraq quoted its casualties as '1640 killed, and 7903 wounded', but claimed to have 'killed or wounded 7600 Kurds', although it did not give a time frame (*Guardian*). Current consensus estimates for the insurrection indicated that Iraq might have lost over 7000 dead and 10 000 wounded, an unusual proportion on general battle averages. The Kurds only admitted to losing some 2000 men, clearly an underestimate. One authority thinks the grand total of casualties for both sides, including civilians, could be '50 000, while up to 250 000 Kurds fled into Iran, and the total number of displaced Iraqi Kurds could be about 600 000' (McDowall, 1985).

In the course of this Kurdish insurrection, at a maximum Iraq deployed no more than 120 000 men, of whom a proportion were detribalised Kurds fighting Kurds. By May 1975 the

number had fallen to less than 40 000, being three divisions
with their supporting arms and services.

Many of the Kurdish refugees in Iran soon began to respond to the amnesty terms offered. Some were resettled, although not necessarily in their former homes, and many were
relocated to camps in southern Iraq. By 31 May it was said that
over 140 000 had returned. Many were detained for vetting,
some being sent to 're-education camps' while others were
released. Later Tariq Aziz, the Iraqi information minister,
admitted 'there had been some executions', and that several
thousands remained in detention. Also, many of the Kurdish
villagers who had remained were evicted from security zones
alongside the Iranian and Turkish frontiers and 'regrouped
into collective settlements'. This was aimed at breaking down
tribal patterns and links and encouraging integration. The
Kurds were forbidden to carry arms, formerly a cherished
privilege.

Security priorities apart, the Iraqi government made an effort to win over the Kurds by building houses, reallocating
land and instituting a rehabilitation programme, its final goal
being to unite the Iraqi peoples into a single nation. The
Baghdad government propaganda machine began to discredit
Barzani, alleging he had betrayed the Kurds, and insisting its
case was against Barzani and not the Kurdish people. Several
senior KDP leaders were brought into Iraq's political and
administrative framework. Ubeidallah Barzani, Barzani's eldest
son, was already working with the government, and Hashim
Aqrawi became head of the 'executive council', a sort of gov-
ernment-appointed 'cabinet for the north'. An efficient and
ruthless security system had produced Iraq's most stable government for several years, which was now girding its loins against
the threat of Iranian expansionism. Its aim was national unity
and economic development, rather that political freedom. Both
the Iraqi government and the Shah of Iran had their secret
agendas.

The Shah had been surprised when the Iraqi armed forces
reactivated their Seventh Offensive, as he had apparently been
expecting a cease-fire to be observed by both sides. He had
not wanted the Kurds to suffer such a resounding defeat and
collapse, anticipating that the 'no win' factor would continue
to distract the Iraqi government. However when the Iraqi

offensive was resumed, the Shah hastened to pull out all his troops and guns from Iraq and abruptly cut off arms and ammunition supplies, to the apparent surprise of the CIA. Prior to this, not wanting Barzani's Kurds to become too militarily strong, for some time he had been curbing ammunition supplies, only sending in 'replacements' upon production of empty cartridge cases.

8 Regional Events: 1976–80

The abrupt collapse of the Barzani Kurdish insurrection in Iraq was a setback to Kurdish aspirations, not only in Iraq but also to Kurds in Turkey and Iran, who had closely followed Barzani's fortunes and misfortunes and had listened to inflammatory exhortations beamed out on insurgent Iraqi radio broadcasts. Many Kurds, some for the first time, became aware of their Kurdish identity and potential. These Kurdish stirrings began to alarm governments.

The strain of defeat and internal differences briefly neutered the Iraqi KDP, and for a short while the writ of the Iraqi government really did extend through Kurdish areas to its northern borders. Such Kurdish activists as remained in Iraq kept a low profile. For the moment it was every man for himself, with survival as the issue at stake. Most Iraqi Kurdish activists heeded advice given by both Barzani and the KDP Central Committee, 'to make for Iran', anticipating that once there they would be able to regroup. However, once they had been herded into refugee camps all political activity was strictly forbidden by the Iranian government, and all contact with Iraq severed.

Inside Iraq hundreds of thousands of Kurds, including many returning under amnesty enticements, were relocated to camps in the south. Rumours abounded of executions, imprisonments and torture. Overtly the Baghdad government was carrying out what it thought was a magnanimous rehabilitation programme, which it was in part, but at the same time it was covertly clearing and forcibly securing frontier areas to block illicit cross-border traffic.

Soon the massive relocation programme and other restrictive measures against the Kurds caused a reaction to set in, and resistance again began to surface. The Iraqi government's intention was to obliterate 'Kurdishness' and encourage national unity. The pro-government 'official KDP', led by Hashim Aqrawi, had to close its Kurdish language newspaper, and Aqrawi was removed from his government position.

When Barzani's resistance collapsed Jalal Talabani was in Syria, where he remained for the time being, the Syrian government – in its hostility towards the Baghdad one – affording him

protection. In June 1975 Talabani formed his left-wing elements into the Patriotic Union of Kurdistan (PUK), and operating from the security of Damascus he set about re-establishing
an active presence in Iraqi Kurdistan. In August 1976 he was
joined by Ali Askari, a former prominent member of the
Ahmad–Talabanj-KDP who had escaped from a southern
internment camp, who became PUK military commander in
the field.

In August 1975 the rump of the KDP held a conference
'somewhere in Europe', attended by 'over 90 personalities'
(*The Times*), in order to analyse their defeat and decide what
to do in future. The Kurdish defeat was blamed on Kissinger
(the US Secretary of State) and the Shah of Iran, both of
whom were said to have betrayed Barzani. It decided to fight
on and avoid any Iranian entanglement. The later (leaked)
secret Pike Report (US House of Representatives Committee
Report on Intelligence), which analysed the Barzani defeat,
attributed it to groundless promises of American assistance and
the deviousness of the Shah.

Mustafa Barzani was now an old, sick and broken man,
despite more flattering journalistic reports, and was in no condition to lead a Kurdish insurgent revival. It was therefore
decided that two of his sons, Idris and Masoud, would jointly
lead the section of the KDP that remained loyal to him. This
became known as the KDP(PL) (Provisional Leadership), which
began to re-establish itself in the Badinan region in northern
Iraq. Another splinter from the rump KDP was the Provisional
Committee, led by Mahmoud Osman, which did not become
active in Kurdistan. After a brief sojourn in Iran, Barzani, his
family and a 'few hundred followers' were taken by ship to the
USA, where he eventually entered a hospital for treatment for
cancer, and so was removed from the immediate scene.

By the end of 1975 the embers of Kurdish insurgency were
again glowing. Groups used guerrilla warfare tactics against
government posts and patrols, avoiding the confrontational
stance that Barzani had favoured in his latter days. In 1976
small Iraqi military operations were launched. For example a
KDP(PL) spokesman based in London claimed that '130 Iraqi
soldiers were killed in renewed fighting in the last two weeks
of August' (*The Times*). Propaganda smoke was again pouring
out from Kurdish Iraqi dissident groups, but there were signs

of fire as well. As both KDP(PL) and PUK elements struggled to re-establish themselves in their former stamping grounds, they came into violent contact with each other. Old patterns of hostility were reemerging.

Sceptical that Iraq would fulfil the terms of the Algiers Treaty, especially regarding frontier clauses, and anticipating ensuing bad relations developing between Iran and Iraq, which could be to their benefit, the Kurds were surprised and disappointed in this respect when the Shah abruptly closed his frontier to all Iraqi Kurds but those returning home.

To attract international attention the KDP(PL) began to take foreign hostages, demanding in exchange for their safe release the return of Kurds and their families from the southern relocation centres and the release of political prisoners. Four Polish engineers, captured in December 1976, were held until March 1977, to be released after two Frenchmen had been kidnapped the previous month. An Algerian was also seized. This caused the Iraqi armed forces to launch another campaign against the Kurds.

Saddam Hussein visited Ankara in March 1977 to try to persuade the Turkish government to tighten up its frontier controls, which had become lax, to prevent arms and supplies from reaching the Iraqi Kurds and to cooperate with the Iraqi armed forces in curbing their activities. Iraq accused both the USSR and Syria of helping Iraqi Kurds, but hesitated to include Turkey in its allegations. Saddam Hussein arranged for a joint Turkish–Iraqi intelligence liaison cell to be established in Diyarbakir, but this did not seem to become effective. Turkey remained suspicious and tended to distance itself from Iraq.

Exasperated, and convinced that Turkey was actually helping Iraqi Kurdish insurgents, in January 1978 the Iraqi government halted supplies through the oil pipeline running from Kirkuk through Turkey to the East Mediterranean commercial port of Yumurtalik, and to Turkey itself. The Turkish economy was in a poor state, and the country was indebted to Iraq to the tune of some $30 million for oil supplies, which it could not pay. Iraq's demand for repayment of the debt and resumption of oil supplies was turned into an allegation that Turkey could not control its Kurds or stop the PUK cross-Turkey supply route, and would not cooperate in closing and securing their joint frontier. Relations between Turkey and Iraq became more distant.

In April 1978 Kurds attacked an army outpost at Mosul, and in the fighting it was claimed that some 30 government troops were killed, This was followed by similar incidents, which left little doubt that insurrection was developing. In June the Baghdad government cracked down on communists, and especially on the Iraqi Communist Party (ICP), which had been part of the National Progressive Front. Government measures included executions and imprisonment. Many communists fled northwards to seek shelter from Kurdish resistance organisations, which added fuel to the Iraqi allegation that they were receiving Soviet assistance.

KURDS IN TURKEY

In Turkey a Kurdish political resistance pattern was developing as activists – wanting to operate openly as Kurds and not to have to pretend to be Turks – realising there was no place for them as such in any Turkish organisation, began to form semi-secret groups of their own. In 1974 the former DDKO was revived as the Democratic Cultural Association (DDKD) with the object of uniting progressive Kurdish movements, but was unsuccessful in this aim. About the same time the Kurdish Socialist Party of Turkey (TKSP) appeared, founded by members of the dissolved Turkish Workers' Party. Its 'Marxist' platform called imprecisely for the liberation of Kurds from 'colonial oppression' and the formation of a Kurdish national democratic front (McDowall, 1985).

In Turkey, as in Iraq, it was difficult to persuade Kurds to come to mutual agreements among themselves, and to stick to them. At one stage the TKSP, whose secretary, Kemal Burkay, operated from abroad, pressed for 'independence' in the form of separate Turkish and Kurdish soviets. Some Kurdish organisations included the expression 'colonial oppression' in their manifestos, a complex left over from Ottoman days.

The one virulent, durable Kurdish political party that came to dominate Turkish Kurdish resistance for many years ahead had been in embryo form since 1972, or perhaps even before, although its official foundation date, now celebrated annually, was 27 November 1978, when it launched its guerrilla warfare campaign against the Turkish government. This was the Kurdish Workers' Party (Parte Krikaranc Kordesian – PKK), which believed in violent revolution against the Turkish regime and 'feudal' Kurds.

The 'Marxist' PKK, founded and led by Abdullah Ocalan, its secretary general, originated with a group of activists known as 'Apocus', and Ocalan became known as 'Apocular', or 'Apo'. The PKK was independent and often in contention with other Kurdish organisations that were developing in the late 1970s. According to one authority the PKK emerged from the extremist left-wing Turkish Revolutionary Youth (Dev Genc) in 1974 and moved from Ankara to Kurdistan in 1979 (McDowall, 1985).

Like many durable, long-time terrorist groups, its origins have tended to become shrouded in mist and legend. I was later told by two who claimed to be founder members that the PKK had begun as an ideological political group, almost a private debating circle (the emphasis always being on the 'armed struggle') that came to be influenced by the writings of Mao Tse-tung and other revolutionary leaders and practised in China, Indo-China and later in Vietnam.

The situation in Turkey's Kurdish south-eastern provinces remained abrasive and confused during 1978, with government armed forces making occasional punitive forays in which buildings and personnel were attacked, or to intervene when Kurdish intertribal and interpolitical fighting and assassinations became too intense. Added to this internal strife, in-fighting between the Iraqi KDP(PL) and the PUK on several occasions spilled over the border into Turkey, where each had its own respective allies, ever eager to join in the fray.

In mid-June 1978 the Turkish media reported that fighting on Turkish territory between the two rival Iraqi groups 'left over 100 PUK supporters dead or wounded'. The following month another report stated that in mid-July the KDP(PL) 'captured over 400 PUK members including its leaders, notably Ali Askari, the PUK military commander, but not Talabani' (*The Times*). From time to time, both Turkish and Iraqi armed forces individually strayed over the joint frontier in hot pursuit, seemingly acting independently of each other.

While Iraq was trying to make its frontier secure, an almost impossible task, Turkey seemed less committed to this objective.

Border areas between Turkey and northern Iraq, and indeed
with northern Iran, were on the fast-growing international drug
route from Afghanistan to Europe. Also, the PUK had beaten
its own route from Syria through Turkish terrain to its elements in Iraq, along which personnel and supplies moved,
apparently with the tacit approval of the Turkish government,
a fact that did not amuse the Turkish army.

REVOLUTION IN IRAN

Turmoil inside Iran had been mounting for some time against
the Shah's oppressive rule, fanned by the inflammatory oratory
of the exiled Ayatollah Khomeini. On 16 January 1979 the
Shah was pushed into exile; on 9 February fierce, confused
fighting erupted on the streets of Tehran and some other
major cities; on the 11th Prime Minister Bakhtiar resigned and
the military made their 'Declaration of Neutrality', signed by
24 generals, of whom eight were executed within days; and on
1 April Khomeini proclaimed Iran an Islamic republic. Political
restraints were removed and over 100 different parties, organisations and groups came out into the open, loudly declaring
their own diverse aims. The historic moment of unprecedented
unity that brought about the downfall of the Shah, once the
deed was done, instantly dissolved, and internal chaos ensued,
in which the mullahs hijacked the revolution.

One group emerging from obscurity was the 'Komala' (the
Revolutionary Organisation of Kurdish Workers and not to be
confused with the previously mentioned 'Komola'), which in
Kurdish means 'organisation'. The Komala had been founded
in 1969 by left-wing students in Tehran, but had been passive
until the revolution (McDowall, 1985). The Komala soon
claimed to have a rising industrial and urban membership, but
it also became active in rural Kurdistan, with some success,
rivalling the KDPI.

Vengeance was wreaked on the Shah's armed forces as generals and senior officers were dismissed or imprisoned, many
being executed. Conscripts disappeared to their homes, but
the large regular element, leaderless and demoralised for the
moment, remained quietly in barracks, while the gendarmerie
stayed at its posts along borders and throughout the country.

Repression by Khomeini, his Islamic Revolutionary Council (IRC) and the some 80 000 mullahs (estimates vary) continued as a myriad of self-appointed revolutionary committees (Komiehs), each with its own armed vigilante force, mushroomed, assumed authority and enforced their local interpretations of Khomeini's edicts.

THE KDPI

The KDPI had survived under Abdul Rahman Ghassemlou, a French-educated socialist who assumed its leadership in 1973, despite being buffeted between Iraqi and Iranian governments. Its platform had been anti-Shahist, and during the Iraqi Kurdish insurrection, when the Shah was supplying Barzani with arms and military aid, its leadership had sought sanctuary and support in Baghdad, while its Pesh Mergas in the field fought against pro-Barzani Iranian Kurdish elements wherever and whenever possible.

When the Iraqi Kurdish insurrection against the Baghdad government resumed in 1974 it expected open condemnation of Barzani from Ghassemlou, but in the curious Kurdish belief that 'today's enemy might be tomorrow's friend', Ghassemlou refused to give it. Consequently he and the KDPI leadership were ejected from Iraq, to survive as best they could in Iran, or in exile elsewhere.

The Kurds in Iran had been kept on a tight leash by the SAVAK system of informers, government bribes and patronage, and turning one tribe against another. Many tribal sheikhs with feudal estates or authority, held at the behest of the Shah, and many others who held sinecure appointments and benefits, did not want the old order to change. Others, not so well blessed, did for ideological reasons, for the opportunity to exploit or for vengeance. The KDPI, which had a longer vision, worked in cooperation with any radical group when it was to its advantage to do so, and sided with 'landless peasants' seeking to become 'landed peasants' by supplanting their feudal masters and assuming their powers. The KDPI also selectively sided with traditional sheikhs in their struggles against each other whenever it suited its purpose, often quickly switching sides at vital moments in the furtherance of dominance.

As central authority collapsed and a power vacuum appeared, Kurds, and especially KDPI members in Kurdish terrain, occupied army barracks whenever they were able, thus acquiring quantities of arms, ammunition and many gendarmerie posts, and dominating towns and villages. The KDPI played its full part in forming self-appointed revolutionary committees to run local affairs in Kurdish areas, finding itself in competition with both the Komala and the left-wing Fedayeen Khalk, the latter having many Kurdish members. Initially they avoided conflict, and in places shared power.

After the Khomeini revolution two leaders became prominent in Iranian Kurdistan. One was Sheikh Ezzedin Hosseini, a Sunni religious authority who lived at Mahabad and gained a wide traditional following; the other was the activist Abdul Rahman Ghassemlou, who claimed his KDPI had over 10 000 Pesh Mergas. Hosseini represented religious authority, and the younger, enlightened Ghassemlou military might. It was an unlikely partnership but it worked well for some time.

Another catalyst appeared on the scene. In the eyes of the Tehran government Sheikh Ezzedin Hosseini was an obscure cleric, a Sunni who had suddenly become dangerous and disruptive, and so it pushed forward a rival Shia leader, Sheikh Ahmad Moftizadeh, to counter him. This brought religious friction into the Kurdish resistance equation, as only a minority of Kurdish tribes were Shia.

Most Iranian Kurds recognised that the Iranian revolution and instability in Tehran presented an opportunity to obtain more political freedom for themselves. In early March Sheikh Ezzedin Hosseini, operating from Mahabad, called a huge 'Kurdish Revolutionary Council' of tribal sheikhs and leaders, said to number about 500, which decided to demand complete autonomy. An eight-point plan, which just left foreign affairs, defence and economic planning in the hands of the central government, was produced and dispatched to Tehran. Nothing was heard for some time, causing anxiety as it was known that Khomeini was preparing a new constitution, in which the Kurds wanted their autonomy to be enshrined. The Kurds were not consulted.

It was true that the new Tehran government had many problems on its hands, but it found time to oppose Kurdish autonomy, as if this was achieved other non-Farsi minorities, including Arabs, Azerbaijanis (Turks), Baluchis and Turkomans, would demand it as well, which would lead to federation – and who knows what else could follow. However right from the start Khomeini and his IRC did not seem to object to limited Kurdish autonomy.

In an effort to cool Kurdish agitation the Khomeini government tried to persuade the Kurds to support the rival Shia religious leader, Sheikh Ahmad Moftizadeh. This did not go down well amongst Sunni Kurds. Khomeini's next move was to stop revolutionary committees issuing arms to non-Farsi individuals. Kurds in Sanandaj immediately protested, demanding their full share of the arms taken from the military, and when this was refused street fighting ensued. On 19 March Kurds seized the military commander of the Sanandaj garrison, occupied part of the barracks and broadcast a rallying cry over the local radio station. The Kurds remained defiant over the period of the Kurdish New Year (Nowruz, on 21 March). Ayatollah Khomeini condemned their action and appealed for them to give themselves up.

The minister of the interior was sent as a negotiator to Sanandaj, which at that time was regarded as the unofficial capital of Iranian Kurdistan. He persuaded them to evacuate the barracks and release their prisoners, giving in return the assurance that Kurdish, for the first time, could be taught in schools. Kurdish had only recently adopted a Latin alphabet, which enabled Kurdish periodicals to be printed. Kurdish had never officially been a teaching medium in schools. This was the first head-on clash between Iranian Kurds and the Khomeini government.

The KDPI – which had taken over the military barracks at Mahabad, the seat of Sheikh Ezzedin Hosseini, who quickly came to be the acknowledged spiritual leader of the Iranian Kurds – found itself opposed by pro-Barzani Iranian Kurds and elements of Barzani's KDP, who were filtering into northwestern Iran. The Komala and the left-wing Fedayeen Khalk also established HQs at Mahabad in order to ensure their share of power. Baneh was another town with joint Kurdish administration, where the KDPI and Komala shared power. Each of these three groups were bent on consolidating their own power bases. The Komala accused the Tehran government of using revolutionary committees, Shia Kurds and pro-Barzani forces against it (McDowall, 1985).

During the weeks following the Iranian revolution, although the Kurds were fighting, quarrelling and striving amongst themselves, they did in fact dominate their whole region, often through Kurdish revolutionary committees or by default as local military garrisons and gendarmerie remained passive. Kurdish voices began to call for autonomy. Beset by a multiplicity of problems and lacking an effective military capability, the Tehran government had perforce to put its Kurdish problem on the back-burner for a while. As the unlikely partnership of Sheikh Ezzedin Hosseini and Abdul Rahmam Ghassemlou continued to dominate the situation, the Tehran government attempted to negotiate with them.

In April 1979 Naqadeh in northern Iran became a dangerous flashpoint when the KDPI, seeking to establish a branch in that mainly Shia town, came into violent confrontation with the local revolutionary committee, which opposed this project. Street-fighting broke out between the KDPI and the revolutionary committee's militia, which was driven out of town. The central government threatened to send troops against the KDPI unless it laid down its arms. On 20 April a cease-fire was signed in Naqadeh. The KDPI backed down on this occasion.

THE PASDARAN

Khomeini began to rebuild a national military capability and, as a first step, on 16 June he formed the Islamic Revolutionary Guards Corps (Pasdaran-e Inqilal-e Islam), known as the Pasdaran, a dedicated Islamic military force. The following month it was ready for action. The armed forces were also put into better shape.

In mid-July a detachment of Pasdaran descended on the border town of Marivan, and in a skirmish drove out the Kurdish defenders. In protest the inhabitants, together with a column of sympathetic citizens from Sanandaj, about 70 miles distant, commenced a demonstration march towards Marivan, some making 'sit-down' protests to block roads. Sheikh Ezzedin Hosseini protested, demanding the release of captured Kurds and refusing the government's offer that Marivan should be garrisoned by equal numbers of Pasdaran and Pesh Mergas. A local stalemate ensued. The Pasdaran settled in several other Kurdish towns, causing friction between them and local Kurdish defenders.

On 17 August a group of KDPI Pesh Mergas attacked and occupied the frontier town of Paveh, driving out the Pasdaran. Pasdaran reinforcements arrived, and in the counter-attack, which was supported by helicopters, lost a score of men before regaining possession of Paveh on the 19th. This was the catalyst Khomeini had been waiting for, and acting upon 'false information' he launched a campaign to put his military imprint on Iranian Kurdistan.

On 18 August Khomeini assumed supreme command of the Iranian armed forces, and ordered the army and the Pasdaran to work together (an unlikely partnership). A general mobilisation order followed. At that time a delegation from Mahabad's Kurdish Revolutionary Committee was in Tehran offering peace terms. The KDPI was proscribed, the arrest of its leaders ordered and Ghassemlou's election to the assembly of experts, to produce the new constitution, was annulled.

An 18-day campaign began in which the Pasdaran and the Iranian army, with artillery, tank and air support, drove militant Kurds from the main towns in Kurdistan back into the hills. The Kurds resisted but their defiance was often only brief, as they were neither armed nor conditioned for urban or siege warfare. The government claimed it was operating against over 50 000 armed Kurds. Ghassemlou admitted he controlled over 10 000 Pesh Mergas, the backbone of the Kurdish resistance.

Paveh, Sanandaj, Marivan, Naqadeh, Jaladin, Miandoab and other towns quickly fell to government forces in the face of such overwhelming odds, the Iranian media deliberately depicting glorious battles and victories at each one. The foreign media reported little signs of heavy fighting, although in Saqqiz, which fell on 26 August, it was reported that the 'dead and injured lay unattended on the streets' (*Daily Telegraph*). The last town to be occupied by government forces was Sardasht on 5 September.

Although they had lost their foothold in all the major towns, the Kurds still retained the freedom of the countryside, in a claimed area of some 78 000 square miles. They reverted to guerrilla tactics, which better suited their capabilities. Ghassemlou declared that the war was just beginning and would be a long one, probably having the recent Iraqi Kurdish insurrection in mind and encouraged by hoped for support from Turkish and Iraqi Kurds. Confrontational defiance in the face of the might of the Pasdaran and a rapidly reviving Iranian army was never a viable, nor a wise option for the Iranian Kurds.

It came of something of a surprise when Khomeini suddenly produced a sledgehammer to crack the weak Kurdish nut, but he had his reasons. Iran had about 1500 miles of joint frontier with the USSR, and he feared a Soviet-inspired and Soviet-supported communist backlash by Iranian left-wing groups, including the KDPI, against his increasingly dictatorial Islamic regime. Kurds and other mutinous Iranian minorities were giving shelter to communists and left-wing activists escaping from the reign of terror in Tehran and other major Farsi cities. A main reason had been to extend his authority in a vulnerable frontier region and to obtain a military victory to boost the morale of his armed forces. Khomeini saw external dangers ahead, and regularised his military conscription system. The much-mentioned 'false information' upon which he overtly acted was that Kurds had attacked the barracks at Sanandaj, taking soldiers, their wives and children hostage, which he accentuated by organising protest demonstrations in Tehran demanding military action.

As the fighting died down Ayatollah Sadiq Khalkhali, with his revolutionary court, arrived on the Kurdish scene, and within days over 70 Kurds had been executed. Amnesties were then extended to most of the Kurds who had fought against government forces, but not to Sheikh Ezzedin Hosseini or Ghassemlou. Low-level guerrilla warfare rumbled on in Iranian Kurdistan.

In the first week of September 1979 Kurdish Pesh Mergas ambushed a convoy in the Doab Pass and 15 Pasdaran were killed. In retaliation, a few days later the Pasdaran massacred '46 Kurdish men, women and children at the village of Garna' near Neqadeh. A government enquiry was instigated, and responsibility admitted (*Guardian*). In early October Kurds in Iran rose once again in insurrection to 'liberate' most of their region. On 8 October Kurdish Pesh Mergas claimed to have ambushed and killed 52 Revolutionary Guards near Sardasht. The Kurdish countryside became dangerous terrain for government forces to tread, and garrisons tended to adopt a defensive stance. A cease-fire was arranged.

Soon Ayatollah Khomeini was ready to negotiate again, and in November 1979 a government delegation visited Sheikh Hosseini at Mahabad. This was followed in December with a proffered fourteen-point settlement, allowing 'self administration', but it was refused as it fell short of Kurdish demands. There was disagreement over the precise area to be included. Kurds wanted to embrace all Western Azerbaijan, but Tehran would not agree to forfeiting control over certain strategic and vulnerable frontier territory. It also refused to grant the Kurds Ilam and Kermanshah, which were inhabited mainly by Kurdish Shias. Negotiations broken down and guerrilla warfare rumbled on.

SEIZURE OF AMERICAN HOSTAGES

On 4 November 1979 the American Embassy in Tehran was seized by Islamic revolutionary students and all inside were held hostage. The initial demand was that the Shah, then in the USA, be handed over to them in return for the safe release of the American hostages. Instead the hostages were held captive for 444 days, while the greatest superpower in the world chafed helplessly and hopelessly. This had a profound effect on the thinking of revolutionary movements, demonstrating the high regard Western nations had for the lives of their nationals and what their worth in the ransom market could be.

BANI-SADR AND THE KURDS

When Abdol Hassan Bani-Sadr was elected President of Iran in February 1980, Ghassemlou and Sheikh Ezzedin Hosseini presented to him another plan for Kurdish autonomy, but this too was rejected. In April, disturbances broke out over the military moving Kurdish families from their villages in order to create security areas near international borders. Fighting ensued at Saqqiz and Sanandaj, the government insisting that the insurgents surrender. This was a time of mounting tension between the governments of Iran and Iraq. Bani-Sadr rushed to Mahabad to see Hosseini, demanding that the Kurds lay down their arms, but the meeting was not an amicable one. The prospect for Iranian Kurds seemed to be one of indefinite armed insurrection, on the pattern of the Iraqi Kurdish one of the 1960s. Ghassemlou again spoke of a long war ahead.

The Kurdish resistance consisted basically of the KDPI, the Komala and the Fedayeen Khalk, supported by groups of mercurial tribes and tribal federations. Hosseini was having difficulty in holding them together. In June he complained that the communist Tudeh was infiltrating the KDPI, and that already several members of its central committee had split away from that organisation. The Pasdaran had by this time come into violent contact with the KDPI. A few days later it was reported that 15 Kurds had been executed at Khoy in Western Azerbaijan for murder and rebellion, having killed a local governor and the officer commanding a Pasdaran detachment after taking them hostage.

THE DEATH OF MULLAH MUSTAFA BARZANI

The famed Kurdish leader, Mullah Mustafa Barzani, died on 2 March 1979 – at the presumed age of 75 – of cancer in a Washington hospital, less than a couple of months after his one-time friend and ultimate betrayer, the Shah of Iran, had fallen from power. He lived long enough to express the view that the Iranian revolution was an opportunity to achieve Kurdish autonomy in both Iran and Iraq. Despite his support for the one-time Kurdish Mahabad Republic, Barzani had never asked for more than autonomy from the various Baghdad governments.

His body was brought back to Iraq by his son Masoud, who had been with him, to be eventually buried at Ushnavia in Iranian Kurdistan. A few days afterwards the grave was desecrated. Interviewed later by Robert Fisk in Karaj (Iran), Idris Barzani stated that his father's body 'had been hurled from the grave', and that he blamed Ghassemlou, whom he alleged had given the order for this deed to be done.

Barzani lived on in legend as a warrior chieftain whose qualities ranged from great to petty and vindictive. A master of tribal warfare and intrigue, his vision above and beyond the tribal scene had been limited. Much of his time had been spent fighting brother Kurds and countering left-wing elements that were forever creeping into the KDP, as witnessed by his quarrels with Jalal Talabani.

Barzani's tortuous relations with the KDPI had continued after his return from the Soviet Union as he did his best to keep it on traditional tribally orientated lines in the 1950s. When it adopted a left-wing stance and policy and came into conflict with the Iranian SAVAK, he handed over many escaping KDPI members to the Iranian authorities. On several occasions Barzani arrested KDPI leaders and delivered them to SAVAK. When the KDPI held a conference in Iraqi Kurdistan, Barzani prevented left-wing delegates from attending.

When receiving military aid from the Shah, Barzani clamped down on KDPI members sheltering in Iraq, who were being bribed by the Baghdad government to fight against anti-Shahist Kurds in Iran, preventing them from crossing or recrossing the Iraq–Iran border. In 1968 Barzani executed a KDPI leader (Sulieman Muini) and handed the body over to Iranian authorities, who displayed it in Kurdish villages (McDowall, 1985).

When the shah was overthrown the Barzani-KDP(PL) and the PUK openly supported the Islamic revolution, which immediately threw them both into hostile contact with the KDPI, itself soon hostile to the new Tehran government. After Mullah Mustafa's funeral the Barzani-KDP(PL) held its ninth congress in Iranian territory. Masoud was appointed leader and tried to placate the 'progressives' by dropping the term 'Provisional Leadership' from the title. It still remained tribal and traditional. With a claimed 3000 Pesh Mergas, Masoud embarked upon warfare against the KDPI, or rather continued his father's bitter quarrel.

However the new KDP alliance with the Islamic regime in Tehran, and continuation of the Barzani dynasty in a leadership position, did not please its 'progressives', who broke away to form the Kurdistan Popular Democratic Party (KPDP), led by Sami Abdul Rahman and Nur Shawis.

KURDISH NATIONALISM IN TURKEY

In Turkey, a civilian government under Bulent Ecevit was formed in January 1978. Apart from major internal unrest amounting almost to open civil war, the new government was faced by severe economic difficulties and a large, burdensome external debt. Turkey had few friends and was struggling to become accepted into the European Economic Community (EEC), only to be met by barely veiled hostility over its invasion of Cyprus in 1974 and criticism of its poor human rights record. Only its NATO membership kept its Western dialogue alive, saving it from becoming a European outcast. Turkey was a NATO frontline state, fielding some 22 infantry divisions, and in Cold War terms it was Europe's south-eastern bastion against potential Soviet aggression. It therefore had to be accommodated, although its application for EEC membership was coolly left pending. Western Europe did not want to get to know Turkey.

Although in 1978 international publicity was mainly centred on violent struggles between right-wing and left-wing major political groups, regions in which Kurds were in a majority were festering into uncontrollable insurrection. In December a state of martial law was declared in 13 provinces, mainly Kurdish majority ones, it being officially stated that over 1400 political murders had been committed that year, and that large quantities of illegal Soviet- and Czech-manufactured arms were pouring into the country through Syria and Iraq to extremist political groups.

The Iranian revolution in February 1979 made the Turkish government wary in case its out-of-control Kurds in the border provinces ignited hostilities with that country. Accordingly, after a demand by independent ministers in the Ecevit government for more effective measures against terrorism and insurrection, on 20 April an agreement was signed in Baghdad between Iraq, Iran and Turkey to cooperate in suppressing Kurkish separatist activities in the border regions of these three countries. In addition the state of martial law was extended in Turkey to include the predominantly Kurdish provinces of Adiyamen, Diyarbakir, Hakkari, Siirt and Tunceli, bringing the number of provinces under martial law to 19, of which 16 were Kurdish (Turkey had 67 provinces).

In the summer of 1979 Turkish security forces launched an intensive campaign against the power centres of the main extremist groups, making mass arrests and exciting the renewed interest of Amnesty International, but with only limited success. Violence escalated and intergroup assassinations increased. This was compounded by terrorist activities, both in Turkey and overseas, by the Armenian Liberation Army, which was struggling for the restoration of Armenian autonomy in eastern areas of Turkey.

In October the Ecevit government fell because of political defections and losses at the polls, to be replaced by a coalition led by Sulieman Demirel. Ecevit had tried unsuccesfully to impose martial law with a 'human face' on the Kurds. Kurdish leaders threatened there would be rebellion in eastern Turkey if their demands were not met, but this was dismissed by government officials, who insisted the Kurds did not have the means to carry out their threat. The military were not so sure.

NATO IN TURKEY

NATO authorities, the Americans in particular, became concerned about the state of potential insurgency in Turkey, which would endanger their facilities in that country. The US Pentagon expressed anxiety over its only radar 'listening and searching' station in the country at Pirincilik (10 miles from Diyarbakir), which was essential for monitoring Soviet territory for the second Strategic Arms Limitation Treaty (SALT-2).

Turkey had upset Western countries in 1974, when its troops invaded the Turkish-inhabited part of Cyprus and stayed there. An arms embargo against Turkey followed and, when the US House of Representatives refused to have it lifted, the 26 NATO (US) bases in Turkey were closed. When the embargo was eventually lifted in September 1978, four such bases, under stricter Turkish supervision than formerly, were opened, and also certain radar-tracking ones covering Soviet air space. The argument over NATO bases in Turkey continued, with Turkey making difficulties over US U-2 aircraft 'spy flights' through Turkish air space.

MARTIAL LAW IN TURKEY

A blanket of official repression fell on much of Turkey, involving curfews, searches and arbitrary arrests, provoking rumours of torture and 'disappeared persons'. Amnesty International reports made horrific reading. Turkish armed forces launched punitive campaigns against insurgent Kurds and the power centres of the other main extremist groups, while political assassinations at times averaged 20 a week.

While both Iran and Iraq recognised Kurds as a separate ethnic race, and treated them as such within their sovereignty, this was still not so in Turkey. This provided the government with the dilemma of how to deal with them separately without recognising their Kurdishness. In April 1979 a Kurdish ex-minister said in public: 'In Turkey there are Kurds. I too am a Kurd'. He was charged with uttering propaganda aimed at weakening national feelings, and was eventually sentenced to two years imprisonment (*Kurdish News and Comment*). This illustrated the rigid government attitude towards its unspoken Kurdish problem.

The Turkish government tried hard to distance itself from inter-Kurdish fighting in Iran and Iraq, which periodically flowed across its borders, and when in September a Turkish newspaper reported that '5000 Turkish Kurds had been recruited to fight alongside Iranian Kurds' (*Hurriyet*), this was instantly denied by military authorities. The denial was disbelieved, especially as it followed an army interception of a convoy of arms destined for Kurds in Iran, then in open conflict with Khomeini's Pasdaran and his armed forces.

Turkish Kurdish insurgent groups had disjointed liaison and gave selective support, including arms, to Kurds in Iraq and Iran who were either struggling against each other or against their respective governments. There was also evidence that small groups of Turkish Kurds, anxious for battle, were crossing international frontiers to fight for or against Kurdish insurrectionary groups, although not in such huge numbers as was alleged by the Iranian and Iraqi governments.

THE SOVIETS INVADE AFGHANISTAN

For sometime the Soviets had been busily involved in Afghanistan, a very backward Muslim country reluctantly shambling into the twentieth century, establishing a series of left-wing puppet presidents who were very unpopular with the insular, conservative inhabitants. When one puppet ruler got out of control, wanting to liaise with the USA, he was eliminated, and Soviet armed forces entered Afghanistan in December 1979 to begin a decade-long, painful and difficult occupation of the country.

Afghanistan immediately became a pawn in the Cold War as the USA began to support the insurgent Mujahideen (Holy Warriors), which in turn attracted the attention of Muslim countries hostile to the USA. Both Iran and Turkey, whose territories adjoined the USSR, became anxious, fearing the invasion of Afghanistan was but a first step against them. The Kurds came into the equation as some had sought, and received, Soviet help and sanctuary. The fear was that the Soviets would begin to manipulate them in order to destabilise Iran, Iraq and Turkey. The converse fear was that the USA might pursue a military option in the region.

The contact between Kurdish resistance groups and the USSR made Western countries suspicious of the Kurds' intentions, and to shy away from them. But the Kurds only approached the Soviets because they had no other country to turn to. The West need not have worried too much, as the doctrines of Marx and Lenin did not penetrate the Muslim-proof armour of the average Kurd, and only rested very lightly on the so-called Kurdish Marxist leaders as an emergency covering. It is perhaps true, however, that some young, detribalised Kurdish leaders were attracted to Soviet communists, admiring their methodical organisation, indoctrination methods and single-minded pursuit of power, and hoped to emulate them for their own purposes.

THE MILITARY COUP IN TURKEY

On 11 September 1980, for the third time since 1961, the Turkish armed forces, which considered themselves to be the guardian of their country, stepped forward again and effected a military coup. A National Security Council assumed supreme power. Admiral Bulent Ulusu, Commander of the Turkish navy, as prime minister formed a government of both military and civilian personnel. A massive wave of arrests followed, which caused most of the violence to decline momentarily, the main exception being in Kurdish regions, where resistance to the central government had become traditional and where 'liberated areas' were appearing adjacent to frontiers, formed by the PKK and other major Kurdish resistance groups.

Many political leaders of all persuasions, including ex-prime ministers, were arrested and a heavy blanket of political repression was laid over Turkey. Selected censorship influenced the media and little reliable hard news came out of Turkey for some time. One newspaper (*Hurriyet*) did manage to report that in the first fortnight after the military coup only 14 people had been killed whereas previously the weekly average had been over 50.

THE SYRIAN FACTOR

Syria was regarded by the US CIA as a state that was fostering terrorism by sheltering a number of international terrorist leaders and their groups. Accordingly Syria was viewed with deep suspicion by Western countries. Its relations with its northern neighbour, Turkey, continued to be poor, mainly because of the dispute over the distribution of the Euphrates waters and because it gave covert shelter and support to the PKK.

Kurds in Syria, said to make up only about 8 per cent of the population (of 8.8 million in 1980, according to the IISS), remained in their communities (some of which were close to the Turkish and Iraqi borders), which had been swelled by waves of refugees. With the tacit blessing of President Hafiz Assad, Syria had become the operating base for Kurdish dissident groups which, owing the length of its borders with Turkey and Iraq, were able to cross them with little difficulty.

The Kurdistan Democratic Party of Syria (KDPS), founded in 1958, had never prospered, being buffeted first by Arab nationalism and then by the ruling Baathist Party, but persecution by governments tended to ease in the 1960s, and in the 1970s some Kurdish land reforms were effected. However the Kurds in Syria were regarded as Syrians and had to serve in the Syrian armed forces.

LACK OF INTERNATIONAL SUPPORT

Generally, still little was known about the Kurds or their problems in the Western world, but such news that did come through about them and their misfortunes caused a vague sympathy to develop for them in some countries, as exiled Kurdish political and cultural groups became active. Silent sympathy was not enough, and had little effect. What exiled Kurds wanted was a patron in the UN forum, but such matters could only be raised by member states, not individual groups. Some governments vaguely smiled on the Kurds and were sympathetic to their cause, but none were willing to take it up and expound it in the UN forum.

The Kurds still inhabited five countries, all with a seat at the UN, but their Kurdish political discontents were regarded as their own domestic affairs. Any UN member nation taking up the Kurdish cause would not only offend the country involved and breach protocol by interfering in its domestic affairs, but would almost certainly arouse hostility in other nations too. In the case of Iraq, for example, such a proposer could cause Arab States to gang up against it on any Kurdish issue, while in the case of Iran the proposer might find itself facing the wrath of the whole Islamic Conference Organisation.

In 1963 Iraqi Kurds had tried to persuade the semi-willing, or naïve, Mongolian Soviet Socialist Republic to bring their case before the UN, but had failed. A few other feeble, unsuccessful attempts had been made, but no country so far had been willing to risk prejudicing its international relations on behalf of the Kurds. Once again in the international field, Kurds found no friends, although some Western countries gave considerable freedom to to their political activities.

9 The Iran–Iraq War

The eight-year Iran–Iraq War began in September 1980, when on the 10th Iraqi troops occupied Qasr Sherin and other Iranian border towns, although Iran dates its commencement from skirmishes on the 4th. On the 17th Saddam Hussein, who had become president of Iraq on 16 July the previous year, abrogated the Algiers Treaty, and on the 20th President Bani-Sadr declared general mobilisation in Iran. Initially Iraq had some tactical successes, but as Iran mobilised its military strength the invading forces were repulsed. Within months a military stalemate set in along a roughly north–south line, loosely coinciding with the mutual international frontier and eventually extending to almost 600 miles. The scene was reminiscent of the First World War, with Iraqi troops holding ever stronger entrenchments and Iranian 'human waves' battering themselves against them, mostly unsuccesfully, in the southern and central sectors. In the northern (Kurdish) sector combat was more fluid.

Anticipating a swift victory, Saddam lacked a well coordinated master plan for the invasion that was flexible enough to cope with unexpected contingencies; his intelligence services underestimated Iranian military potential, being misled by Western media reports of the alleged total collapse of Iranian armed forces; the anticipated rising of the Arab population of Khuzistan (Arabistan) province did not occur; nor did the anticipated internal collapse of the Islamic government. On the contrary, invasion by traditional Arab enemies enraged and tended to unite the Iranian people. Instead of quickly concluding a limited opportunity operation, Saddam found himself enmeshed in a long, dragged-out war.

Kurdish reactions in both Iran and Iraq ran true to form, as both sought to exploit the Iran–Iraq War to their own particular advantage, only to find that they in turn were being used by the Tehran and Baghdad governments. Both Iran and Iraq bribed the other's Kurds, the Baghdad government paying Iranian Kurds to fight against the Tehran government, while the Tehran government bribed Iraqi Kurds to fight against the

123

Baghdad government. Kurdish resistance groups and tribes continued to pursue their own domestic enmities regardless of their notional nationality. Meanwhile hundreds of thousands of Kurds were conscripted into the Iranian and Iraqi armed forces to fight against each other on the battlefield.

In Iranian Kurdistan, Kurdish resistance groups more or less retained the free run of the whole region, gained in their almost unopposed rising in October 1979, as the Iranian army was still basically inactive, feebly trying to remain intact and retain its weaponry, with only the new aggressive Pasdaran trying to impose its authority. Having already gained a foot-hold in a few Kurdish cities and towns, the Pasdaran made renewed efforts to bring the region under its control. Fighting erupted for possession of towns, including Bokan, Mahabad, Piranshah, Sanandaj and Urmiya, some changing hands more than once.

The Islamic government in Iran still distrusted the army, a distrust ingrained from shahist days, and was reluctant to use it in an internal security role. In any case Khomeini had decreed that the army's task was simply to defend the country. Since the February revolution of 1979, Kurdish resistance groups and regular army units had tended to keep their distance, each being content to live and let live. The initial heady days of free-for-all looting of military armouries for arms and ammunition were past, although opportunity in this respect, no matter how small, was never overlooked. Military liaison officers regularly travelled through Kurdish territory across the border to Van and Diyarbakir in safety under unofficial Kurdish protection, and to a degree so did commercial international traffic.

However Kurdish resistance groups had a special hate for the Pasdaran, seeing them as the real danger, and continued to operate guerrilla tactics against them. Instances of Pasdaran trucks being ambushed, with attendant Pasdaran casualties, were frequently reported. Accordingly Sheikh Ezzedin Hosseini, still based in Mahabad, offered to fight to drive all Iraqis from Iranian territory, provided the Tehran government pulled the Pasdaran out from the Kurdish region. This offer was rejected and the Pasdaran continued 'mopping up' operations, with increasing support from the army, which was perforce dragged into the fight against insurgent Kurds.

THE KDPI SPRING OFFENSIVE: 1981

The KDPI remained in the pay of the Baghdad government, which wanted it to become more active against Iranian forces in the north and so attract military attention away from the central and southern fronts. Accordingly, on 15 January 1981 the Iraqi army launched a minor operation across the Iranian border to seize the crossroads frontier town of Nowdesheh, where Ghassemlou established his HQ and supply base with routes back into Iraq.

Beginning in April 1981, Ghassemlou launched a three-month spring campaign, which had some success. The Pasdaran were ejected from a number of Kurdish towns, including Bokan, Mahabad, Piranshah, Sanandaj, Saqqiz and Urmiya. After a summer pause, in September a reinforced Pasdaran force, now openly supported by the army with guns, tanks and helicopters, hit back viciously and managed to eject Kurdish resistance fighters from some of the towns, but not all.

As the Kurds were settling down for the winter, the Iranian government launched a surprise month-long offensive against them, mustering some 4000 Pasdaran, headed by the newly formed 'Zulfiqar' army commando brigade. Bokan fell, as did Mahabad, Urmiya and other towns, although government claims were disputed by the Kurds. Fighting spilled over into Turkey and Iraq as Pesh Merga were driven from villages west of Lake Urmiya. Some local tribes, including the Herkis and Baghazadis, were fighting against the KDPI, having been bribed by the Tehran government, as were elements of the Iraqi KDP.

Still retaining freedom of movement in the countryside and a foothold in some towns, KDPI Pesh Mergas struck at Pasdaran HQs in the winter months, particularly in Bokan, Piranshah and Sanandaj. In December, when a Kurd working for the government was killed in Mahabad, the Pasdaran sealed off part of the city, burned down houses and ran riot, killing at least 12 people and injuring about 30. A five-day protest strike by Kurds followed. Battle communiqués issued by both sides verged on the ridiculous, but international media consensus estimates were that during this November offensive over 4000 casualties occurred, including over 400 dead, which indicated the ferocity of the fighting on both sides. Ghassemlou claimed that in three years his KDPI group had lost 5000 personnel, including civilians, both in the fighting and 'before execution squads'.

When Ghassemlou briefly stopped fighting the Tehran government, offering to side with Khomeini if the Pasdaran were withdrawn. Two factions broke away from the KDPI: one led by Abdul Karim Hussami, based in Baghdad and already working with the Iraqi government to overthrow the Khomeini regime; and one led by Abdul Ghani Balourian, working to the same end but operating inside Iran while receiving money and aid from Baghdad. The Komala, advocating the overthrow of Khomeini, supported Sheikh Hosseini, who belonged to no political party and relied upon his religious prestige for his popularity and influence. Hosseini refused any involvement with the Iraqi government.

In Nowdesheh, Ghassemlou sat back to plan a spring 1982 offensive, intended to recapture Mahabad and Urmiya and to establish a broad 'liberated zone' as a probable springboard for anti-Khomeini resistance that was developing. In spite of his setbacks and losses in 1981, Ghassemlou could still muster a probable 11 000 full-time Pesh Mergas and up to 30 000 part-time, locally-based militiamen. The KDPI was the armed core of the Kurdish resistance in Iran, and had been for the past three years or so, all other groups being lesser or auxiliary.

Both Ghassemlou and Hosseini travelled to Western Europe to lobby support, and also to visit Bani-Sadr, who, following his impeachment in June 1981, had fled to France, where he plotted against the Khomeini government. Bani-Sadr set up the National Resistance Council (NRC), which held its first meeting in France in April 1982 with Bani-Sadr in the chair. He was reluctant to form a government-in-exile but said he might return to operate in 'liberated zones' in Iranian Kurdistan, Ghassemlou claiming he already held about 60 000 square kilometres. Khomeini was convinced the KDPI and the Komala had joined the NRC, and said so, but he was wrong. Bani-Sadr did not approve of separatism and therefore did not come to any agreement with Ghassemlou. Formed in Paris in October 1981, the NRC was a loose coalition of anti-Islamic government groups, including the KDPI. The National Resistance Movement (NRM), led by Shahpour Bakhtiar, briefly a prime minister to the Shah, was also based in Paris, having been launched in August 1981.

IRANIAN PRESSURE: 1982

In April 1982 Ghassemlou launched his planned spring campaign, which was at once countered by the Iranian military spring offensive, the army by this time being fully involved in the battle against Kurdish insurgents. The Iranians were successful, clearing Pesh Merga before them, establishing an HQ at Urmiya and bringing Bokan, Mahabad, Saqqiz and Sanandaj more fully under control. On 26 June a Kurdish attack on Mahabad was repulsed with some loss of life.

After the discovery of the Ghotbzadah plot of April 1982, in which the foreign minister had schemed to take over the Islamic government by force, the roles of the various Iranian security forces were redefined. The Komitehs, police and gendarmerie were placed under the Minister of the Interior, the army's task to defend the country's borders remained, while the Pasdaran stayed as a separate entity, charged with 'guarding the revolution and preventing plots', which included crushing Kurdish resistance.

After a summer break, in September Iranian troops and the Pasdaran resumed their offensive against the Kurds in northern Iran, concentrating on closing KDPI supply routes. They success fully seized and held a 40-mile section of the Sardasht to Baneh road, which ran almost parallel and close to the Iraqi Kurdish frontier, and this disrupted KDPI supplies from Iraq.

HOSTAGE TAKING IN IRAQ

In northern Iraq, when the Iran–Iraq War began there was no cease-fire and the KDP, now in collaboration with the Iraqi Communist Party, continued its attacks on military targets. Both the KDP and the PUK were settling back into their old stamping grounds and were seeking to increase the amount of territory under their individual control by attacking each other whenever opportune. In a clash with Iraqi troops at Haj Omran on 25 November 1980, KDP Pesh Mergas suffered casualties but claimed to have captured a large quantity of weapons, 'including two tanks'. According to its London spokesman they also killed '52 Iraqi soldiers' (*Guardian*).

Although the Barzani-led KDP and the PUK were the two

dominant Kurdish resistance groups in Iraq, other smaller ones existed and still more began to appear, some soon to sink into anonymity. One such was the Kurdistan Socialist Party (KSP), led by Mahmoud Osman, which vaguely supported the KDP and gained notoriety by kidnapping and holding Western Europeans. The American hostages who had been held by Iranian revolutionary students in Tehran since 4 November 1979 were suddenly released on 21 January 1981, immediately after out-going President Carter handed over to Ronald Reagan, who had assumed the presidency of the USA on 20 January 1981.

One of the first hostages taken in Iraq – on 20 January 1981 by the KSP – was Michael Powell, a British engineer working on the Dukan Dam. Powell was held in remote mountain territory near the Turkish border. Initially a large ransom was demanded, together with the release of Kurdish detainees. The kidnapping attracted wide publicity in the Western world but the British government did not respond, sticking to its principle of refusing to negotiate with terrorists. Three Austrian construction workers were seized in November, two Frenchmen in April 1982, and in June eight Yugoslavs and three West Germans were taken hostage. Not all countries followed the British line. Three Indian and three Lebanese hostages were released quietly, little or nothing being offered by way of explanation by the negotiators, as were the Austrians, Yugoslavs and others in due course. The British long-term hostage was eventually released in June 1982.

Hostage taking had international media priority interest, beginning with the American hostage drama in the Tehran embassy and followed by the saga of the Western hostages in Lebanon. Some, but not all, of the hostages seized by Kurdish resistance groups also briefly became the subject of international headlines but they were generally given lesser coverage, except by their own national press, normal press facilities being absent in the liberated zones of Kurdistan.

Two Frenchmen were kidnapped in February 1982 by the ICP, who were operating under the shelter of the Kurdish resistance, but were soon released due to the intervention of the French Communist Party. While Kurdish hostage taking usually gained some publicity, little was known generally of the Kurds and their cause. In June the following year three more

Frenchmen, an Austrian and a West German were captured, and not released until 20 July 1984.

In Iraq, despite considerable Kurdish anti-government activity the Kurdish Autonomous Regional Council – formed in 1974, with its 10-man executive and 50-member assembly situated in Arbil – remained in being but possessed little real power. Only 'one law had been passed in eight years' (*Daily Telegraph*). The Council were required openly to support the ruling Baathist Party.

THE AUTUMN 1982 CAMPAIGN

During 1981 and the first part of 1982 the Kurds in Iraq improved their position considerably, and Iraqi troops were unable to prevent them from establishing 'liberated zones'. Many roads in Kurdistan were closed to all but military convoys and were 'protected' by troops positioned in forts at intervals. The KDP, operating in the Ruwanduz area, and the PUK, around Suliemaniyeh, continued to fight each other as and when the opportunity arose, as well as against government forces. The Baghdad government feared that any successful Iranian offensive would bring Iranian troops up to the Iraqi Kurdish border, and therefore some 50 000 troops were deployed to contain Kurdish activity, the troops being drawn from the main battle fronts facing the Iranians.

The Iraqi government offered large sums of money to persuade its Kurdish tribes to lay down their arms, and also used bribery and intrigue to weaken the KDP and the PUK, which both suffered from defections. Several small Kurdish splinter parties had appeared since September 1980. At the same time the Baghdad government was trying to gain the cooperation of Kurdish resistance groups – government civil expenditure to Kurdish areas increased and the status of the Autonomous Regional Council was emphasised. A great many Kurds were serving in the Iraqi armed forces, and more were required. However the government was simultaneously and quietly continuing its programme of 'Arabisation', closing Kurdish political and cultural centres and schools, including Suliemaniyeh University. Kurdish publications were frowned upon.

In the heat of August 1982 the Iraqi army launched an

operation, ostensibly to quell an uprising of 12 000 Kurds in northern Iraq, although in reality it was to eliminate liberated zones. The Baghdad government feared that the Iraqi Kurds would attract the support of the Syrian and Turkish governments if Iraq suffered reverses in its war with Iran. The prize would be the Kirkuk oilfields and the oil pipeline from them through Turkey to the Mediterranean oil terminal. Although the government claimed it had inflicted huge losses on the 'rebels', little was achieved in this offensive, which soon stumbled to a halt.

THE NATIONAL DEMOCRATIC AND PATRIOTIC FRONT (NDPF)

In June 1982 a Kurdish coalition was formed in Iraq, composed of groups opposed to Saddam Hussein, mainly the PUK and the KSP (but including the ICP but not the KDP). The Iraqi Kurds by this time claimed to have established effective control of much of the provinces of Arbil, Kirkuk and Suliemaniyeh. The PUK had been gaining ground at the expense of the KDP and was training KDPI members, who like itself were fighting against the Tehran government. The KDP was still working with and receiving aid from the Tehran government, and was fighting in the field alongside the Pasdaran in Iranian Kurdistan.

In August the KDP and the PUK came to an agreement to respect each other's territory and for each to live and let live in their own regions, but this was only recognising reality as each had other significant enemies to cope with. This agreement was conditional on the KDP severing its links with Iran, and was therefore a non-starter. The KDP still had its large base at Karaj, some 30 miles from Tehran, but was feeling insecure as its Iranian paymasters – now that the Pasdaran was having success in reducing Kurdish resistance activity in Iran – were indicating that the KDP should think about reorientating its energy towards destabilising the Iraqi regime.

IRANIAN OFFENSIVES: 1983

During the winter of 1982/3 there was a general stalemate on the battlefields of Iran and Iraq, where combatants had reached a strategic impasse position. Iraq was strengthening its entrenched, elongated defensive system, designed to resist the anticipated 'human wave' attacks in the coming spring. Both Iran and Iraq gave attention to their Kurdish territories, which they were never able to control completely. In the spring and summer of 1983 Iran launched three large offensives that drove the KDPI Pesh Mergas from certain areas.

In Nowdesheh, Ghassemlou was making ready to launch a spring campaign to recover the Kurdish cities and territory he had lost the previous year, but was beaten to it by the Iranians, who launched their own 'cleansing' campaign in the second week of March, well ahead of the KDPI. The Iranians probably mustered over 150 000 men, making up four army and six Pasdaran divisions. These were directed by regular army staff, now back in their old role and taking over an ever-increasing part of the planning side of the war. 'Liberated zones' between Saqqiz, Mahabad and Bokan were soon overrun.

Belatedly launched, Ghassemlou's offensive was roughly jostled aside by the Iranian operation. He eventually had to back away and revert to guerrilla tactics, his Pesh Mergas in many cases hastily going to ground for their own survival. Ghassemlou had overreached himself and miscalculated his moves. Furthermore his intelligence must have been faulty, as he virtually fell into a trap from which he only narrowly escaped. His attempt to use conventional tactics had failed. Politically astute, Ghassemlou did not always display the qualities required by a successful general. However the KDPI did have some minor successes, and their hovering presence in the Mahabad area caused the government to 'execute 59 Kurdish sympathisers' in that city (*The Times*).

In July one of Iran's main operations against the Iraqi main defensive line included a thrust into the wide Ruwanduz Valley, just inside Iraqi Kurdish territory near the border town of Haj Omran, which was dominated by the Mount Marmand massifs. The valley was a main supply route for both the KDPI and the Iraqi PUK operating inside Iran, in which were located the KDPI HQ, base camps and families of Pesh Mergas. One authority (McDowall, 1985) states that there were about 15 000 well-armed Pesh Mergas in the area.

A two-division Iranian force, containing an 800-strong group of Barzani's KDP (listed as 'Muslim Iraqi combatants'), seized Haj Omran on the 22nd but was halted as Iraq rushed in reinforcements. Fighting in the valley (recorded in regional annals as the Battle of Mount Marmand) continued until the 29th, when through exhaustion it died down, leaving the Iranians in possession of Haj Omran and part of the valley. Many KDPI Pesh Mergas were captured by the Iranians although many escaped, some abandoning their families. KDPI and PUK Pesh Mergas taken by the Iranians were handed over to the KDP detachment to suffer a sad fate. Iraqi troops took the opportunity to seize about 8000 members of the Barzani tribe, mainly families and including Ubeidullah Barzani, Mullah Mustafa's eldest son, who were encamped in the valley. They were transferred to detention camps in the south and for a long time nothing was heard of them, rumours circulating that Saddam Hussein had eliminated this batch of his enemies.

The Iranians moved the Iraqi KDP base from Karaj to Haj Omran, part of the Ruwanduz Valley and the adjacent areas they had seized, technically handing over this Iraqi territory to the Iraqi opposition Supreme Council of the Islamic Revolution of Iraq (SCIRI). SCIRI was led by Ayatollah Mohammed Bakr Hakim, an Iraqi opposition Shia leader backed by Khomeini, and was allowed to open an office in Haj Omran. The Iraqi Dawa, a major constituent of SCIRI, was allowed to operate in this 'liberated' part of Iraq.

In mid-October 1983 Iran launched another major offensive against Iraq on a wide front, one prong being directed at the Panjwin sector, about 80 miles south of the Haj Omran 'bulge', again with KDP support. The object was to make limited inroads into Iraqi territory for propaganda purposes, to cut Kurdish resistance supply routes, and to remove Iraqi guns that had both Baneh and Marivan within their ranges. Suliemaniyeh lay some 30 miles to the south-west of Panjwin. Iranian forces pushed into the Panjwin valley, fighting hard for tactical peaks alongside it. By the 29th, when fighting died down, they had penetrated more than 15 miles but had not succeeded in occupying the town of Panjwin, although they had managed to disrupt Kurdish resistance border-crossing points.

As the war with Iraq had disappointingly stabilised, Iran, realising its military weakness, sought to develop its footholds in Haj Omran and Panjwin as bases for the anti-Saddam Hussein SCIRI to muster internal forces to overthrow the Iraqi leader.

TURKISH HOT PURSUIT

In Iraq, Saddam Hussein was also concerned about his Kurdish problem, having insufficient troops to spare for a major campaign to bring them to heel. He was also concerned about the rate of Kurdish desertion from his armed forces. In January 1983 he complained that over 48 000 Kurds had deserted, and in March he offered them an amnesty if they would return, promising they would not be sent to the main battle fronts; but this had little effect. Later he claimed that 26 000 had accepted and returned.

Saddam Hussein was also concerned about the continuing flow of oil through the trans-Turkey pipeline, which together with its parallel oil road ran through an area in which the PUK was dominant, being guarded by about 15 000 Jash. Apart from a few minor instances the Jash had been generally been left alone by resistance groups. Turkey obtained handsome transit revenues from the pipeline and oil for its own refineries, and was therefore keen that the flow of oil from Kirkuk should continue. On the Turkish side of the border a strong protective sleeve had been placed round the oil road and pipeline, consisting in places of depopulated areas, minefields and free-fire zones.

In February 1983 Turkey approved an increase in the flow of oil through the pipeline, and the following month signed an agreement with Iraq for joint security measures, which included allowing Turkish troops to enter Iraqi territory in 'hot pursuit of rebels'. On 25 April Turkey launched its first operation into Iraq, penetrating ten miles and scooping up hundreds of subversives, including many PUK and KDP personnel as well as its own fugitives. Iran was none too pleased as it freed more Iraqi soldiers to face Iranian fronts. Turkey kept a low profile over its cross-border activities as its government did not want to agitate further its own restless Kurds.

Subsequently Turkey launched a similar operation, again with Iraqi cooperation and again catching hundreds of subversives. This raid had a particularly devastating effect on the PUK as several of its leaders and many Pesh Mergas were detained and handed over to the Iraqi authorities; some to be executed. Talabani bitterly alleged that since 1976 until the end of 1983 over '1400 PUK members had been executed by the Baghdad Baathist regime' (*New York Times*).

On 14 September 1983 a Turkish military aircraft crashed in northern Iraq. The two pilots successfully bailed out but were captured by the KSP, which intended to hold them hostage. Turkey immediately mustered a military force and uttered dire threats, including its intention to hand over any detained 'subversives' to either the Iraqi or the Iranian government, whichever wanted them most. The Turkish airmen were instantly released. Turkey had made its point. For the moment the Kurdish hostage saga was suspended and oil continued to flow through the pipeline towards Turkey.

TALABANI TURNS HIS COAT

Fate had been against Talabani during 1983, causing him to make secret contacts with the Baghdad government. On 10 December this resulted in a cease-fire agreement that suited both Talabani and Saddam Hussein, under which Talabani would speak for all Iraqi Kurds. Saddam Hussein wanted Talabani to join his National Progressive Front but Talabani prevaricated. The PUK was being squeezed by three regional powers – Iraq, Iran and Turkey – and the pressure was endangering survival. Saddam still had some 50 000 troops tied up in Iraqi Kurdistan. Iranian successes at Haj Omran and Panjwin, and their superior numbers, brought fears that they would eventually break through Iraqi defences and flood into Iraqi Kurdistan to seize control of the Kirkuk oilfield and pipeline. Talabani chose what most probably seemed to him to be the best survival option, preferring the Baghdad regime to the Iranian one.

Talabani's accord with Saddam Hussein gave him both

breathing space and a new lease of life, as he was given arms and money to defend Iraqi Kurdistan from the Baghdad regime's enemies. In his turn Talabani made a number of autonomy demands, a few of which were accepted by Saddam, but not all. In return Saddam wanted much greater Kurdish cooperation in the war effort against Iran. Talabani successfully brought about the removal of his enemy Hashim Aqrawi (who was leading the pro-Baghdad KDP), and also the removal from government of the hostile (to him) small Kurdish Revolutionary Party. An argument arose over Kirkuk, Talabani wanting a share of its oil income to improve local Kurdish housing and education, while Saddam wanted to devote all of it to his war with Iran. Saddam told Talabani, 'Do not insist on Kirkuk being a Kurdish town, and we shall not insist on it not being a Kurdish town' (McDowall, 1985). The two men both understood and used each other. It was said that PUK collaboration enabled the Baghdad government to free 'four to six divisions based in Kurdistan to fight Iran' (*Guardian*). This was probably an overstatement, visualising more smoke than fire.

IRANIAN KURDISTAN: 1984

In February 1984 Iran dispatched a two-brigade force, supported by KDP elements, from Nowdesheh towards the Iraqi Dardani Khan Dam, near the confluence of the Qala Dasht and Sirwar rivers and the source of up to 40 per cent of Iraq's normal electricity supply. After three days fighting the force was within six miles of the dam and had occupied a claimed '40 square miles and killed 75 Iraqis' (*Guardian*). Penetration raids were not yet within the capability of the Iranian army, which was more conditioned to 'human wave' tactics at that time. The main objective of the operation had been to block Iraqi roads leading south, which it partially did, and also to bolster the morale and position of the KDP in Iraq, now that the PUK was fighting on the government side.

By the beginning of 1984 Kurdish resistance 'liberated zones' in Iran were being smothered by overwhelming military manpower. However the Pesh Mergas were by no means inactive, despite facing some 250 000 Iranian troops spread out along a front extending south from Urmiya to Qasr Sherin and supported by some 12 000 Pasdaran, who were seeping outwards from population centres into the countryside, choking freedom of movement. A few KDPI leaders and Pesh Mergas were making their way into Iraq for sheer survival. In some areas KDPI and Komala militiamen went to ground – returning to their villages, hiding their weapons and merging into the population. The theory was that they would stand down for the time being, and that just a few would remain ready for local opportunity activities.

Thousands of Kurds were in detention in Iran, thousands had been displaced and thousands more had been forcibly resettled in the south, while most Kurdish chiefs, seeing which way the wind was blowing, made their peace with the central government. The KDPI leadership felt that the 'water was being drained away from the guerrilla fish', as large numbers of rural Kurds were giving up the struggle owing to a shortage of food, fuel and medicines as a result of the government's 'economic campaign' against them. Sheikh Hosseini sent emissaries to Western capitals pleading for assistance, but none was given. In Tehran it was triumphantly announced in February 1984 that the Kurdish insurrection 'was practically eliminated', and that since the February revolution of 1979, 27 000 Kurds had died as a result of their struggle against the central government, of whom only 2500 were fighters. This was a very premature assessment.

In June Iran launched a two-pronged attack around Lake Urmiya, in the course of which it was claimed that several KDPI leaders were killed. This was followed in ensuing weeks by other operations against Kurds in the areas of Sardasht, Marivan, Qasr Sherin and Kermanshah. The Iranian armed forces soon found that although they controlled the Haj Omran area (in Iraq), which should have led to the severing of the Kurdish insurgent supply line from Iraq, old mule-track routes over the mountains had again come into full use, thus enabling the KDPI to return to a guerrilla offensive.

Later, in the Hawraman region (south-west of Panjwin), the KDPI and the Komala began to fall out, the Komala apparently having expected a full share of KDPI supplies received from Iraq. In November, when a KDPI military commander was killed by Komala members, a spate of fighting broke out between them.

The Tehran government now wanted to rid itself of the Barzani KDP as it felt it no longer had any need for it in Iran. Pressure was therefore exerted to persuade the KDP to move completely into Iraq and take on the PUK in battle. The Barzani brothers, Idris and Masoud, who were operating fairly successfully in northern Iraq, were hesitant in case this would lead to complete severance of their supply line back to Tehran, and perhaps total abandonment by the Iranians.

IRAQI KURDISTAN: 1984

During 1984 in Iraq, most of the fighting in Kurdish territory was between government troops and the KDP, even though Talabani's PUK was being armed and paid by Saddam Hussein to combat the Barzani-led group. Talabani's negotiations with Saddam Hussein over autonomy rumbled uneasily on, being disrupted in March when a number of Kurds were executed for draft-dodging and desertion in Suliemaniyeh and Dohuk, while in an incident at Arbil University several Kurdish students were killed. Intermittent fighting spasmodically continued between PUK and KDP Pesh Mergas.

In August Iraq launched a three-brigade force of some 15 000 men, supported by the PUK, in an effort to dislodge the KDP from the area of Zakho and Dohuk. The KDP obtained cross-border support from Kurds in Turkey, but the Iraqi army was not helped by the Turkish army on this occasion, as had been anticipated, it being said that Iran had persuaded Turkey not to intervene as it would seem that Turkey was siding with the Baghdad government against that of Tehran. The following month on Radio Kurdistan the KDP claimed successes in the northern Badinan region. In September Said Karim, a senior PUK military commander, was killed in an ambush by the KDP, as allegedly were Talabani's brother and his family.

Turkey did not like the PUK–Baghdad government partnership. On 15 October 1984 the Turkish foreign minister visited Iraq and told Saddam Hussein that if he did not dissolve the partnership the oil pipeline would be closed down and the Turkish frontier shut tight against Iraq. Turkey, alarmed by PUK activities and its liaison with Turkish Kurdish resistance groups, had noted how Turkish Kurdish fighters had flooded over the Iraqi border in August to support the KDP. Turkey feared that the PUK, which still claimed it could muster 10 000 Pesh Mergas, would disrupt the oil pipeline, while KDP Pesh Mergas might flood across the Iraqi border into Turkey to aid dissident Turkish Kurds in their fight against Turkish security forces. Saddam hastily sought an arrangement with the Turkish government, and on the 18th Talabani claimed he had broken off negotiations with the Baghdad government. Saddam Hussein, who could have told another story, was silent on this occasion.

By this time Saddam Hussein was already receiving military assistance from the USA, the USSR and France, and covertly from Britain. He was still at war with Iran and Turkey was a vital supply corridor, so another Iraq–Turkey cross-border agreement was hastily concluded. The PUK again found itself in conflict with the Baghdad government, being supported this time only by Syria as both Baghdad and Tehran had cut off funding and aid.

In Western Europe, on 27 September 1984 fighting had broken out in the Iranian embassy in The Hague, as Kurdish activists attempted to stage a sit-in occupation in protest against Iranian government actions against Kurds, and also to attract international attention. Shots were fired before the demonstration was broken up by the Dutch police.

The same month Iranian Kurdish opposition groups in Western Europe claimed that Iranian troops were expelling whole communities of Kurds from mountain villages around Sardasht. The Iranian government responded the following month with a self-satisfied statement claiming that recent operations in Kurdistan had been highly successful, leading to the surrender of large numbers of 'rebels', including senior KDPI officials; and that the offer of an amnesty to all militant Kurds who refrained from participating in attacks would now be extended to all resistance fighters.

THE HOSTAGE FACTOR: 1985

In Iraq, on 13 February 1985 Saddam Hussein announced a general amnesty that was to include all his political enemies at home and abroad. This was immediately rejected by the communists and by the Dawa, which had gained for itself a reputation for deadly international terrorism, including aircraft hijacking and hostage holding. Mohammed Baqer, leader of the Dawa and based in Iran, demanded that Iraq immediately hold free elections and accept the return of thousands of Iraqis who had been deported under the pretext that they were Iranian nationals.

The Dawa, or more properly the Hizb al-Daawa al-Islamiya ('the Islamic Call'), had emerged in the Iraqi Shia holy city of Nejaf in the late 1960s. In the 1970s it had demonstrated against Baathist governments, for which some Dawa members were executed, after which it took to terrorism, attracting international fame. When in exile, Khomeini had lived in Nejaf from 1964 to 1978 and had influenced the Dawa, whose militant arm was known as the 'Iraqi Mujahideen'. When the Iran–Iraq War began the Dawa sided with the Khomeini Islamic Revolution, causing Saddam Hussein to impose a death penalty for Dawa membership; over 30 having already been executed by Baghdad regimes.

In early March 1985 – in the Haj Omran pocket, which was occupied by Iranian supported forces – the vendetta between the KDPI and Komala flared up. A KDPI attack on Komala positions reputedly resulted in over 50 Komala deaths. This was followed by a Komala reprisal raid on the town of Marivan, held by Ghassemlou's men, in which at least ten were killed. In these two skirmishes between the two rival dissident organisations, apart from casualties inflicted, prisoners were taken and were said to have been executed, perhaps tortured first according to rumour. In April the KDPI was expelled from the Iranian opposition NRC owing to its seeming willingness to negotiate with the Tehran government.

In May, in Iraq the PUK claimed successes in action in the Kurdish region, but it was also involved in hostage taking. It was reported to have seized 26 foreigners working in the country, allegedly on defence-related projects, who would not be released until their respective governments and companies agreed not to undertake such work without PUK permission. They were mainly East Europeans, but also included Chinese, Japanese and Korean technicians. Governments were contacted by the PUK and urged to persuade Baghdad to abandon its harsh and repressive rule against the Kurdish people, and especially 'to abandon its policy of erasing total villages' (*Guardian*).

The following month the PUK released six Bulgarian hostages, claiming that it still held 20 more. On 29 October it announced that it was also holding two Soviet technicians. Little was revealed about this ongoing hostage saga, nor of the precise demands made and how releases could be effected, nor even confirmation of identities. The parties involved often negotiated in secret in order to avoid interference by governments on points of principle. It was widely rumoured that sums of money, sometimes very large sums, changed hands, but the PUK's demand for international publicity for their cause was often almost muted.

In Iran, during the last days of June the government began a fresh offensive against the Kurdish resistance, the Pasdaran playing a full part. In one clash, in July near Baneh, a KDPI senior military commander (Karim Aliyar) was killed, but during August the KDPI claimed to have killed over '50 Pasdaran' (*The Times*).

Amnesty International was kept busy in both Iraq and Iran during the year. In August it received a letter from the Baghdad government confirming that in February and March 1985 it had 'executed six KDP members, ten relatives of Ayatollah Bakr al-Hakim (of SCIRI), and some Christians', all of whom were accused of carrying weapons and of sabotage.

KURDISH LIBERATED ZONES: 1986

In Iran, many frontier crossing points into Turkey and Iraq had been jointly dominated by the KDPI and the Komala, the two organisation sharing the tolls extracted, which formed a large part of their incomes. However in January 1986 all vestiges of harmony and cooperation between them finally broke down, after which they were at daggers drawn. Komala was the class enemy of the KDPI and this could no longer be concealed, despite common strategic objectives. This was particularly embarrassing to Sheikh Hosseini, who lived in one of the Komala-run tented villages and wanted to be friends with both. The Pasdaran were aiming to eliminate the Komala first if possible, and already in the Sardasht region 66 villages had been evacuated to prevent the Komala from 'communising' them (*New York Times*).

In northern Iraq, in mid-February Iranian troops – mainly Pasdaran, supported by the Barzani-KDP – emerged from the Panjwin Bulge and moved eastwards along the Suliemaniyeh Valley towards Kirkuk, occupying a string of villages before turning northwards towards Chwarta to occupy a ridge of peaks overlooking the town of Suliemaniyeh. Not only was Iraqi aerial counter-activity neutralised by bad weather, but on 1 March Iraq had to withdraw a mountain brigade from the area as it was urgently needed at the Fao front in the south. This enabled the Iranian force to occupy the garrison town of Sitak on the 2nd, and to invest Chwarta. The following day Iranians shelled Suliemaniyeh for the first time in this war, inflicting civilian casualties. Iran claimed it had occupied another 25 square miles of Iraqi territory, and alleged that Iraq had dropped chemical warfare bombs on Baneh.

Farther north, Kurdish-liberated zones were reputed to already encompass most of the territory to the north of a line from Dohuk to the Haj Omran Bulge. The KDP was reported to be better equipped by this time, having some Chinese-made mortars, Soviet SAM-7s, a few small US artillery pieces and plenty of Kalashnikovs, the majority having arrived from Syria and Libya. It was also reported that Iran had 'lent' the KDP some sophisticated guns, enabling them, with Iranian assistance, to shell Iraqi bases such as Zakho, the main base for troops protecting the oil road and pipeline into Turkey. The pipeline now ran underground, protected by wire, mines, electronic sensors and other other devises, with concrete forts every few hundred yards, manned mostly by the Jash. Kurds still farmed land to the east of the road, but Arabs had been armed and brought in to farm on the west side. However the main deterrent was fear of Turkish invasion and reprisal, Turkey having about 30 000 troops poised along the border.

At the beginning of May Iraqi government forces mounted an operation to try to split Kurdish-liberated zones and sever 'rebel' communications between Zakho and the northern Badinan region. They fought for five days but failed to reach the Turkish frontier. Iranians and their KDP allies were again on the attack, and on the 15th they captured the town of

Mangesh near Mosul, a key point on the oil road that had been under siege for some time. Iran claimed to have 'captured 800 prisoners, and enough arms and ammunition to hold the town for two years' (Islamic Republican News Agency). This was not a hard-fought battle as the majority of the local Kurdish militia either deserted or defected to the attackers. Iraqi attempts to regain Mangesh were not immediately successful.

This new aggressive Iranian policy, replacing the former hit-and-run guerrilla warfare normally favoured by the KDP, had been decreed by Khomeini, who was in the process of admitting that his early hope of a Shia rising in Iraq was fading and that it would be better to concentrate on activating Iraqi Kurds against their Baghdad government.

NATIONAL LIBERATION ARMY OF IRAN

In June Masoud Rajavi, the Iranian exiled leader of the NRC (who had expelled the KDPI from his organisation), arrived in Iraq with about 1000 followers, whom he formed into the National Liberation Army of Iran (NLA(I)). He was welcomed by Saddam Hussein and allocated a 'sector' in the war against Iran. On the other side of the fence, the Iranian authorities tried their best to persuade the PUK and the KDP to work together amicably, but with little success, although a meeting between leaders was sponsored in Tehran in November, at which time the KDP was also persuaded to consider possible cooperation with SCIRI. The Iranian government expressed dissatisfaction with SCIRI when it held a conference in Tehran in December, and especially with the terrorist activities of its constituent, Dawa, as it did not want to extend the war, nor to unnecessarily antagonise Arab countries. SCIRI's proposal to found an Iraqi government-in-exile foundered, and the following year it was replaced by the revamped Iraqi Leadership Committee.

In August Ghassemlou, leader of the KDPI, visited London to raise support, saying that he anticipated a large Iranian attack the following month. He believed Khomeini had reached the height of his unpopularity, and that '95 per cent of the 3000 or so military bases and outposts the regime has set up in Iranian Kurdistan lead us to understand that if our guerrillas do not harass them, they will not bother us. In fact we have trouble only with the remaining 5 per cent, where religious fanatics still manage to dominate the men under their command' (*The Times*). Claiming that his 10 000 men in the field were tying down 200 000 Iranian troops, Ghassemlou admitted that he had succeeded in 'rolling back areas under government control, because the government had switched more troops south for the big battle with Iraq'. He also confirmed that his main source of aid was Iraq, and that Khomeini was very much against Kurdish autonomy.

Throughout the year the PUK slowly expanded its domination, which latterly included the successful defence of Mahwat against Iraqi army assaults. In riposte, Iraqi aircraft staged numerous bombing raids on Kurdish villages and settlements that were thought to harbour resistance fighters, the PUK claiming that its ranks were swelled by Iraqi army deserters. Western journalists who managed to reach liberated zones confirmed the bombing raids, and also reported that Pesh Mergas made frequent raids into towns to procure money and weapons. A curfew remained in force in much of the Kurdish region, and government officials were allocated military escorts. On several occasions the Baghdad government falsely claimed that its army units, assisted by the Jash, had regained control of the whole Kurdish region.

On 28 December 1986 some 400 Iraqi opposition leaders, including Talabani and Masoud Barzani, met in Tehran to patch up their quarrels. Syrian and Libyan representatives were also present. It was resolved to escalate the military struggle against the Baghdad regime; and also to establish a standing military committee, which would include Iranian representatives.

DISJOINTED OPERATIONS: 1987

In February 1987, in furtherance of its new policy of launching smaller attacks to make smaller but persistent gains in mountainous terrain, Iran, supported by the Barzani-KDP, launched a small operation from the Haj Omran Bulge westwards along the Ruwanduz valley towards Arbil. This did not penetrate very far, although Iran claimed to have destroyed many Iraqi radar facilities. The following month Iran made another similar thrust along the same valley, this time with the intention of seizing the more strategic heights overlooking it; but again it did not seem able to penetrate very far. International journalists, flown in to witness this 'success', recorded that the column had advanced only about 12 miles.

Differences had begun to surface in both operations as there seemed to have been reluctance on the part of Iran's ally, the KDP, to cooperate fully. KDP objectives did not always coincide with those of Tehran. It was suspected that both the KDP and the PUK, while eager to accept selected help, were not keen on turning their Kurdish homeland into a major theatre of war, nor on it becoming flooded with Pasdaran, whom they regarded with suspicion and fear owing to their vicious campaign against the KDPI in Iranian Kurdistan, and because of Khomeini's rigid opposition to Kurdish autonomy. Nevertheless, through sheer necessity Iran continued to use the Kurds as best it could, and the Kurds to use Iran. The KDP was now led by Masoud Barzani, his brother Idris having died from a heart attack in Tehran on 1 February 1987 – Masoud was the more positive leader of the two.

The next joint Iran–Iraq Kurdish PUK operation began on 13 April, the PUK mustering some 2000 Pesh Merga for an all-night attack on Suliemaniyeh and claiming to kill over 600 Iraqis. Iraq reacted by bombing a number of Kurdish villages in the area in an attempt to regain positions, allegedly using chemical weapons (Islamic Republican News Agency). Iraq denied using 'gas bombs'. This incident coincided with a visit to Baghdad and Tehran by a United Nations fact-finding team investigating allegations of the use of chemical weapons.

In spring 1987 the Iraqi army embarked upon a series of clearing operations in its Kurdish terrain that lasted through into the summer. Inhabitants were removed from areas close to frontiers in order to create 'free-fire zones' and allow unhindered military mobility. This aroused resistance, some coordinated by the PUK, which resulted in many clashes, the PUK claiming that Arbil, Zakho and Dohuk were virtually besieged. In August the Iraqi government announced that its army was in 'full control of border areas in the north', and denied reports that a 'major war had been raging' in Iraqi Kurdistan for the past four months.

On 14 September, acting alone, the KDP claimed it captured

Kani Masi, the northernmost base of the Iraqi army, and could now 'seriously' challenge government control of the oil road and pipeline. However it had to evacuate hastily a few days later in the face of an Iraqi counterattack. The Kurdistan Socialist Party, based in Syria, alleged that Iraq had summarily executed eight Kurds from Suliemaniyeh province in June in an attempt to curb Kurdish nationalism.

Hostage taking was still being practised by the PUK, which on 3 October kidnapped three Italian engineers, demanding the cessation of Italian aid to Iraq and the withdrawal of Italian warships from the Gulf (Italy had sent eight warships to escort merchant ships). The Italian government ruled out any deal with the kidnappers, but the three hostages were eventually quietly released in February 1988, Talabani claiming that Italy had agreed not to supply arms to Iraq. On 3 November 1987 the PUK announced it was holding nine hostages: six Chinese and three Filipinos. Presumably others previously held had also been quietly released.

On 2 December Saddam Hussein announced yet another amnesty, this time aimed at enticing the return of Iraqis abroad, even those accused of political crimes or sentenced to death. On the 17th Iran launched a minor offensive in the Panjwin valley area near Mahwat and occupied several Iraqi positions, some of which were completely undefended or manned. Success was due to the element of surprise, as military activity had virtually ceased as winter had set in.

A UN Resolution (number 598) of 20 July 1987 had called for a cease-fire in the Iran–Iraq War, but there was little sign of this emerging. However Iranian 'human wave' attacks had subsided, as to an extent had the 'wars of the cities', in which each had bombarded the other's population centres with SCUD ballistic missiles. As the year ended the frustration of military stalemate was manifesting itself in an increasing use of chemical weapons, allegedly by both sides.

Already in March 1986 the UN had condemned Iraq for using chemical weapons, since when there had been two more complaints from Iran of their use by Iraq (in April and May 1987). Also according to Amnesty International, on 24 November Iraq had dropped 'thallium poison when trying to kill 40 Kurdish separatists', of whom allegedly three died and three were flown to the UK for examination. The prospects for 1988 looked grim.

10 Kurdish Resistance in Turkey

Meanwhile in Turkey, Kurdish resistance had smouldered on, although its activities had been overshadowed by other powerful and active Turkish political groups hostile to the government, and to each other. Political turmoil and violence had threatened to swamp that unfortunate country until the 1980 military coup, when activists were detained, forced to go underground or into exile. Abdullah Ocalan, leader of the PKK, escaped into Syria. For some time Syria had been providing Ocalan with covert support to destabilise the Ankara government. Ocalan was now able to operate, almost openly, from Damascus, and his activists were allowed sanctuary and training facilities in the Lebanese Bekaa Valley, nominally under Syrian military occupation. Not all major Kurdish resistance groups were so fortunate.

The PKK differed from other Kurdish resistance organisations in that right from the beginning it was dedicated to achieving its vague objective of 'Kurdish independence' by means of 'armed struggle'. Most Kurdish parties professed to be working for their objectives by non-violent means. Like the PKK, many Kurdish resistance parties had their own shadowy beginnings, now blurred by legend and propaganda. Student groups in universities in major cities were urban in character and outlook, being influenced by famous revolutionary leaders and thinkers, and had little in common with Kurdish peasants in the mountains or those tied to feudal acres.

Although Ocalan professed to favour Marxist–Leninist philosophy, it is probable that he paid more attention to the practical aspects of Mao Tse-tung's theory of initially generating revolutionary warfare in the countryside and developing the revolution from that basis. The concept of 'guerrilla fish swimming in the water of the people', rather than hounded like rats in city sewers by security forces, was the one adopted by the PKK.

Ocalan now misleadingly states that he founded his PKK in

1978, which is probably the year he took the decision to establish his revolutionary organisation in rural surroundings and desert the cities: his student-based Apocular group dates back to at least 1972.

KURDISH GROUPS IN TURKEY

By this time there were at least seven other active Kurdish resistance groups in Turkey. They were mainly left wing (and illegal as of October 1981, when all political parties were dissolved by decree) and all operated independently underground. Some even fought each other, although temporary alliances were occasionally formed for a time, usually due to opportunity or expediency. This was a typical Kurdish situation, little understood by the outside world, nor indeed properly by the new Turkish military government. The seven identified groups were the following:

- The Cultural and Democratic Revolutionary Association (DDKD), which was formed from associations in Ankara, Istanbul and Izmir. Its programme was independence for all Kurdistan (including territory in Iran, Iraq and Syria and the USSR).
- Ozgurluk (Freedom), which sought an independent Kurdish state within a Turkish federation.
- The Kawa (named after a mythical Turkish hero who slayed mythical monsters) was Maoist and anti-Soviet and sought the independence of all Kurdistan. It was split into two factions, one pro-Chinese and one pro-Albanian. After the military coup in Turkey some 47 Kawa members were arrested and charged with 14 murders. The Kawa had links with Kurdish groups in Iran, and it was said that its weapons were those seized from Turkish right-wing activists.
- The Kurdish Communist Party (KCP) was pro-Soviet and called vaguely for Kurdish independence.
- The Kurdistan Democratic Party of Turkey (KDP(T)) was the most moderate politically, with tribal philosophy and support. It had links with the Iraqi KDP and sought autonomy within Turkey.
- The Partisans of Kurdish National Liberation (KUK) splintered

from the KDP(T) in 1977 and was seeking 'independence' within a socialist Turkey.

– The Rizgari, which sought independence for all Kurdistan as the route to revolution throughout the Middle East with a wider, anti-Soviet vision. (I am indebted to David McDowall for this information.)

The two main non-Kurdish active political organisations in Turkey, which were antagonistic to one another and the government, were the left-wing Devrimci Yol (Dev Yol) (Revolutionary Way) and the right-wing National Action Party (NAP), of which the Grey Wolves was the military arm. Another powerful group was the Islamic National Salvation Party (NSP), which was seeking to turn Turkey into an Islamic republic.

Islamic fundamentalism, as propagated in Iran, did not appeal to either Turks or Kurds, who were mainly Sunni. In addition the Kurds were opposed to Iran for its base treatment of its Kurdish minority.

The new military government certainly clamped down hard on political activists, swamping insurgent towns and areas with troops and making mass arrests, which calmed the situation for a while. In March 1981 the military authorities claimed that 'all terrorist and extremist organisations in Turkey have been exposed', that many of their leaders had been arrested while others had fled the country. However it was officially admitted that several 'extremist secessionalists, mainly left-wing groups, remained active amongst the predominantly Kurdish population in south-east Turkey' (Government press release). All detained were handed over for trial by military courts.

In November 1981, martial law authorities stated that since the 1980 coup a total of 43 140 people had been detained on suspicion of terrorist or illegal political activity, that 29 929 were still in custody, and that there had been 282 violent deaths in the course of anti-terrorist activities (*The Times*).

In Diyarbakir the following month a mass trial of 447 PKK members and suspects began. They stood accused of 'separatism and setting up tribunals', of murdering 243 people, including 30 members of the security forces, and of committing atrocities. The prosecution demanded death sentences for 97 of them, alleging that 27 PKK members had been killed by their own organisation. It also alleged that the PKK trained its members in squads of 50 for violent campaigns, and that it prepared false passports. The prosecution stated that over 1500 PKK members and suspects were in custody awaiting trial, and that about 1000 were on the 'wanted list', including Ocalan (*Hurriyet*).

This provides a fair idea of the magnitude and intensity of PKK resistance. It also shows that the strength of the PKK had been abruptly reduced from several thousands to a probable 1000, or less according to some authorities. The speed with which the army had moved had taken the resistance activists of all groups – left, right and Kurdish – by surprise. It also indicated that Ocalan was a harsh disciplinarian who thought little of executing his own members when they failed him, was a survivor with a flair for intelligence by managing to evade the army net, was a good organiser and administrator rather than a redoubtable frontline fighter, and had been having some success with his 'fish and water' strategy.

Later (in July 1982) the Turkish government stated that since September 1980 – the date of the military coup – its security forces had seized '804 000 illegal firearms'; adding almost as an afterthought that the reason for mounting the military coup was that 'political violence had got out of hand'.

CROSS-BORDER PROBLEMS

Busily trying to clean up the Kurdish insurgency in its south-eastern provinces, the Turkish government was concerned about its mountainous, lawless 'open borders' with Iran and Iraq and the fact that groups of Kurdish 'rebels' crossed them freely to gain sanctuary as well as to conduct raids back across them. Turkey was seeking a common approach to this problem with the two other countries, both of which had their own Kurdish problem. This was slow to come about, largely for reasons of suspicious caution and national pride over sovereign territory. However some cooperation emerged more by accident than design, but blind eyes were still conveniently being put to telescopes.

In March 1981 the Turkish army launched a series of punitive operations against its Kurdish insurgents, mainly in Hakkari province adjacent to Iran, forcing many 'rebels' to seek sanctuary on the Iranian side of the border. About the same time Iranian armed forces were clearing their Kurdish terrain northwards and westwards from Mahabad, and some Turkish Kurdish groups were pressed between the two national forces. Frontier incidents occurred, and on occasions Iranian troops crossed into Turkey in 'hot pursuit'. Little was said about this as the end result was invariably satisfactory to both governments.

When the Iran–Iraq War began in September 1980, seeing a great opportunity to increase its trade with both countries, the Turkish government made an effort to secure the main, trans-frontier mountain road routes into them. By the end of 1981 the Turkish army stated that these frontiers were 'strongly patrolled, and cross-border communications secured', adding somewhat apologetically that 'illegal cross-frontier traffic has *almost* stopped' (*Hurriyet*).

KURDISTAN OVERSEAS RESISTANCE

Political repression in Turkey under a military government caused resistance to blossom and develop overseas among the ever-growing Turkish labour diaspora, of which Kurds formed a sizable proportion. Cultural and social centres and clubs began to appear in many Western European capitals and some major cities, some of which were fronts for political parties. There were, for example, about 1.8 million Turkish 'guest workers' in Western Germany and another 150 000 in West Berlin. Freed of the constraint of official Turkish non-recognition of Kurds as a separate ethnic community, Kurdish social centres also sprang into existence, many of which became politically orientated. Major Kurdish resistance groups dominated some of them. For instance the Frankfurt-based Komar (Association of Kurdish Workers) had direct links with the Kurdish Ozgurluk, while the National Liberation Front of Kurdistan (ERNK), based in Cologne, became the overseas wing of the PKK. Some centres changed allegiances, and there was infighting for dominance.

The several Kurdish social centres and clubs in Western Europe reflected the divisions in Turkish Kurdistan, being individualist in policy and action. However there was some common ground – all aimed for some form of separatism and all were against the Turkish military government. Most agreed to stay clear of the Iran–Iraq War, considering that neither of the governments were worthy of support because of the way they had treated their Kurdish populations in the past, alternately using them and then casting them aside when no longer needed. It was considered that they were once again attempting to repeat this process for their own selfish benefits, and to the ultimate detriment of Kurds.

In the politically free atmosphere of Western Europe, Kurdish (and Turkish) aspirations, opinions and views were openly discussed at these centres, and at some Kurdish news sheets were published and distributed. The PKK was quick to exploit these conditions and developed an overseas propaganda section, originally based in Cologne, which sought and gained the ear of the Western media. Accordingly the Kurdish cause was emphasised, as were the less palatable aspects of military and repressive measures taken by the Turkish government. Ocalan had a flair and a taste for publicity. He occasionally called news conferences in the Bekaa Valley and Damascus, gave press interviews selectively and wrote articles for his news sheets, often using the pseudonym 'Ali Firkat'. He explained what was really happening in Turkey, and especially in the south-eastern provinces, thus circumventing Ankara's censorship restrictions. Accordingly the PKK forged ahead of rival Kurdish organisations as its activities became known in the Western world.

FRONTIER CHAOS: 1983

In January 1983 Turkey and Iran revived their 1954 Joint Observation Committee, which had not met since 1979, to keep a watch on their Kurdish frontier tribes, some of which were involved in smuggling and the looting of trucks carrying goods between Turkey, Iran and Iraq. This problem concerned all three governments, and as Iran and Iraq were at war with each other, they liaised through Turkey. These frontier regions were described as 'areas where armed bandits roamed at will' (*Hurriyet*). Turkish Kurdish groups, especially the PKK, were making full use of them to establish sanctuaries in which to rest and hide their arms.

One authority identified three distinct government-hostile Kurdish groups operating in the mountainous frontier regions. The first consisted of certain tribes (two were named – the Qoraysha and the Yussufan) that allegedly controlled arms smuggling routes. The second was the nationalist Sheikh Said organisation (named after the Turkish Kurdish leader who was prominent in the 1920s), which concentrated on printing and distributing Kurdish-language pamphlets and propaganda, written Kurdish being proscribed in Turkey. The third was the Komala-Azadi, a branch of the Iranian Komala, which, having links with the Turkish PKK, concentrated on disruptive guerrilla activity (*Sunday Times*).

As gestures of goodwill to Iran and Iraq, Turkey expelled or handed over many Kurdish refugees. In May 1983, when Turkish military incursions were made into Iraq, the Ankara government handed over about 1000 'wanted' men to Iran, and in return received about the same number of 'wanted rebels' from the Tehran government. These measures tended to curb, but not cure, the lawlessness and insurgency in border regions.

During 1983 the EEC, viewing the military regime in Ankara with disfavour, withheld economic aid to Turkey. However the USA doubled its military allocation to that country, which had become so much more important to NATO after the Iranian revolution and the Soviet invasion of Afghanistan. NATO (but in fact the USA) had six bases in Turkey, one at Incirlik, which supported a US squadron with a nuclear-strike capability. During the summer Turkey refused to allow these bases to be used to ferry American military materials to the Lebanese army, or as transit facilities for American troops in Lebanon. This small gesture of Turkish defiance from American influence was for domestic consumption, but it was also a warning to the USA not to push demands too far.

BACK TO CIVILIAN RULE: DECEMBER 1983

On 23 December 1983 Turkey formally returned to civilian rule. In the 6 November election Turgut Ozal gained 211 seats out of 400 in the Grand National Assembly for his right-wing Motherland (Anavatan) Party. The National Security Council, led by General Kenan Evren and formed in September 1980, was dissolved, to be superseded by the President's Council, headed by 'President' Evren. Martial law remained in force.

During the period of military rule Turgut Ozal had been deputy prime minister, and was regarded as the architect of Turkey's 'politics of the East'; that is, directing Turkish industry to the Middle East and moving Turkey into the Arab world in the 1980s.

Turkey pursued its struggle against its Kurdish insurgency with vigour, still relying on mass arrests, mass trials and enforced relocation, supported by punitive campaigns. Concern was shown about the lack of central government control over the Kurdish populations in Iran and Iraq. Turkish warplanes frequently flew over Iraqi Kurdish terrain, allegedly with Iraq's foreknowledge, and there was a suspected sharing of the intelligence gathered by this means. In March 1983 Turkish troops again crossed the Iraqi border after the two governments had come to an agreement on the issue.

Before this, on 13 January 1983, a third hunger strike by Kurds had begun in Diyarbakir after the death of seven Kurds. A fourth hunger strike by over 100 Kurds, protesting against torture and systematic beatings, began on the 21st in the same prison. On the 28th, 92 PKK and other Kurdish leaders were sentenced to imprisonment. Later, on 2 April, an official report indicated that '63 092 people had been imprisoned under martial law regulations, and that 53 had died in custody'. Still in April a mass trial ended with 39 Kurds being sentenced to death for attempting to establish a separate state. This puts the Turkish response into perspective.

THE PKK DECLARES WAR

Meanwhile Abdullah Ocalan, in his sanctuary in Damascus, had been busy planning, scheming and preparing for a more active phase against the Turkish army, which had dealt his once flourishing PKK organisation such disastrous body blows in 1980–1. Since this major setback, shattered by mass detentions and exoduses, surviving Kurdish resistance groups had been on the defensive, remaining underground in the south-eastern provinces. Insurrectionary activities were largely retroactive. Underground, PKK members began to recover confidence and flex their muscles. Still convinced that the armed struggle was the only way to obtain Kurdish independence, Ocalan had been recruiting and training field commandos in the Bekaa Valley in Lebanon. He was now ready to carry the war to the enemy; that is, the Ankara government and its army. It is believed he began his aggressive campaign with a small nucleus of about 100 commandos.

THE PEOPLE'S LIBERATION ARMY OF KURDISTAN (ARGK)

Ocalan's 'field army' became known as the 'People's Liberation Army of Kurdistan' (ARGK), and its guerrillas began their offensive against the Turkish security forces on 14 August 1984 with a diversionary attack on Sirvan. The following evening two groups, each about 40-strong, entered and took over the towns of Semdinli (Hakkari province), just 15 miles from the Iranian border, and Eruh, some 25 miles north-west of Sirnak. The two towns were over 120 miles apart. The ARGK remained in the towns for over an hour, during which time it released Kurds held in prison (in Eruh), executed alleged collaborators, destroyed records and warned the people against collaborating with the Turkish security forces. It then departed, taking hostages with it. Eye-witnesses said the ARGK was well organised and disciplined, knew exactly what it had to do, and had its own attendant medical teams. The PKK was back in business.

These ARGK attacks took the military authorities by surprise as the south-eastern provinces had been relatively quiet during the summer. Since 1982 the army had been experimenting with 'Korucu', or 'village protectors'. Villagers were armed, and paid, to protect themselves against 'anti-government bandits'. As this seemed to be developing well, the army began blending them into a militia network in the eight Kurdish frontier provinces. A certain amount of security complacency had been setting in, a point the PKK had noted as its intimidation threats against Korucu members to abandon the village defence force had become ineffective.

Hastily the army launched Operation Comfort, which was a back-up for the Korucu. Small, well-armed mobile commandos, often with helicopters, were dispatched to follow, search out and eliminate the insurgent groups responsible for the attacks on the Korucu. The ARGK groups involved had disappeared, most probably withdrawing over the frontier into Iraq. Turkish helicopter-gunships searched for them in vain. The liberal use of helicopter-gunship fire, the abrasive attitude towards Kurds generally, and the brutal measures used to obtain information had the effect of arousing insurrection rather than quelling it. This made the task of the army more difficult and hazardous, as army bases, buildings, convoys and patrols became insurgent targets. The Turkish government later confirmed that the ARGK had shot down an army helicopter. Summer heat caused Operation Comfort to tail off without having achieved success.

OPERATION SUN

All remained quiet until October, when the ARGK struck again. On the 3rd it ambushed and killed three members of President Evren's military escort. This was followed on the 10th by another ambush near Cukurca, close to the Iraqi border, when the ARGK killed eight soldiers of Prime Minister Ozal's military escort. Both VIPs were touring Kurdish areas, and the fact that they had been targeted alarmed the military authorities, who immediately launched Operation Sun in response. This developed into a cross-border excursion into Iraq.

In the Grand National Assembly on the 17th Ozal confirmed that Operation Sun had just been completed, that a border strip of Iraq, some '15 kilometres wide', had been occupied with Iraqi consent, and that '805 arrests had been made'. He omitted to add that those detained had either been brought back to Turkey for trial or had been handed over to the Baghdad government.

Ozal also stated that his Foreign Minister, Vahit Halefoglu, when on a visit to Baghdad, had negotiated a fresh cross-border agreement that enabled Turkish troops to enter Iraq, to penetrate 'up to five kilometres' and to remain for up to three days, without prior notice. It is thought this was an understatement as it was believed that Operation Sun had carved a swathe into Iraq some 18 miles deep and 30 miles wide.

Turkey angled for a similar cross-border agreement with Iran, but was rebuffed by Prime Minister Hussein Husavi, who loftily replied that Turkey's 'security problems were its own' (Islamic Republican News Agency–IRNA). Later (June 1985) it was claimed by Turkish authorities that the Tehran government had invited Turkish security forces into Iranian territory in the frontier area.

By this time several parts of the south-eastern provinces were again alive with insurrection, which replaced sullen, passive resistance and non-cooperation. The ARGK was not the only active organisation, but to the government the ARGK seemed the most vigorous and dangerous. Walls in towns and villages were daubed with the initials of the DDKD, Kawa or the PKK, often with apt slogans attached. As intimidating threats were often ignored by the Korucu, the ARGK began to take more ruthless measures, such as killing civilians, including women and children, often when the Korucu were absent from their villages. Soldiers searching for arms also chose to visit villages when the men were away in the fields at work.

THE CONTINUING MANHUNT: 1985

During most of 1985 the Turkish army operated an intensive manhunt in the south-eastern provinces for active subversives. Priority was given to the ARGK, although other active Kurdish insurgent groups were pursued with equal vigour, especially the Kawa and the DDKD. Army manhunts resulted in numerous clashes and casualties occurred on both sides. These intensive tactics were a strain on the army, as often several had to be in motion at the same time. Exhaustion, coupled with frustration that such considerable energy was being expended to produce such small results, caused their intensity to decline. In May the Turkish Minister of the Interior, Yildirm Akbulut, admitted that Turkish security forces were 'fighting a limited guerrilla war against Kurdish separatists' (*The Times*).

After a fairly uneventful summer – which the army described as a successful period, claiming that '97 subversives had been killed and 309 captured' – man-hunting searches supplemented with punitive operations were resumed in the autumn. It was claimed that over 1000 subversives were netted within a three-week period. This activity was said to have been prompted by the urging of the Tehran and Baghdad governments after some of their frontier posts had been attacked by Kurdish insurgents. Many of those detained were handed over to Iran or Iraq. It was rumoured that both the Iraqi KDP and the PUK were liaising with the ARGK in the lawless frontier regions.

In March the Syrian government, whose army was deeply immersed in the Lebanese problem, somewhat reluctantly signed an anti-terrorist agreement with Turkey. Syria sheltered some '50 000 Turkish Kurdish refugees', some of whom the Ankara government would have liked to get its hands on. Syria again refused to agree to a hot-pursuit clause, so Turkey insisted that the security fence along the Syrian–Turkish border be electrified, studded with warning gadgets, and protected by mines and patrols in order to prevent PKK guerrillas from conducting raids into Turkey. This issue had been avoided by the Syrians so far, whose relations with Turkey were not of the best, and whose secret agenda was probably to allow this destabilisation to continue. Ocalan still sheltered in Damascus and his men still trained in the Bekaa Valley. However work on the security fence got under way, and in return Syria gained some amelioration in its Euphrates waters dispute with Turkey.

Mass trials of subversives continued in Turkey, attracting overseas media attention and that of Amnesty International. Some had been long underway, with periodic judgements that sentenced scores to death and hundreds to long-term imprisonment. The Turkish government was alleging that ARGK guerrillas were receiving training in camps in Iran, Iraq, Syria and 'some North African countries'. This was probably correct, but while in Iran and Iraq these activities might have been beyond the control of the central governments, this was not necessarily so in the other countries mentioned.

Thanks to its competent propaganda section the PKK was becoming known internationally and regarded as the predominant Kurdish resistance group in Turkey, which in fact it was rapidly becoming. The multifarious deeds of other active groups tended to remain in media darkness, and so less was was known of their organisations, leaderships and activities, other than what was patchily revealed at the several long-drawn-out mass trials. Some of the revelations may have been accurate, although some allegations and confessions were suspect.

THE OLAF PALME AFFAIR: 1986

Although Kurdish exiled communities in Western Europe did their best to remain well within the law of their host countries, wanting their approbation and support rather than reprobation and repression, it was long-suspected that some Kurdish extremists were involved in an underground struggle amongst themselves There were 'disappearances', often barely noticed by civil authorities, but occasional and more noticeable assassinations and attempted assassinations tended to cause Western governments some unease. Turkey was still politically disliked in Western Europe, a heritage of its military regimes, its current political repression and poor human rights record. Only NATO could find a good word to say on that country's behalf. Consequently there was bemused sympathy for resident Kurds who seemed to be in rebellion against their harsh, unjust Ankara regime, as the massed trials and Amnesty International reports seemed to indicate.

Some light was thrown on murky Kurdish activities when on 28 February 1986 Olaf Palme, the Prime Minister of Sweden, was shot and killed while walking in a Stockholm street. The police were baffled as to the identity of the killer, and the motive. The eye of suspicion roamed widely, but unsuccesfully. To the surprise of many, Kurds were mentioned as prime suspects.

In July a Turkish newspaper (*Hurriyet*) propounded its own theory. It stated that the assassin was Hasan Hayri Guler, a PKK member who had travelled to Stockholm by way of Denmark with orders to kill Palme, and that a Syrian diplomat, codenamed 'Besir', had smuggled the gun into Sweden for him. This was said to be a revenge killing, and that a PKK tribunal in Damascus had sentenced Palme to be executed after finding him responsible for the death of a PKK militant in Uppsala (Sweden). Initially the Stockholm police chief had said that Kurds 'topped the list of suspects' and four were arrested. They were later released as the state prosecutor insisted there was insufficient evidence to convict them.

The PKK office in Stockholm was raided by police, who stated there was a 7000-strong Kurdish community in Sweden, including about 30 PKK activists. The PKK's rift with Sweden had begun in 1984 when a PKK leader was refused asylum, and this was followed by the imprisonment of two Kurds for the murder of two PKK defectors. Enquiries dragged on fruit- lessly until February 1987, when the government ordered the 'Palme Affair' to be sidelined.

In March 1986 Ater Sait, a PKK representative, accused the Turkish authorities of greatly understating the losses sustained by the army since August 1984, when the ARGK aggressive campaign began, claiming that at least 1500 Turkish soldiers had been killed. Government figures for the period were 84 soldiers, 125 guerrillas and 66 civilians killed. In November these figures were amended by the Minister of Information, who admitted that in the two-year period '440 people, includ- ing 180 civilians, had been killed in clashes between the secu- rity forces and insurgents' in the frontier provinces. He also confirmed that since the 1984 hot-pursuit agreement there had been over 20 Turkish air strikes on 'insurgent camps in Iraqi territory', as well as two land excursions. This was an example of constant PKK questioning of government state- ments and statistics, the answers being widely distributed to the Western European media.

MORE TURKISH AIR STRIKES

The first Turkish air strikes into northern Iraq admitted since 1983 occurred on 12 August 1986, when ten aircraft attacked alleged Kurdish insurgent camps near the border. This was in response to an ARGK ambush near the border village of Ortabag, near Uledere (Hakkari province), in which 12 sol- diers had been killed. This Turkish attack followed the pub- lication of a decree amending martial law and emergency regulations to authorise 'hot pursuit' into neighbouring coun- tries. Prime Minister Ozal boasted that this would show that 'these bandits will be pursued until their hiding places are destroyed', adding 'If need be we will do so again'.

However the Turkish air raid was criticised by Iran as a violation of Turkish neutrality in the Iran–Iraq War, and the Turkish Foreign Minister had difficulty in reassuring the Tehran government that it had been undertaken only 'to defend the territorial integrity of Turkey', and that it was within the 1984 agreement. He admitted that some 200 people had been killed in the attack. Iran had previously protested (in September 1985) when Turkish warplanes had bombed Iraqi border villages. Even so relations were generally good over frontier issues, both having the same objectives in mind, and therefore touchy sovereignty feelings did little to interfere with commercial business.

A pro-Kurdish Istanbul newspaper (*Gunaydin*) reported on 22 August that the air raid had been followed by a major ground operation, but this was officially denied by Ozal the following day. During September there was a marked increase in army activity in the frontier provinces.

Turkish neutrality was again called into question by Iran following reports in the Turkish media in October that Turkey planned to occupy the oil-rich Kirkuk region of Iraq, should Iraq be defeated in its war with Iran. This was emphatically denied by the Turkish Foreign Minister in a written statement.

THE KURDS IN TURKEY

The situation for the Kurds in Turkey had improved little, although some claimed it was softening to appease EC sens- ibilities. The use of the Kurdish language was still illegal, al- though in practice it was used on the streets in Kurdish provinces, but not allowed in schools or government offices. Some Kurdish publications were sold openly and Kurdish songs were permitted at weddings and similar functions. Men who addressed election rallies in Kurdish were still put on trial, and Kurdish children still had to be given Turkish names, as did Kurdish villages. The government said that well over a million people who claimed to be Kurds could not speak Kurdish, such as those born in towns and attending Turkish schools. Some Kurds admitted that the government's assimilation policy was beginning to work. However Kurds remained non-citizens in Turkey, although many insisted that in the cities there was goodwill between Turks and Kurds and little trouble between the two communities. Some expressed doubt about this.

Kurds generally complained that the government was de- liberately neglecting Kurdish provinces, both administratively and economically. There was a higher rate of illiteracy and unemployment than in non-Kurdish areas, and a dearth of hospitals, doctors, clinics, schools and good roads. The difference was noticeable to a visitor. In response the government pointed to its major $20 billion South-East Anatolia Project, which was designed to ameliorate Kurdish poverty and improve their poor economy. By the turn of the century the project aimed to complete 21 dams and 17 hydro-electric plants in order to irrigate some 16 million hectares and generate some 7600 million megawatts of electricity. Originally expected to be completed by 1988, the project was running well behind schedule.

Kurds pointed out that the planned extra irrigation and electric power would only affect four of the nine south-eastern provinces, and would chiefly benefit large landowners rather than the average peasant. The structure of Turkish society away from the large towns revolved around the power still wielded by large landowners (aghas) and religious sheikhs, which had been the Ottoman way of balancing power in border regions. It was said that Turkish society was the 'most antiquated and brutally inequitable' in the Middle East (*Middle East*).

THE TURKISH ECONOMY

Self-sufficient in food, some 53 per cent of its workforce being engaged in agriculture, Turkey was struggling slowly into the industrial age. The government was anxious to earn hard currency to enable it to develop economically, and was having difficulty in breaching some EC markets. Its largest overseas trading partner was West Germany, Iran and Iraq – due to their war with each other – having fallen to second and third place, respectably. Despite insurgent terrorism in border areas, heavy commercial road traffic continued to roll between Turkey and the two warring countries, the Iraqi trans-Turkey oil pipeline was producing handsome revenues for the Turkish government, and large expatriate workforce remittances were a welcome addition to the economy.

Turkey had four major oil refineries but as yet only a trickle of its own oil, it being estimated that its current consumption was about 350 000 barrels a day while its production was barely 50 000 barrels a day. Turkey's south-eastern provinces accounted for most of its domestic production, but only 12 out of its 47 oil fields were producing more than 1000 barrels a day (Strategic Survey, IISS). In late March 1986 Ozal visited Baghdad, and in July an agreement was signed between Turkey and Iraq to increase the flow of oil along the trans-Turkish oil pipeline from one million to 1.5 million barrels a day. Discussion began with Iran for a trans-Turkish pipeline to the Mediterranean.

THE ARGK VERSUS THE KORUCU: 1987

Following an ARGK attack at the beginning of March 1987 on the village of Acikyol (Mardin province), in which nine people, mainly members of the Korucu, were killed, Turkey mounted a major security operation along its border with Syria – the raiding party had breached the security fence. Two days later another ARGK attack was launched, this time on the town of Sirnak, in which over 34 civilians were killed, again mostly Korucu. Turkish aircraft bombed three villages in northern Iraq that were alleged to harbour ARGK guerillas, claiming to have destroyed them.

During the first part of 1987 the ARGK intimidation campaign met resistance from the Korucu, who were supported by landowners and conservative elements of Kurdish society. Not all Kurds, especially those in the countryside, were by any means in favour of participation in armed violence against the central authority. Most were primarily concerned with eking out a living, although many favoured recognition of themselves as Kurds and the freedom to use their own language and follow traditional Kurdish customs. As Korucu groups ignored repeated threats and warnings to disband, the ARGK commenced a campaign of retribution against them.

On 20 June the ARGK attacked the village of Pinarcik (Mardin province), again breaking through the security fence from Syria. They caught the authorities completely by surprise, took over the town for two hours and 'killed 31 out of the 80' Korucu members before departing. This was said to be the worst attack of this type since 1984. It had repercussions, as the army was blamed for the delay in responding to the emergency.

The Pinarcik massacre brought to a head differences between Prime Minister Ozal and the armed forces. It had been long suspected that the army had been independently running its own campaigns against insurgents in its own way, with only a minimum of civilian control and consent, and without informing Ozal of what was happening. Ozal complained that the first he knew of such attacks was by reading of them in newspapers. He faced up to the army and a fortnight later cancelled his attendance at a meeting of the military National Security Council, flatly refusing to approve the army's choice for the appointment of chief of staff. This and other measures brought the army to heel, but to a limited extent.

In the first week in July similar ARGK attacks were made on two villages – Pecenek and Yuvali in Mardin province – in which over 30 Korucu were killed and other casualties were incurred. These were prestige attacks as Ozal was touring the area at the time. Again the attacks had been launched from Syria, where ARGK training camps were still based. Ozal once again tried unsuccesfully to pressure the Syrian government into accepting a Turkish hot-pursuit agreement.

The only success Ozal had in this respect had been in 1985, when following border security talks with Syria, that country had extradited five PKK members and reportedly closed down several ARGK border camps, but that had occurred at a point of high political tension, when Syria feared Turkish aerial retribution. Perhaps Ozal again used threatening language, as ARGK attacks from Syria declined and more attention was given to making the security fence a better obstacle by adding additional watchtowers.

Syria admitted that Ocalan was still in Damascus, but insisted he was a legitimate political refugee who could not be extradited. In June, Ocalan had boasted in an interview in *Serwebun*, which was circulated in Western Europe, that he would soon have a permanent presence in Turkey, which indicated perhaps that he did not have one as yet, and that Turkish army 'manhunt' tactics were having some success in preventing the ARGK from 'swimming in the sea of the people'. Since 1980 the ARGK had been steadily forced out of its strongholds in the 'lowlands' of Turkish Kurdistan, towards mountainous border areas.

Similar ARGK attacks were made on the Korucu in villages near the border during the second part of 1987, launched mainly from Iraqi territory. These included one at night in

October on Cobandere (in Siirt province), in which 13 Korucu and four 'bandits' were killed and the body of another was taken away by the attackers. Villagers were lectured by the ARGK and warned not to cooperate with the government in future. However the Korucu managed to hold together as the army's response time improved.

In other instances the ARGK entered villages in order to make examples of individuals. During September in a village named Gunesli, when villagers refused to reveal the where-abouts of a man being sought for execution, twelve people were killed, some allegedly dying under torture. This was again a prestige incident as President Evren was touring the vicinity. In Bingol the commander of the Korucu was dragged out and shot, the villagers being mustered to witness his salutatory death. Numerous other clashes between insurgents and the security forces in the south-eastern provinces were reported.

THE TURKISH PEACE ASSOCIATION

Formed in 1977, the Turkish Peace Association had been set up to monitor human rights in Turkey, in accordance with the Helsinki Human Rights Accords. It was neither effective nor influential, even though it worked with Amnesty International, and its investigations were deliberately hindered. In May 1987 a number of its members were arraigned and imprisoned, accused of 'spreading communism and seeking to overthrow the constitution'.

ACTIVITIES IN WESTERN EUROPE: 1987

Since the revelations of the Palme Affair, the West German authorities had become alerted to Kurdish illegal activities, to the extent that at the beginning of August 1987 members of the Chief Prosecutor's Office in Bonn raided '39 locations' in an attempt to secure evidence that organised Kurdish terrorist groups were operating in West Germany. It was stated that since mid-1984 there had been five known murders of Kurds, two attempted murders and six arson attacks on Turkish premises (Official press release). Allegations that the PKK was using legal Kurdish associations, such as the ERNK and the Komar, were mentioned. At the ERNK Cologne office, police seized thousands of secret PKK documents, including lists of members, locations and activities.

West German police raids and seizures caused a wave of Kurdish protest actions across parts of Western Europe. Generally, the Kurds in West Germany were discontented, complaining they had not been given the minority status enjoyed by the Turks. Protesting Kurds blockaded the State Assembly in Hanover; in Stockholm and Athens they occupied the offices of Lufthansa Airlines. In Amsterdam they occupied the offices of Amnesty International, refusing to leave until officials agreed to supply them regularly with lists of Kurds held in detention in Turkey, and also protesting against the refusal of the Dutch authorities to give them a copy of a letter the Dutch Foreign Minister was sending to the Turkish government about the Kurds' lack of human rights. Protesting Kurds also occupied the West German consulates in Liège and Zurich.

This unexpected bout of Kurdish protest simmered down after a few days, but the West German police now knew they had a Kurdish terrorist problem on their hands. The PKK was exporting its struggle to host countries, in the course of which the Kurds began to lose the sympathetic tolerance they had received towards their cause so far.

TURKISH POLICIES: 1987

In November 1987 Ozal's Motherland Party (ANAP) was returned to power in a general election, which meant that Turkish policies would continue much as before. Ozal was still keen to take his country into the EC. His application had been accepted in April, with only Greece dissenting. However the EC dragged its feet. In July Ozal lifted martial law from the last four provinces, leaving just the lower grade state of emergency in being. This did not move the EC either, which was concerned about journalists having been sentenced to imprisonment for mentioning 'Kurdish separatism'.

The Council of Europe passed a resolution in which it blamed Turkey for the Armenian Massacres of 1915–18, and called on the Turkish government to recognise its 'Kurdish problem'. In

January 1988 Turkey signed the Council of Europe's agreement on the Prevention of Torture, having been criticised for not doing so when other council members had signed in November 1987.

In the first week in January 1988, in Paris a West German diplomat (Siegfried Wielspitz) was murdered. The finger of suspicion pointed at the ERNK as one of its pamphlets was found on the body; however it denied the accusation. It was suspected to have been a grudge killing as it appears the diplomat had been somehow involved with the police raids of August the previous year, and with the confiscation of money found in searches of PKK premises. When a West German aircraft crashed near Izmir on the 2nd, the PKK was again suspected of involvement, which was also denied.

THE KURDISH INSURRECTION: 1988

Mass trials and verdicts, followed by prison protests, continued to generate unfavourable international publicity for the Turkish government. For example in February 1988 20 PKK members were sentenced to death by a Diyarbakir military court, and the same month some 2000 Kurdish prisoners in the same city prison mounted a 10-day hunger strike, demanding improved conditions. Some were granted, including the right to converse in Kurdish with visiting family members.

Throughout 1988 the Turkish army spasmodically continued its manhunt tactics, which largely prevented the ARGK from carrying out Ocalan's stated aim of establishing a permanent presence in the country. Cross-border ARGK raids continued, provoking aerial retribution on border sanctuaries in Iraq and Iran, but not Syria.

By this time the character of the Kurdish insurrection was changing, as the left-wing, educated, youthful and energetic Kurdish leadership in exile, mainly PKK members, seized control of events, elbowing other insurgent groups aside. A certain amount of infighting occurred for influence and territory. Landowners and tribal sheikhs sheered away from the new Kurdish PKK leadership, as did many Kurds with vested interests in stability. Harsh repressive measures were enabling the

Turkish army to at least contain the Kurdish insurrection, but not to defeat it.

Previously, in mid-1987 a regional governor (Hayri Kozarcloglu) had been appointed with almost absolute authority over eight Kurdish provinces in order to concentrate security resources and prosecute the war against the Kurdish insurgents. He was having moderate success, although this was largely concealed by the PKK propaganda section and Western European 'Turkey watchers' with human rights abuses in mind.

The Korucu increased to over 40 000 and became slightly better armed, some villages having army helicopters on call. Improved Syrian–Turkish border security more or less blocked the ARGK's route from the Bekaa Valley into Turkey, forcing guerrillas to enter though Iraq, and more recently through Iran as well. These mountainous detours, through which commercial routes ran, were heavily infested with troops and patrolled by aircraft, as well as being subjected to occasional military joint operations.

Belatedly the ARGK had begun to gain a foothold in northern Iranian territory. The Tehran government was unhappy about what it saw as Turkey's pro-Iraqi stance. Trade between Turkey and Iran continued, but Prime Minister Hussein Musavi's visit to Ankara had not been a success as he had refused to make the customary homage visit to the Ataturk mausoleum, opting instead to go to Konya, a centre of Shia fundamentalism. Iran, feeling severely the strain of its war with Iraq, was becoming nervous and touchy.

THE PKK OFFERS A CEASE-FIRE

In early June 1988 in the Bekaa Valley, in an interview for an Istanbul newspaper, Ocalan offered a cease-fire to the Turkish government if it would recognise the PKK. Should this offer be rejected he threatened to mount attacks on Turkish towns and politicians. The Istanbul court suppressed the article, but the contents were leaked on a worldwide basis. The Turkish government ignored the offer, believing it to be an admission of weakness.

Ocalan was perhaps under duress from his host government,

which feared a major Turkish military invasion into the Bekaa Valley was in preparation. This would have destabilised Syria, and perhaps brought down the government. Syria, like the Kurds, had no real friends at that time. Also, the Syrian government feared Turkish manipulation of the Euphrates waters, should open hostilities erupt between the two countries.

On Ocalan's part, his insurrection was not going as well as he had hoped in Turkey. His ARGK had far more members in prison or on trial than he could muster in the field. He also knew that while Turkey, Iran and Iraq were all willing and able to give covert subsistence support to the others' Kurdish insurrectionary groups, in order to keep them alive and active against their central governments, there was a distinct limit as to how far any of them would go. None were in favour of an independent Kurdish entity. Ocalan knew that if he lost his valuable Bekaa Valley foothold he would be unlikely to obtain another in any country contiguous to Turkey. He knew the value of his ARGK to Syria, but also knew its limits, and that when it came to the crunch all Kurds were expendable. His cease-fire offer was a measure of expediency.

11 Between Wars: 1988–90

On 13 March 1988 an Iranian force of some 20 000 Pasdaran, supported by Barzani-KDP Pesh Mergas, advanced from the the Panjwin Bulge towards the Dukan Dam in Suliemaniyeh Province to capture the Kurdish village of Khormal, six miles inside Iraq. The objective was to gain a swathe of territory from which to launch a step-by-step approach into the major northern Iraqi valleys – a most sensible course. The Iranian Pasdaran then moved on to the Kurdish town of Halabja (nominal population about 60 000, which would include adjacent villages). The area garrisoned about 1500 Iraqi troops, who in the next 48 hours were surrounded. According to Pasdaran sources (personal interviews), realising they were heavily outnumbered, cut off from contact with their own troops and that there was little hope of reinforcements arriving, the Iraqi troops surrendered 'without a shot being fired'. They were hastily evacuated to Bakhtaran (in Iran) some 180 miles distant, where Western journalists were allowed some access to them. The Pasdaran insisted that the Kurdish inhabitants of Halabja had welcomed the invaders.

When the Iraqi troops had been removed from the scene the Pasdaran units moved away from Halabja, some pushing on to the shore of Lake Dardani Khan, where they took up positions overlooking the Dukan Dam and its hydro-electric power station. Iraqi aircraft had already flown over the area, but so far had not attacked. Aerial retaliation was expected. The remainder of the Pasdaran camped some distance from Halabja. Pasdaran sources said that 'about half the inhabitants had fled from the town', but that their Pasdaran allies, the KDP Pesh Mergas, had remained there. Iraq gave a different version of this incident, insisting there had been 'three days hard fighting' before the Iraqi force was overcome.

On 16 and 17 March Iraqi aircraft made several sorties, bombing Halabja and nearby villages and using chemical weapons that included mustard and sarin nerve-gas bombs. According to some reports tabun nerve-gas bombs were also deployed. Probably up to 5000 people were killed or injured by chemical means, mainly Kurds. The precise figures are still subject to debate.

On the 19th a small number of Western journalists, issued with gas-masks, were flown in two helicopters from Bakhtaran to see for themselves the scene of the devastation and report the facts to the world. A few survivors were flown out to Western hospitals as further proof that chemical weapons had indeed been used. These attacks were condemned by Western governments. The US State Department denounced Iraq for 'grave violation of the 1925 Geneva Protocol outlawing the use of gas weapons'. Kurdish activists staged protest demonstrations in Western Europe, the USA and even the Soviet Union. A UN resolution condemned Iraq for using chemical weaponry. Similar Iraqi violations had been reported previously, as had ones allegedly committed by Iran, but little real international interest had been taken in them. Suddenly chemical warfare in Iraq and Iran became a major issue.

The Pasdaran said the bombing had been Saddam Hussein's deliberate revenge operation on the Barzani-KDP Pesh Mergas – who were in the pay of the Tehran government – for their participation in the seizure of Haj Omran in 1983.

In April Ozal, concerned that the Iran–Iraq War was escalating into a chemical warfare dimension, visited Baghdad in an attempt to bring it to an end, but was unsuccessful. Heavy Western odium fell on Saddam, who was personally held responsible for the Halabja disaster. Anxious to be accepted into the EC as a good European, Ozal would have liked to have become a peacemaker. He certainly wanted to avoid being seen as a collaborator.

THE IRAN–IRAQ CEASE-FIRE

Suddenly and unexpctedly, on 18 July 1988 the Iranian government accepted the year-old UN Resolution 598 for an immediate end to the eight-year Iran–Iraq War. Two days later Ayatollah Khomeini made his famous speech, in which he portrayed acceptance of the ceasefire as 'more deadly than taking poison'. At once Javier Perez de Cuellar, the UN Secretary General, sent UN teams to Baghdad and Tehran to negotiate its implementation.

The Baghdad government greeted Iran's decision with great suspicion and continued air attacks deep inside Iran, while the Iraqi-based NLA(I) – the military arm of the NRC, led by Masoud Rajavi – pushed into Iran to capture and briefly hold two towns near Kermanshah. Iran responded by attacking Iraqi forces east of Basra. Saddam insisted on direct negotiations with Iran, which was refused. On 1 August the UN published evidence indicating that Iraq had recently stepped up its use of chemical weapons, with cyanide and mustard gas being used against Iranian troops and civilians.

On the 8th the UN Secretary General announced that the cease-fire would come into effect on 20 August 1988, which opened the way (on the 17th) for the deployment of a 350-strong multinational peacekeeping force to be positioned at strategic points to monitor the truce. On the 25th Iranian and Iraqi representatives met in Geneva to begin talks. The Iran–Iraq War had at last ground to a halt, largely through exhaustion. Forward troops remained in position facing each other, but the cease-fire held with only minor breaches.

THE KURDISH REACTION

The cease-fire came as a complete surprise to the several Kurdish insurrectionary groups. They were nonplussed, as it is doubtful whether any of them had seriously thought beyond this point. Circumstances had conditioned Kurdish groups to live for the day, to be alert in seizing opportunities in changing scenarios, and to cope with setbacks and disappointments. Kurds thought tactically rather than strategically, probably because loyalties were flexible. Leadership attitudes clashed, some remaining tribal and rural while others inclined towards extreme revolutionary doctrines, organisations and methods.

The governments of Iran, Iraq, Syria and Turkey also seemed to have given little thought to what they would do about their rebellious Kurdish minorities after the cease-fire, other than to beat them into submission. As the guns fell silent, the initial thought of the various governments was to increase the volume of trade between them, especially across joint frontiers. Thoughts must have centred around a joint clean-up of the frontier 'bandit' areas to facilitate the flow of trade. The problem remaining was that the cease-fire had not restored normal relations between Iran and Iraq.

There was no clear victor to call the shots, nor vanquished to fall meekly into line, which tended to rule out viable joint operations. Therefore each had to deal with their Kurdish minorities in their own limited way. Both Iran and Iraq faced the dilemma of whether to continue paying subsidies to their Kurdish proxies, and what to with them in a changed situation.

The Kurdish resistance pattern remained the same bizarre one in which Kurdish groups were fighting both as proxies and against each other. The Tehran government still supported the Iraqi KDP, and perhaps also the PUK to a much lesser degree, in their struggle against the Baghdad government; while the Baghdad government was paying the KDPI to fight the Tehran one. In addition these Kurdish groups were at odds with each other. In Iraq the PUK and the KDP were at daggers drawn, while in Iran the KDPI and the Komala were at each other's throats. All these active Kurdish groups were in conflict with those Kurdish populations that had quietly accepted central government control, and among which they ruthlessly marched and countermarched, demanding shelter, extorting or wreaking vengeance. The Kurdish insurrectionists were as disunited as ever.

In March 1988, during a visit to London Jalal Talabani stated that the Iraqi army was mounting a spring offensive in northern Iraq, both to clear the border regions and to concentrate the mountain Kurds around Arbil, Dohuk, Kirkuk and Suliemaniyeh so that they might be better controlled. Iraq had already used chemical weapons on Kurds in the Balisan and Jaffati valleys on 26–8 February (*The Times*). The army was continuing its routine containing action.

The Iraqi army began its real campaign against Iraqi Kurds on 25 August, operating from Zakho and mustering some 30 000 troops with supporting tanks, artillery, planes and helicopters. This caused Masoud Barzani to call on the UN to outlaw chemical warfare operations and to persuade Iraq not to use chemical weapons on some '150 000 villagers living alongside the Turkish border' (KDP release issued in Berlin), alleging that Saddam Hussein was launching a deliberate 'war of genocide'.

The Iraqi offensive caused a flood of Kurdish mountain

refugees to seek sanctuary in Turkey, but the border was closed against them. After initial hesitation, and wary of his image as a good European, on 1 September Ozal offered 'conditional temporary refuge for the fleeing Kurds' (*Kurdish Life*) and to establish refugee camps, pointing out that all this must somehow be paid for with international funds. Ozal was a good weatherman, who had an eye to economic opportunity.

Within days a reputed 50 000 Iraqi Kurdish refugees entered Turkey through the Cukurca border post. Another border crossing point was opened at Uzunde, and then three refugee camps were established away from the frontier near Diyarbakir, Silop and Yuksekova. By the end of the first week in September an estimated 90 000 refugees had entered Turkey, with a further 45 000 waiting to cross, some being prevented from doing so by Iraqi troops. Belatedly Iran, seeing which way the international wind was blowing and also wanting to be once again accepted into the international family of nations, offered to accept Iraqi Kurdish refugees, although Turkey remained their preferred destination.

On 6 September Saddam Hussein offered an amnesty to all Iraqi Kurds, inside or outside the country, which was rejected by Kurdish resistance leaders. Later the Baghdad government claimed that 11 000 Kurds had returned from Iran and 20 000 from Turkey. At a media conference in Ankara, the Iraqi ambassador to Turkey claimed that 'the Iraqi army now controls the full length of the Turkish border for the first time in 123 years' (*Daily Telegraph*). The Turkish Foreign Minister, Mesut Yilmaz, stated that the exact number of Iraqi Kurdish refugees in Turkey was 56 377.

Suddenly, on 9 September Ozal changed his mind and closed his frontier to Iraqi refugees, stating that over 60 000 refugees were already living in five tented camps near the border with Iraq, and that he needed $300 million to take care of this problem.

Ozal was alarmed by the huge influx that was pouring into his country, and by the implications this might have for his own Kurds, notably the ARGK, which he held responsible for attempting to blow up a bridge near Bingol on the main railway link between Turkey and Iran. He feared that the ARGK and other insurgent Kurdish groups would take advantage of the confused situation and launch a major campaign against government forces. Ozal cancelled his hot-pursuit agreement with Iraq and would not allow Iraqi refugees to mix with Turkish Kurds, isolating them in their camps.

On 14 October Iran too closed its doors to Iraqi Kurdish refugees, and asked Turkey not to send any more. Apparently Turkey had been quietly pushing some of the refugees into Iran, which alleged that at least 20 000 had arrived in this way with the full knowledge of the Turkish government. The UNHCR stated on 20 September that '51 000 Kurdish refugees had fled from Iraq into Turkey'.

In Iraq the army's campaign against the Kurds continued during the autumn, and it was alleged that chemical weapons were used on several occasions. The first such attack since August was said to have occurred on 11 October near Kirkuk, with another on the 14th near Suliemaniyeh, when over 50 Kurds died. The Iraqi government repeatedly refuted these allegations. General Adnam Khairallah, the Iraqi Defence Minister, denied using chemical weapons, insisting that it would be counterproductive to do so during an army advance, Few believed him. One authority (the London-based Organisation of Human Rights in Iraq – OHRI) stated that a team of American doctors working in Turkish refugee camps had found ample evidence of chemical weapons having been used. Anti-American demonstrations were subsequently mounted in Baghdad. The OHRI also stated that Iraq held 400 000 political prisoners, including 120 000 women. It was said that 'gas and extermination tactics' had caused the Kurdish exodus. Areas of northern Iraq became depopulated and devastated.

SADDAM HUSSEIN'S BIG MISTAKE

Saddam Hussein's decision to use chemical weapons against his Kurds was one of his biggest mistakes, as the horrific aspect of this form of warfare drew universal attention to the plight of the Kurds and put them really in the spotlight for the first time. It is probable that if he had carried out his punitive operation in northern Iraq using only conventional weapons, comparatively little notice would have been taken of it. Fearing a westward spread of Iranian fundamentalism in the region, since 1986 the American administration had been building up good relations with Iraq in the hope it could become a barrier against the spread. Several nations traded with Iraq, including the USA, France and Germany, and continued to do so, and Britain refused to suspend trade credits to that country. Governments remained more interested in commerce than Kurds, feeling perhaps that the developing, universal, pro-Kurdish euphoria might soon pass.

Iraq's use of chemical weapons against Iranians in the latter stages of the Iran–Iraq War had elicited little real protest from the West. Khomeini and his repressive and bloody Islamic regime was the main Western bogeymen, with Saddam Hussein as a lesser enemy in Western eyes. Over the years the world had been largely indifferent to Kurdish misfortunes, but this time the scenario of Kurds fleeing before Saddam's hail of mustard, cyanide and nerve gases suddenly hit consciences and aroused international concern on a massive scale. From this moment onwards Saddam Hussein became known as the 'monster' who had bombed his own people with mustard and nerve gas at Halabja. He was painted black with indelible paint.

To the discomfort of regional countries with Kurdish minorities, Western governments loudly expressed concern over the fate of the Kurds. The last thing these countries wanted was an international spotlight on their Kurdish problems. Embarrassed, the USA – reluctant to lose a possible Iraqi barrier against Islamic fundamentalism – shuffled responsibility on to a somewhat reluctant UN. Madame Mitterrand, wife of the French President, publicly took up the Kurdish cause and visited Kurdish refugee camps, but she was a lone crusader as the attitude of Western governments remained correct, cool and non-committal.

THE IRAQI KURDS: 1989

Throughout the autumn of 1988 the Iraqi army continued its campaign against the Kurds. It was suspended during the winter, to resume again in spring 1989, only to be briefly halted during April when the government brazenly mounted an international arms exhibition, which attracted many international visitors. A senior Iraqi religious leader, Imam Mohammed Delgaii, visited Baghdad to plead for some amelioration for his

Kurds, but was promptly imprisoned. This was a difficult time for the several Kurdish groups that had been in receipt of proxy pay from opposing governments, their main fears being that they would be abandoned and their funding terminated, and that Iranian and Iraqi armed forces might combine to bring them to heel. In the absence of positive new policies, Kurdish proxy groups retained their funding from their principals for the time being.

By June 1989 mass relocations of Kurds were underway from the 'Qala Siza, Taswasrab and Raniya areas, involving some 300 000 people' (*The Times*), The government's explanation was that they were being moved to more modern villages with better facilities. A security zone was created alongside the Iranian frontier, up to 40 miles in depth, in order to deprive the KDP and PUK of the support of Iran and local tribes and villages.

Villages in the security zone were razed and it was made a prohibited area, parts of which were free-fire zones. Kurds living near the zone were uprooted and replaced by Iraqi Arabs, who took over their agricultural holdings. Some Egyptian migrants were brought in and paid to work some of the depopulated land. Saddam Hussein planned to Arabise the entire Kurdish region. The first stage was to resettle Kurds into closely supervised 'cluster camps' around Irbid, Mosul and Suliemaniyeh. Such Kurds as were allowed to remain in their villages had no freedom of movement, nor were they permitted to engage in agriculture. Resistance was negligible, largely through the fear generated by Saddam's chemical weapon attacks, which had affected even the most hardened Pesh Mergas of the KDP and PUK, who barely retained their entity and mobility.

THE IRAQI KURDISTAN FRONT

The Iraqi Kurdistan Front (IKF), which had been mooted in mid-1987 and given a boost by the Halabja chemical weapon attack, held its first meeting in June 1989. The KDP, the PUK, the Iraqi Kurdistan Socialist Party (KSP), the KPDP, the Iraqi Communist Party and the Islamic Movement of Iraqi Kurdistan (IMIK), although diverse in themselves, were brought together under the umbrella of the IKF to oppose the Iraqi Baathist government.

The spokesman for the IKF (Hushier Zibari, a member of the KDP) stated that its aim was self-determination for the people of Iraqi Kurdistan, claiming that it already had over 100 000 members, most of whom were abroad in exile, especially in West Germany, 'where our numbers are greatest'; others were in refugee camps in Turkey. The policy was to continue to attack military and economic targets in Iraq, and to take political action in Europe. He complained that the Iraqi government's talk of liberalisation was 'only window-dressing to hide the truth from the world'. The spokesman denied both that the IKF was an Islamic movement and that Iranian troops were fighting alongside the Pesh Merga, even though it did contain the IMIK, but admitted to receiving aid from Iran (*Daily Telegraph*). Behind the façade of the IKF, constituent groups continued to operate individually as before and to establish their own political organisations in Europe, largely for fund-raising purposes. Liaison and centralism seemed to be minimal.

THE IRANIAN KURDS: 1989

In Iran, the Pasdaran were tightening their grip on Kurdish territory but they continued to meet resistance. Ghassemlou boasted that his KDPI was tying down about 250 000 Iranian troops, which was probably an accurate figure, but since the Iran–Iraq cease-fire this number could be quickly increased. Ghassemlou admitted there was no military solution to his struggle, that autonomy was the best solution, and that he was willing to negotiate. There was silence in Tehran. Khomeini, who had been against any form of separatism, died in June. Ghassemlou said he had a faint hope the new regime would look favourably on Kurdish autonomy, but he was soon disabused. The new Tehran government would have nothing to do with him, and the Pasdaran, now largely withdrawn from the battle fronts, was able to pay more attention to its responsibility for internal security, increasing its pressure on the Iranian Kurds.

THE ASSASSINATION OF GHASSEMLOU

On 13 July 1989, in an apartment in Vienna, Abdul Rahman Ghassemlou, leader of the KDPI since 1973, was assassinated, together with two senior colleagues. This great blow debilitated the KDPI. The meeting in Vienna had been arranged by Iranian agents, but the Iranian government denied complicity, insisting that it was to arrange a visit by Ghassemlou to Tehran to discuss the Kurdish problem. Khomeini, who disliked Ghassemlou, had died over a month previously. As an Iranian official at the meeting had also been shot and injured, rival Kurdish resistance groups were included in the list of suspects, but few doubted the culprit was the Iranian secret service.

Ghassemlou was succeeded as Secretary General of the KDPI by Sadegh Sarafkandi, who was himself assassinated on 18 September 1992 in a restaurant in Berlin, together with three senior members of the KDPI. It appeared as though the Iranian government was running a secret assassination squad to help it control its Kurdish insurrectionary activities.

THE PKK: 1989

In Turkey, at the beginning of 1989 the Turkish army captured three senior PKK commanders. Following their interrogation some 4000 alleged PKK activists and ARGK guerrillas ware arrested, which the army boasted accounted for the major part of the ARGK organisation in the field. The ARGK struck back in May with a series of hit-and-run attacks in the Judi mountain range, and the following month struck at targets within 15 miles of Siirt. The army admitted that the insurrection had escalated in Siirt province, but insisted it had waned in the other Kurdish areas. Over 100 000 troops and gendarmerie were still being deployed against the ARGK and other active Kurdish groups in the south-eastern provinces, but as there was a sprinkling of activists among the Iraqi Kurdish refugees, troop deployment had to be readjusted.

The Kurdish insurrection by this time was taking on the character of a comprehensive national revolt under PKK leadership, which had largely eclipsed, smothered or absorbed its main rivals, the surviving ones being reduced to minor local activity. In the course of an 80-day period in the summer the army admitted it had lost 45 soldiers in clashes with the ARGK, but said it had killed 45 PKK members, and that 23 civilians had also died in the skirmishes (official report). The ARGK was now obviously short of trained manpower, one source indicating it had as few as 300 (*New York Times*), which caused it to raid villages in order to press-gang recruits, some quite young, as evidenced by its casualties.

By this time ARGK tactics were undergoing a change. Previously it had joined in with zest in tribal rivalry so as to increase its domination. In the course of related activities sometimes whole villages were wiped out, and massacres occurred, which in turn provoked counterterrorist action by the security forces, both of which were condemned in the media, their reputations in this respect gaining widespread odium. Leaders of the PUK and the KDP had criticised these tactics, causing Ocalan to switch to military and economic targets only, the exception being that his campaign against the village Korucu continued. The Turkish media reported all major incidents, which tended to curb the activities of the security forces and the ARGK, both of whom were angling for public support and esteem.

Overseas, foreign patronage of the PKK seemed to remain as solid as ever, several governments having secret agendas unfavourable to Turkey. Iran, for example, resented Turkey harbouring anti-government Iranian exiles, and for its solid front against Islamic fundamentalism, while Syria remained dissatisfied over the distribution of the Euphrates waters. Ocalan still operated with considerable freedom from Damascus, while rebuilding his ARGK, so badly decimated, in covert training camps in the Bekaa Valley, and latterly in Iran. The Turkish government had repeatedly failed to make hot-pursuit or other mutual security agreements with either Syria or Iran against Kurdish activists in the frontier areas.

The main source of PKK funds remained the Kurdish 'guest workers' in Western Europe, but this was beginning to be supplemented by increasing involvement in drug trafficking in Western Turkey, which was on the main illicit international drug highway into Europe from Caucasia and some southern Asian states. Allegations were made in Turkey, and repeated in the media, that while Turkish soldiers were pursuing and searching out ARGK activists, Turkish customs officials were accepting bribes to facilitate the westward flow of drugs.

THE ARGK: 1990

The PKK remained committed to its 'sustained people's war', and in the field the ARGK intensified its activities during spring 1990. Ocalan was disappointed by his lack of success in internationalising the Kurdish struggle, being thwarted to some extent by Turkish government censorship, which denigrated Kurdish insurgent activities as acts of terrorism. Despite the efforts of the PKK propaganda section, most nations continued to regard the Kurdish struggle in Turkey as a domestic problem. In turn the Turkish army was frustrated at the lack of identifiable targets, and invariably had to take reactive rather than proactive action, which became manifested in attacks and brutal measures against people in towns and villages.

HEAVY CENSORSHIP

During March and April 1990, unrest in the Kurdish south-eastern provinces escalated, until it was likened in some sections of the Turkish media to the Palestinian intifada, then in progress in the Israeli-occupied territories of Palestine. It was reported (Anatolian News Agency) that 91 people died in March as a result of the Kurdish insurrection, as opposed to only five in March the previous year.

This prompted the army-dominated National Security Council to outline a package of security measures, which President Ozal had to adopt. These mainly involved stricter press censorship, extended prison sentences and heavy fines for breaches of security regulations, and gave further authority for relocating Kurds. Ozal had been elected president in November 1989 on the death of Evren, and was attempting to develop a presidential style of government.

Turkish political parties tacitly agreed to the implementation of these new measures 'in the national interest', although there was unspoken reluctance in some cases. However a howl of protest came from publishers, editors and journalists, several of whom went underground to avoid imprisonment, and several periodicals ceased publication. Permission was refused to print periodicals that in the past had shown sympathy with the Kurdish cause.

The army launched punitive operations to try to eliminate ARGK commando groups, but they were hard to locate and even harder to pin down. However in one attack on 9–10 April near the village of Dymakya (Hakkari province), it was claimed that 21 'rebels' were killed, including 'Dr Baran', described as the leader responsible for planning ARGK operations from Syria. Up to 15 civilians also died in the incident.

RUPTURED RELATIONS

In April 1990 a West German television documentary was shown, which claimed that West German security services had uncovered up to 30 Turkish secret police, posing as diplomats, who were 'spying on the 1.5 million Turks in that country' (*The Times*). There were diplomatic repercussions, and '15 diplomats' were hastily withdrawn from the Turkish embassy in Bonn. In return eight West German diplomats were expelled from Ankara. The Turkish government complained that the TV programme had threatened the security of all its diplomats in West Germany. This rumpus took a little while to simmer down. It was a serious blow to the good European image Turkey was trying to develop in order to ease its entry into the EC and other West European organisations, which on the whole were still reluctant to accept it owing to its repressive regime and poor human rights record. Turkey was only prepared to bend so far.

THE ARGK OFFENSIVE CONTINUES

The Turkish army continued its relocation tactics, but was finding it increasing difficult to recruit Korucu village guards, whose numbers had reputedly fallen to 25 000. In June an example was made of a village near Catak (in Van province), where the inhabitants had refused to join the local Korucu. All were relocated and their houses destroyed (*Middle East*). In another

instance the same month, more than 25 inhabitants of the
village of Cevrimi, near Sirnak, were killed in a dispute with
the army. The government blamed the ARGK, while the PKK
blamed the Turkish army. It was accusation and counteraccusa-
tion, and invariably there was a lack of sufficient evidence to
determine which had been the aggressor. Invariably the victims
were Kurdish civilians.

In July the ARGK claimed to have killed over 80 Turkish
soldiers, including ten officers and 30 village guards, to have
destroyed three helicopters and to have inflicted over 50 casualties on the Turkish army in the Uludere region. For their
part the Turkish army, while admitting to having lost eleven
soldiers, insisted it had killed 43 'rebels' (*Middle East*).

In October 1990 a minister of state (Mehmet Kececiler), in
a statement in the Grand National Assembly, called for the
immediate execution of almost 200 political extremists who
had been sentenced to death. No executions had been carried
out since 1983 and there were now 287 people in prison awaiting confirmation or commutation of their death sentences
(official figures). This state of affairs was much criticised by
opposition politicians and the Turkish media. Kececiler's statement was said to have been a gambit to speed up legal decision-
making and have all such sentences commuted in order to
improve Turkey's international image (some had been sentenced in the early 1980s, *Middle East Economic Digest*), but it
was more likely to have been prompted by the wave of assassinations – already numbering more than twenty – of Turkish
politicians that year.

IRAQ OCCUPIES KUWAIT

Suddenly and unexpectedly, on 2 August 1990 Iraqi armed
forces occupied Kuwait. Saudi Arabia asked for US military
assistance, US troops landed in that country, and a military
confrontation built up into an American-led coalition of some
29 national contingents, Iraq becoming an Allied enemy.
Saddam Hussein remained defiant, refusing to withdraw his
troops, and the confrontation intensified as Allied forces accu-
mulated strength and sophisticated weaponry in an eyeball-to-
eyeball stance.

President Ozal was quick off the mark in siding with the Allies. He allowed Turkish NATO air bases at Incirlik and other places to be used by the Allies for aggressive military purposes, but did not contribute Turkish troops to the Alliance. With a shrewd eye to the future, he cooperated with the USA, the prime mover in the Alliance, but let it be known that he was expecting to be rewarded in due course. Ozal had his eye on the northern Iraqi oilfields. Already Turkey was the third largest recipient of US foreign aid (after Israel and Egypt), due to its vital position in NATO. The US forgave Turkey a $7 billion debt and increased the Turkish allocation of textile imports to the USA (probably at the cost of some 20 000 American jobs).

Iran watched warily from the sideline. Turkey immediately closed its frontier with Iraq, but not with Iran, with whom it continued to trade. The Turkish army continued its pressure against the ARGK, and extra troops were moved towards the Iraqi border, both to overawe the Kurdish population and to be ready to move into Iraq in conjunction with any Allied strategic plan to occupy as much of northern Iraq as possible, should an opportunity present itself. If is believed that the comparatively small Turkish subsidy to the KDP was continued, presumably in case its services, or neutrality, were needed in the future.

THE KURDS REMAIN PASSIVE

In August, when Iraq invaded Kuwait, the Iraqi Kurdistan Front coalition decided to stop all guerrilla activity against the Iraqi army in northern Iraq. However Jalal Talabani, the leader of the PUK, rushed to Washington to seek American support for his own group to rise up against Saddam Hussein, but his offer was ignored by both the US State Department and the CIA, which were after bigger and more reliable fish. Talabani was cold-shouldered in the USA.

The CIA then approached the IKF coalition with an offer to arm it so that it might fight against Iraqi government forces. This was considered at a meeting in Damascus in November, when its leaders decided that, in return, the IKF should be granted international recognition, such as the Palestinians had obtained, with observer status at the UN. President Bush was not prepared to go that far. That month the wandering Talabani visited several European and Arab capitals, saying that Iraqi Kurds would not join 'any foreign forces' to fight against the Iraqi government. In short, Kurdish groups in northern Iraq remained nominally passive during the Kuwait crisis and Gulf War.

THE GULF WAR

The Allied–Iraqi confrontation dragged on dramatically until 16 January 1991, when the Allied air offensive against Iraq began, followed by a ground offensive on 24 February. Hostilities formally ended in a cease-fire on 3 March, with the resounding defeat of Iraq. This Gulf War, as it became known, introduced new destabilising factors into the region.

12 Kurdish Safe Havens: 1991–92

At the time of the Gulf War over 200 000 Kurds were serving in the Iraqi armed forces, some in Kuwait. Once the Iraqis had been ejected from Kuwait a Kurdish desertion problem appeared and magnified instantly, with Kurdish soldiers rushing homewards whenever possible. The turmoil in Iraq, its defeat by the Allies, the Shia uprising in the south and the apparent helplessness of the Baghdad government, which was expected to fall at any moment, proved to be too big a temptation for the majority of Kurdish servicemen to resist.

Urged on, as they thought, by the Western Allies, the 'Kurdish uprising' began with small groups of Kurds taking over small towns in their areas and local administrative HQs, the rebels pushing aside government officials, police, local enlisted levies and Iraqi Arab troops. Overnight hordes of Kurds became Pesh Mergas, and within a few days whole areas fell to them. They were less successful in larger towns and cities, most of which had sizable military garrisons, and although the government lost control of whole sectors of some of them, such as Arbil, Kirkuk and Suliemaniyeh, government troops were able to hold out against the overnight Pesh Merga invasion.

The Kurdish uprising was a spontaneous outbreak of insurgency, which had not been ordered, nor desired, by Kurdish political leaders – it had in fact taken them by surprise. As they were unable to stem it, they made capital, joined in, and swam with the insurgent tide. Some Iraqi Kurdish leaders had a sort of love–hate relationship with the Baghdad government, merely demanding a form of autonomy and simply wanting a good working partnership with it.

The Jash, the around 30 000 strong government-employed paramilitary auxiliaries who guarded oil pipelines and facilities, defected almost to a man, while Kurds from villages in the mountains swarmed into the valleys and onto the plains, and then into cities and towns. Apart from the Jash and military elements of the KDP and PUK, which had a semblance of discipline and expertise, the waves of overnight Pesh Mergas were mobs of untrained, excited and slightly bewildered volunteers, lacking a leadership structure. Exiled Kurdish organisations issued propaganda communiqués claiming overwhelming success in the capture of major cities. These claims were wildly overoptimistic, but large parts of Kirkuk were in Pesh Merga hands by 12 March.

The PUK and the KDP joined in the propaganda battle, alleging that the Baghdad government was deploying troops, aircraft, tanks and guns against them, which was untrue at that moment; and also that 80 000 Iraqi soldiers had been captured, which might have had more foundation in fact. Later, exiled Kurdish organisations alleged that Iraq was again using chemical weapons against the Kurds. Masoud Barzani called upon the USA, Britain, France, Saudi Arabia and other countries to press for UN intervention, but initially there was faint response. The Allies too had been taken aback by the sudden Kurdish uprising, feebly complaining that Saddam Hussein was acting in breach of UN Resolution 687, which outlined the cease-fire conditions, but this was prompted more by his campaign against his southern Shias than against his Kurds, who according to their communiqués appeared to be doing quite well.

THE KURDISH EXODUS

By the third week of March 1991 Saddam Hussein had broken the back of his Shia uprising and was able to turn his attention to the Kurdish uprising in the north, sending troops, aircraft, assault helicopters, tanks and guns to crush it. He appointed General Kamel Hassan, who had been prominent in punitive operations against Kurdish dissidents during 1987–8, to be his defence minister, with a remit to repeat the lesson that had just been inflicted on the southern Shias

With all guns blazing, the General set about his task with great zeal, and by 18 March had regained possession of Kirkuk, while other smaller towns fell before him like dominoes. Suliemaniyeh took a few days more. By 1 April he had recaptured Arbil, Dohuk and Zakho. The speed of the government's victory was largely due to lack of Kurdish opposition. This was hardly believable, as Kurds had the traditional reputation of being fierce mountain warriors who had at times (but not always) acquitted themselves well in the 14-year long revolt (1961–75), and in previous uprisings against central authority. Indeed Hassan had anticipated stubborn resistance.

Masoud Barzani of the KDP said that he had 'inspected four lines of defences between Kirkuk and Suliemaniyeh'; but when the Iraqi army 'put in its attacks the Pesh Merga abandoned them without firing a bullet', and the whole Kurdish front collapsed (*Middle East*). Only a few veteran Pesh Merga briefly put up resistance at a few strategic points, one at Koreh (between Salahuddin and Shaklana) being specially mentioned. In this wholesale retreat, both Talabani and Barzani were left with only small groups of their own Pesh Mergas as bodyguards.

Barzani said 'If it were not for the respect I owe to the memory of my father (Mullah Mustafa Barzani, leader of the 14-year revolt) I would have thrown away my red turban'; the red turban being the traditional head-dress of the Barzani tribe (*Middle East*).

However the underlying reason for the collapse of the Kurdish uprising was the realisation that the West had no intention of intervening on its behalf, and so the heart suddenly went out of the resistance. The abrupt Kurdish withdrawal was also put down to the fact that the main body of overnight Pesh Merga volunteers lacked military structure, discipline and expertise, and sufficient modern arms, while the Jash became more interested in looting than fighting, and Kurdish military deserters from the Kuwaiti battlefield had already seen enough of war. All feared vindictive retribution in the form of chemical warfare, and in some areas whole families fled their homes.

Government successes were broadly confirmed by Masoud Barzani, who alleged that in the process over 50 000 Kurds had been killed, and 'around three million' had fled into the mountains, as part of a 'tactical withdrawal to escape the government's programme of genocide and torture against our people' (*The Times*).

Barzani's estimate of the number of refugees was exaggerated, but there was no doubt that a great multitude of Kurdish families had been set in motion, whole communities fleeing before Saddam's vengeance and barbarity. Later it was more accurately estimated that some 300 000 Kurds had initially fled into Turkey and a further 200 000 into Iran, and that during the exodus some 1500, including many women and children, had died through cold and hunger – winter still had a firm grip on the Kurdish mountains. Mass ethnic cleansing was in progress.

Revelling in the euphoria of their victory in the Gulf War and influenced by their desire to bring home their armed forces as soon as possible, for a while the Western Allies took little notice of this major Kurdish disaster, as indeed it appears they had barely noticed that of the southern Shias while it was in progress. All the Allies seemed disinclined to become involved in Iraqi internal affairs. Surprised and displeased that the Kurdish refugee problem should mar his victory and indicate that it had perhaps been incomplete, Present Bush avoided the issue. A White House spokesman later let it be known that the president had been advised by his Arab allies not to intervene to save the Kurds (*The Sunday Times*). Only slowly and reluctantly did the USA, Britain and France wake up to the plight of the Kurds and bestir themselves to do something about it.

Meanwhile Saddam Hussein, discouraging foreign intervention, insisted that all foreign aid should be channelled through the Iraqi Red Crescent. Eventually, under Allied pressure, he was persuaded to allow 50 foreign non-governmental aid organisations into Iraq, but they operated as individual units and were met by a blank wall of non-cooperation from Iraqi authorities at all levels. The already overburdened UNHCR hesitated to become involved, pointing out that it already had a huge disaster in Africa on its hands, where a probable 27 million people were starving. Disaster relief efforts were also handicapped to a degree by the Turkish and Iranian attitudes towards the Iraqi Kurdish problem.

SAFE HAVENS

The plight of the Iraqi Kurds was presented to the world by harrowing and emotive TV pictures of Kurdish women and children starving or freezing to death in the mountains, causing Western viewers to ask their embarrassed leaders what they were doing about this urgent problem. Except under strict and selective conditions, TV cameras were barred from southern

Iraq, where Saddam Hussein had quickly regained control, shutting off that region from international view. However, large stretches of Kurdish territory were still beyond the physical writ of the Baghdad government, into which venturesome foreign TV crews and journalists were able to penetrate and report the true situation. Television pictures resulted in an avalanche of 'Kurd Aid'.

The French were the first to respond positively, raising the issue at a UN Security Council meeting on 2 April. The UN was jogged into approving Resolution 688 (on the 5th), demanding that the Baghdad government halt its repression and allow relief workers access to Kurdish refugees. Germany's Foreign Minister, describing Iraq's actions as 'genocide', called for intervention; and on the 6th Austria called for the creation of a UN buffer zone to protect the Kurds. On the 7th President Ozal of Turkey repeated this idea, but insisted that the 'buffer zones' be inside Iraq (and not inside Turkey), in which Kurdish refugees could be mustered, temporarily housed and fed. On the 8th the EC approved a British suggestion for 'UN safe havens' in northern Iraq to protect the Kurds. This idea was pushed hard by John Major, the British Prime Minister, much to the annoyance of President Bush, who was initially against any form of intervention. This jostled him into activity as he did not want to be pushed aside by Western Europeans from his leading role in his undefined 'new world order'.

On 10 April Bush changed his policy of non-intervention in Iraq (which he had restated on the 5th), and issued an 'injunction' against Iraq to cease all military activity north of the 36th Parallel, a line just south of Mosul and Arbil (excluding the oil-producing area around Kirkuk), northwards to the Turkish border, demanding that Saddam keep his troops south of that parallel. Bush created a virtual 'security zone', which became an Iraqi 'no fly zone' when it was monitored by Allied combat aircraft. However the expression 'safe haven' came into common currency, another slight annoyance to Bush. The British labelled the project 'Operation Provide Comfort', while the Americans insisted on referring to it as 'Operation Poised Hammer'. Bush denied there was any rift between the USA and its West European allies. Perhaps there was no actual rift, but there was certainly rivalry and one-upmanship.

Already on the 7th the Allies had begun dropping food, blankets and even tents by parachute onto makeshift refugee camps along the Turkish border, manned by the Turkish army, notably at Cukurca and Isikeren. The Turkish military contribution was to establish an HQ with 1000 infantrymen at Silop, some 30 miles inside Turkey. On the 14th the Turkish authorities announced that owing to adverse conditions they would be moving some 200 000 Kurdish refugees to prepared camps near Silop. Although the government, and especially the Turkish military, was reluctant to allow Iraqi Kurds of any sort into the country, it was under the glare of the international TV spotlight and wanted to be seen as a good European, and a very obliging and humane one too.

On the 16th Bush authorised American troops, under an American general (General Shalikashveli), to organise encampments in northern Iraq for some 300 000 Kurds, this to ensure their safety and coordinate relief supplies and the Allied monitoring aerial cover. The following day Allied troops moved into northern Iraq. This Allied military presence gave a sense of security to Kurdish families, some of whom were still sheltering on mountainsides, and thousands of them were persuaded to return to their homes. The irony was that American troops were quitting southern Iraq (the last leaving by 8 May), and Bush was authorising them to march into northern Iraq. He covered himself by asserting that this was just a temporary humanitarian measure, and gave the date of their withdrawal as 15 June.

During the third week of April about 800 Iraqi military personnel moved in on the northern city of Zakho, where a safe haven was being established, but in the face of the threatened use of military force against them by the Americans, British and French, they withdrew; all that is except '50 policemen'. By the 25th there were over 7000 American and 900 British troops in northern Iraq organising relief camps for refugees. Kurd Aid was in full progress, but so far the UN had stood aside.

SADDAM HUSSEIN'S AMNESTY

At an RCC meeting on 4th April Saddam Hussein had concluded that 'Iraq has totally crushed all the acts of sedition and sabotage in all the cities of Iraq' (*Middle East*), and granted an amnesty to all Kurds involved in the uprising, except those accused of murder, rape and acts of treason. The following day Masoud Barzani rejected the amnesty offer, mainly because it coincided with reports that thousands of Kurds living in and around Baghdad were being rounded up and detained. Kurdish leaders were now accused of having treasonable contacts with foreign countries. When visiting Arbil on the 18th, Saddam repeated his amnesty offer to the Kurds, which was officially extended by the RCC. Occasional reports still surfaced of clashes in and around Baghdad between Kurdish insurgents and the security forces.

KURDISH NEGOTIATIONS

At secret talks between the Iraqi government and Kurdish leaders, lasting several days, it was agreed that the unofficial cease-fire would continue while political issues were discussed. On 23 April Barzani had said that his KDP wanted a 'protection zone', administered by the USA, Britain and France, as part of any peace agreement. The following day Jalal Talabani of the PUK announced that Saddam Hussein had agreed in principle to grant a measure of autonomy under the 1970 agreement. Talabani appealed to Kurds to return to their homes, saying, 'We want to stay in Iraqi Kurdistan, not leave it' (*Middle East*).

This was confirmed by the Iraqi Prime Minister, Sadoun Hammadi, who said that the four main Kurdish political groups (in the IKF), had come to an arrangement amongst themselves during secret talks. But on the 27th this was contradicted by Talabani, who said that some aspects of autonomy had still to be resolved. As usual the Kurds were in disagreement with one another. The two other Kurdish groups mentioned were the KDPD, led by Sami Abdul Rahman, and the KSP, led by Rasoul Marmand – it seems that the ICP had been dropped from the IKF.

Negotiations continued spasmodically until 15 May, when Talabani commented that democracy remained the main obstacle to an accord. Three days later Barzani claimed that the Baghdad government had accepted Kurdish demands, including the separation of the ruling Baathist Party from the state, freedom of the press and free elections.

Talks faltered over the issue of Western assistance to the

Kurds, and a point emphasised by Talabani was that any agreement made with the Baghdad government would have to be underwritten by the Western Allies. An Iraqi offer of 16 June was that Kurdish leaders suspend their links with the West and side with the ruling Baathist Party against Shia insurgents and other 'artificial organisations', meaning exiled anti-Saddam groups, in return for a joint Iraqi–Kurdish administration over Kirkuk, and exclusive Kurdish control over Arbil, Dohuk and Suliemaniyeh. This caused Kurdish disagreement, as Masoud Barzani seemed ready to sever Western links while Talabani was not.

In northern Iraq there was friction between Allied personnel and government troops. For example, on 9 May it was reported (*Guardian*) that Iraqi troops had fired on American aircraft near Mosul; while near Dohuk on the 13th, in a series of mini-clashes near Sarsank, British troops had killed an Iraqi soldier. In its first timid venture the UN agreed to send a ten-man observer team to Dohuk to monitor the safety of refugees. On the 22nd the Allied forces concluded an agreement with the Baghdad government to withdraw all troops from Dohuk to allow the restoration of essential services to that area.

THE WITHDRAWAL OF ALLIED FORCES

On 21 June the three Western Allies involved had a change of policy, and halted the withdrawal of their troops from northern Iraq, asserting they would remain until the Kurdish population received assurances of their safety. The USA was trying to form a rapid deployment force, to be based in southern Turkey, to ensure continued protection for Iraqi Kurds.

Figures released on 1 June indicated that about 13 000 Kurds had perished before reaching the safe havens, and that up to 7000 additional refugees, mainly women and children, had died in mountain refugee camps along the Turkish border. After closing their refugee camp in Cukurca on 3 June, the Turkish authorities issued some figures, reporting that 25 000 Kurdish refugees were refusing to leave the Turkish camp at Silop, and that a further 12 000 were still being accommodated in other camps in Turkey.

The tension between Bush and Saddam subsided somewhat and troop withdrawal recommenced, to be completed by 15 July, even though there were increasingly numerous clashes between Kurdish Pesh Mergas and government forces across northern Iraq. The commander of the US forces in northern Iraq denied that the Allies were abandoning the Kurds to their fate, but admitted that 'Operation Poised Hammer is on the verge of being finalised'.

After the Allied troops had been withdrawn, a multinational rapid deployment force (RDF) was formed in July to deter Iraqi troops from advancing into the Kurdish 'no fly zone', positioned in southern Turkey. A nominal 4600 troops were based at Silop, mostly Turkish. As it was not called upon it was stood down in September, but its air element remained in being as a 48-warplane deterrent force, based at Incirlik and Pirincilik and backed by aircraft on a US aircraft carrier in the Eastern Mediterranean. On 21 September the Turkish government announced that the use of the two air bases would be extended for another three months, but this was only to apply to air force personnel and their equipment.

While the Turkish government strove to please its West European allies, it also sought desperately not to offend its Middle East neighbours any more than was absolutely necessary, especially Iraq, with which it had had lucrative trade agreements prior to the Gulf crisis, and which it wanted to resume as soon as possible. Turkey was a reluctant ally in the Bush–Saddam Hussein confrontation. Ozal's eyes were on Brussels as well as Washington.

KURDISH FRICTION WITH BAGHDAD

Friction increased between government forces and Pesh Mergas wherever they came into contact and there were several armed clashes. For example, in July 1991 there was fighting in the Suliemaniyeh area, which resulted in another fairly large Kurdish migration farther into the mountains and 'safe havens', and again in September, when after a series of clashes in the Kirkuk region about '55 000 Kurds' fled northwards (UN estimates). Officially, UN representatives complained that Kurdish leaders were persuading their people to remain in the mountains, partly to pressure the UNHCR into continuing to provide food and aid, but additionally, if possible, to provoke international intervention on their behalf. Kurdish refugees did not take much persuading as they all feared Saddam Hussein's retribution.

In August both Talabani and Barzani met Ozal. All gained an international photo-opportunity to boost their causes, and Ozal took the opportunity to demonstrate sympathy and concern for the Kurdish refugees in his care. He was careful to emphasise that he would not be in favour of a Kurdish entity in Iraq. Both Talabani and Barzani still maintained offices in Ankara (*Kurdish Life*). Ozal's critics contrasted his seeming solicitude for Iraqi Kurds with that for his own Kurds. When both Iraqi Kurdish leaders said they intended to fight against the Baghdad government, the USA smiled on them and the CIA arranged a trip to Washington for them to see the US Secretary of State, James Baker, who made them vague promises of support as long as they adhered to this policy.

Iraqi Pesh Mergas pursued the armed struggle against government armed forces, and incidents between them became more frequent and deadly. A major one occurred on 7 October, when it was alleged that Kurds 'shot dead 60 unarmed soldiers' near Suliemaniyeh (*Middle East*), and although a ceasefire was announced the following day, on the 9th government guns shelled that city and the Kurdish towns of Kifri, Kalar and Maysan.

KURDISH AUTONOMY TALKS

Negotiations between the two major Iraqi Kurdish leaders, Talabani and Barzani, and the Baghdad government had continued fitfully through July and August, the two disagreeing over what was acceptable and what was attainable. Talabani now demanded an autonomous area comprising about '80 per cent of the historical Kurdish region' (*Middle East*) (being about twice the size of the area held by Pesh Mergas), and Kurdish control over their own security services. Rather than risk the total collapse of the negotiations, which could only lead to an intensification of guerrilla war, Barzani thought it might be better to accept the original Iraqi offer, despite uncertainty over the status of Kirkuk, as he did not think Baghdad would make any more concessions. Talabani embarked on another round of visits to Western European capitals in order to drum up support, but found that interest in the Kurdish cause was waning: international TV cameras were pointing elsewhere.

Several Kurdish personalities were anxious that an autonomy agreement be signed as they anticipated becoming 'ministers' in an autonomous framework, and thus publicly acknowledged as leaders of their own factions; their secret fear being that they would lose their leadership status. A draft agreement was reached on 20 August, which included provisions for the resettlement of Kurds and the creation of a Kurdish executive and legislative council for the proposed Kurdish Autonomous Region (KAR). Just previously (on the 14th) the Iraqi government had demanded the withdrawal of all Turkish armed forces from northern Iraq, an ultimatum made more threatening, especially to Pesh Mergas, by reports of Iraqi troops concentrating around Kirkuk. Talks were suspended on the 30th. Disagreement between the Western-orientated Talabani and the more tribally orientated Barzani increased, until on 29 October Barzani challenged Talabani to an electoral test to see whether there should be a more favourable autonomy settlement, or whether the Kurds should again revert to armed struggle.

AN ECONOMIC BLOCKADE

When negotiations over Kurdish autonomy stalled, the Baghdad government imposed an economic embargo against Kurdish territory, withdrawing administrative staff and government employees from schools, hospitals and offices in the Kurdish region. Those who remained receive of no salaries or wages, nor were pensions or allowances paid. The Iraqi army established a fortified containing line across northern Iraq along the 36th Parallel. Soon shortages of food and fuel became acute.

After futile meetings between Kurdish leaders and government ministers, on 12 November the Kurds announced they were withdrawing all Pesh Mergas from south of Arbil in exchange for the lifting of what had become a three-week economic blockade, which was hitting Kurdish families hard. Fearing that the Pesh Merga evacuation of villages south of Arbil heralded an Iraqi military offensive on that city, on the 17th some 200 000 Kurds (UN figures) fled northwards in anticipation of imminent attack. The Baghdad-imposed economic blockade continued.

Masoud Barzani met Saddam Hussein in Baghdad, and although this resulted in some amelioration of the blockade, he set a deadline of 23 December for the total lifting of the embargo. Failure to do so would mean Kurdish reversion to military action. Kurdish leaders agreed to appoint an inquiry into the alleged massacre of 60 Iraqi soldiers (in October). In return the government exempted Kurds from swearing allegiance to the Baathist Party.

WINTER 1991–2

As winter began in northern Iraqi Kurdistan, and snow fell in the mountain areas and on the 'safe havens', the Baghdad economic blockade began to bite deep. The UN Military Co-ordinating Council estimated that 'at least 800 000 Kurds were at risk' of starvation and hypothermia. The UNHCR wanted to pull out, as the task ahead seemed so great and resources so meagre. Limited economic help was arriving across the border from Iran, but Barzani was embittered by the small trickle, complaining about the parsimonious attitude of the Tehran government, which during '16 years residence' he had served so well, especially during the Iran–Iraq War.

Barzani wanted to accept the autonomy offered by the Baghdad government, even though it was a poor offer that excluded Kirkuk, Sinjar and Khaniqin. He reasoned that if the Allies relaxed, lost interest or had their attention diverted elsewhere, Saddam Hussein's troops could enter Kurdish terrain and advance to the Turkish frontier within 48 hours. Talabani did not agree with him: they differed on several major issues.

A spokesman for the UN Inter-Agency Humanitarian Programme for Iraq and Kuwait stated, in Geneva on 7 January 1992, that a minimum of $145.3 million would be needed to protect and assist the Kurds over the ensuing six months. In

February the UNHCR reported that Iraqi Kurdistan was on the point of collapse, with 'hundreds of thousands' of people facing starvation owing to the Iraqi economic blockade, compounded by heavy snow blocking roads linking it to Iran and a Turkish truck drivers' strike. The UNHCR was proposing to withdraw its representatives in April 1992, while other UN personnel and the UN military observers were due to leave in June.

The Turkish truck drivers' strike had resulted from pressure by the Turkish authorities to refuse to pay the tolls levied by Kurdish Pesh Mergas on oil brought into Turkey from Iraq through Kurdistan. Each of the two major, and some minor, Kurdish groups, 'had a piece' of the Iraqi embargo line, and imposed tolls on all traffic they allowed to cross from Iraq. These levies were the only income they had and were used to buy food and other essential items, and to enable them to administer their own local fiefdoms. The Turkish government had no wish to succour Iraqi Kurds in this manner, but as it badly needed oil from Iraq it eventually had to compromise.

THE KURDISH DEMOCRATIC FRONT

Masoud Barzani, as chairman of the Kurdish Democratic Front (KDF), an eight-party coalition of Kurdish groups that had come together in opposition to Saddam Hussein, and as the son of the famous Kurdish guerrilla leader, had immense influence, especially amongst the tribes, but he had to carry the more sophisticated PUK along with him in major decisions. On 11 January 1992 Barzani announced that the autonomy talks, which had been stalemated for some time, would be suspended.

In early February, turning away from Baghdad, Barzani secured an agreement with the Turkish and British governments that Allied aircraft would continue to provide Kurds with protection against attack by Iraqi forces. In March, as Chairman of the KDF, Barzani had talks with British, French and German leaders, who assured him of continuing Western support for Kurdish autonomy. On the 12th the EC condemned the 'siege imposed on the Kurds' by Saddam Hussein. By this time Iran, having changed its policy, was supplying larger amounts of food and fuel to the Iraqi Kurds in order to undermine Saddam's embargo.

IRAQ TESTS THE ALLIES

In early March there was renewed fighting in northern Iraq, and by the end of the month it had become obvious that Saddam was concentrating troops just south of his embargo line, preparatory to launching an operation across it. On 5 April, responding to an attack by Iranian combat aircraft against dissident Iranian Kurds inside Iraq, Baghdad resumed air patrols along the embargo line, and for the first time since the Gulf War Iraqi planes penetrated north of the 36th Parallel into the 'no fly zone', which had come into effect in August to protect the Kurds.

During early April, Iraqi troops facing Iraqi Kurdistan were strengthened, and surface-to-air missiles and radar tracking equipment were deployed. Saddam was testing the Allied reaction to the skirmishing between his forces and the Kurds. However on 14 April a strong warning was issued by the USA, Britain and France, which caused Saddam to back down. His troops and equipment were withdrawn southwards, and his planes ceased to fly north of the 36th Parallel.

KURDISH ELECTIONS

As differences of opinion arose within the eight-party KDF, especially between the KDP and the PUK, its leaderships agreed to hold a general election in Kurdish-controlled territory for a completely new 'Kurdistan National Assembly', and for a national president. It was also designed to end the decision stalemate caused by each of the eight parties having an individual veto. In particular, Talabani – who was now advocating a form of federalism, which he thought would give a semblance of nationhood, instead of simple autonomy – was at personal odds with Barzani, whom he accused of wanting to accept a very much reduced autonomous area.

The existing Kurdish executive and legislative councils in the Kurdish Autonomous Region, created under the legislation of

1974, had not been operating since the Gulf War. Dates were set for the general election but there were postponements, some frivolous, one being because a consignment of indelible ink to stamp on individuals' hands when they voted (to prevent multiple voting) had been found not to be indelible. The election was finally held on 19 May 1992, the poll being organised by an electoral commission headed by a Kurdish judge (Amir Hawsizei) and supervised by international monitors. Saddam Hussein declared the election illegal, but under Allied threats had been powerless to prevent it from taking place.

Five places in the 105-seat assembly were reserved for Assyrian and Christian minority parties, otherwise only the KDP and the PUK won sufficient votes to obtain seats. The KDP obtained 45.4 per cent of the votes cast (437 833), gaining 51 seats, and the PUK obtained 43.9 per cent (423 833), gaining 49 seats. It was agreed between the two leaders that each would have 50 seats, as a one-vote majority could easily cause deep rifts as well as stultifying policy and administration. The voting turnout was good, and it was estimated that some 30 000 people had still to cast their votes when polling stations closed at midnight. There were some allegations of irregularities, but the international monitors said they were not widespread enough to have affected the result.

The four other political parties taking part in the election, but which obtained insufficient votes (7 per cent) to obtain a single seat, were: the KSP, led by Mahmoud Osman; the Kurdish Islamic Party, led by Othman Abd al-Aziz; the KPDP, led by Sami Abdul Rahman; and the Iraqi Communist Party, led by Rajim Ajina.

In the presidency contest Barzani obtained 44.6 per cent of the votes and Talabani 44.3 per cent, so it was decided that a second election for this office should take place. The president of the assembly would be the 'commander-in-chief' of the unified armed forces and would lead any negotiations with the Baghdad government, but would not have power of veto over legislation.

The USA gave a cautious welcome to the Iraqi Kurds' election success, noting public and private assurances that the leadership would only deal with administrative issues and would not move towards separatism. The governments of Turkey, Iran and Syria were less enthusiastic, fearing its effect on their own restless Kurdish minorities. Turkey protested that the KDF had gone beyond the 1974 legislation, and warned that 'Iraq's territorial integrity must be preserved'. However the Turkish government did approve – but not without internal opposition – a six-month extension of facilities at the Incirlik and Pirincilik air bases for American, British and French aircraft to continue their 'protective' monitoring flights over northern Iraq.

Later (7 September) the KSP, the KPDP and the Kurdish Democratic Independence Party, due to their lack of success at the polls, merged to form the 'Kurdistan Unity Party' (KUP), with the aim of establishing an independent Kurdish state.

THE KURDISH NATIONAL ASSEMBLY

The new Kurdish National Assembly (KNA) held its inaugural meeting in Arbil on 4 June 1992, when Hassan Kanabi (PUK) was elected chairman and Jawhar Namiq Salim (KDP) became speaker, while Fuad Maasum (PUK) was asked to form the first government. The executive council was renamed the 'ministerial council', policy committees were established, and a delegation formed to visit European capitals to obtain support. The KNA met again on 4 July, when Fuad Maasum presented his cabinet, saying his first priority was to restore law and order.

July was a troubled month for the Kurds, one in which there was increased friction between Pesh Mergas and government forces, and numerous explosions (allegedly instigated by the Baghdad Mukhabarat), especially against UN aid workers, and their vehicles in an attempt to drive all 'foreigners' from the blockaded Kurdish-governed region. The UN–Iraq Memorandum of Understanding, under which some 600 UNHCR personnel, protected by 500 locally enlisted guards, operated in the Kurdish region, had expired at the end of June.

The KNA was in dire economic straits owing to the increasingly tight Iraqi embargo – Iraqi troops at checkpoints were searching all Turkish trucks going into Kurdistan and removing any food or medicines. It was said that over 150 000 Iraqi troops were manning the embargo line, including three Republican Guard divisions (*Middle East*). Talabani, who had taken over negotiations with Iran from Barzani, secured an agreement with the Tehran government to allow the free movement of oil, machine parts and other items into the KNA area, but in return Tehran demanded that the KNA prevent any dissident Iranian Kurdish groups within Iraq from operating against Iran from Iraqi Kurdish territory. This was a complicated demand, imperfectly carried out.

Explosions continued. A mysterious one on 4 July near a police HQ at Kirkuk (outside the KNA area) reputedly caused over 400 casualties. On the 6th Danielle Mitterrand, on a fact-finding tour, escaped with only minor injuries from a car-bomb explosion near Suliemaniyeh, in which four people were killed, and the following day a gunman shot and killed a UN guard in a remote part of Kurdistan.

The KNA was desperately striving to turn a multi-group guerrilla movement into an autonomous administration. A main problem was that although the various groups still collected tolls from trucks entering their local territory, they were reluctant to hand the money over to the central administration, which needed it to pay its employees and establish a unified army, police force and frontier service. Another problem was persuading the various Kurdish groups to dissolve and disarm their militias, which they were loath to do.

The KNA proposed the formation of a 60 000-strong 'unified army' and a 40 000-strong police force, as a minimum, a suggestion being that arms would be bought from Pesh Mergas. It was claimed that the KDP had about 150 000 Pesh Mergas and the PUK about 90 000, although it was not possible to substantiate these probably over inflated figures. Both the KDP and the PUK refused to cooperate, retaining all the dues they collected, while their respective Pesh Mergas remained armed and mobilised. On 16 September the KDP and the PUK jointly announced they had placed their militiamen under a single command, but in practice this meant little. Despite previous promises by Western nations to help establish an administration, the Kurds complained that now they had achieved one, no help was forthcoming.

A confidential UN report leaked to a British newspaper (the *Guardian*) warned that unless Saddam Hussein lifted his economic blockade on the Kurds, especially in relation to fuel supplies, and resumed cooperation with international agencies, the Kurds faced another 'unbearable winter'.

A FEDERAL SUGGESTION

The KNA approved a motion on 4 October calling for the creation of a 'Federal state within a democratic pluralist Iraq'. This marked a departure from the usual autonomy theme and was condemned by Turkey, which feared it could represent a first step towards separatism and would encourage its own PKK movement. This surprise KNA decision caused the foreign ministers of Turkey, Iran and Syria to meet in Ankara, where they made their hostile views quite clear.

THE OPPOSITION INC

After holding its Vienna conference in June 1992, the opposition Iraqi National Congress (INC) organised another one in September in Salahuddin, near Arbil in KAR territory – the first to be held on Iraqi soil. This had been prompted by the SCIRI, which was concerned by the high profile the INC was gaining at its expense in Western countries. Over 70 delegates from 33 opposition organisations attended, including representatives from Iran, Saudi Arabia and Syria, who had absented themselves from the Vienna conference. Delegates agreed to form a 'Federal Iraqi government', which was to have a 'three-man presidency' (consisting of a a Kurd, a Shia and a Sunni), an executive committee and a 174-member assembly. SCIRI expressed discontent with its one-third share in this proposed government.

THE TURKISH FACTOR

So far Turkey had gone along with the wishes of the Allies regarding Iraqi Kurds, often against internal opposition, but President Ozal was determined to make what capital he could of the situation. In August 1992 he invited both Talabani and Barzani to Ankara to discuss extending the Allied protective 'no fly zone' down to the 34th Parallel, which would encompass the Kirkuk oilfields. This alarmed the Arab allies, who suspected that Turkey was simply trying to regain direct influence over that area. Ozal had frequently commented since the Kuwait crisis began that the Turkish border with Iraq was not satisfactory. Ozal was also suspected of having designs on Mosul, a project that was thought to be supported by the shadowy 'Mosul Vilayet Council', a political group whose aim was to 'liberate' northern Iraq from Baghdad rule and unite it with Turkey.

On the other hand Prime Minister Demirel wanted a rapid normalisation of relations with Iraq, and to resume trade with that country as soon as possible. In particular he wanted the trans-Turkey oil pipeline from Iraq to be reopened, it being estimated that Turkey had lost over $600 million in oil revenues during the Gulf War. Resumption of normal trading relations with Iraq would mean that the Allies would lose the use of the Incirlik air base, which was essential to monitoring patrols over the Iraqi 'no fly zone'. It would also probably deprive the UN of its northern route into Iraq. Both Ozal and Demirel were disappointed by the lack of tangible rewards from the Allies for siding with them in the Gulf War, and also disgusted by their lack of support for Bosnian Muslims in the Balkan conflict.

However both Turkish leaders were deeply concerned about their own unresolved Kurdish problem, and the fact that ARGK guerrillas were still being harboured in northern Iraq, from where they launched raids into Turkey. Iran, with its lesser but still unresolved Kurdish problem, was similarly concerned about ARGK sanctuaries and border raids. In September Iran agreed to cooperate more fully with Turkey to eliminate the ARGK, and other Kurdish insurgents, from their mutual border areas. It was estimated that over 10 000 ARGK guerrillas were encamped in the Hakurk mountain border region of Iraq. This was deeply resented by all hostile Iraqi Kurds, as was the fact that Turkish combat aircraft carried out routine cross-border strikes against them (*Middle East*). Armed clashes frequently occurred between Turkish and Iraqi Kurdish guerrillas, especially over tolls on trans-frontier commercial traffic.

On 4 October the KDP and the PUK issued an ultimatum to the PKK to quit Iraqi territory by the following day, in the hope it would pull its Pesh Mergas out quietly. This deadline was extended several times as the PKK showed no signs of complying with it. Fighting between the PUK and the ARGK began. In retaliation the ARGK enforced a blockade along the stretches of the Iran–Iraq–Turkey border that it controlled, which prevented 'hundreds of trucks a day' from crossing from Turkey into Iraq with supplies (*Middle East*). The PUK–ARGK fighting was inconclusive, but eventually on the 27th a PUK spokesman claimed that the PKK had agreed to stop launching raids into Turkey from bases inside Iraq.

TURKISH INTERVENTION

Meanwhile the Turkish government – which had mounted a series of counter-ARGK operations in its south-eastern provinces during the summer and autumn of 1992 – lost patience, and on 16 October began a 'limited' air and ground offensive, involving about 5000 troops, into Iraq to root out ARGK camps north of Zakho and Dohuk. This caused the ARGK guerrillas to concentrate mainly in the Hakurk valley. Determined to eliminate these ARGK base sanctuaries if possible, Turkey expanded its operation, which soon came to involve over 20 000 Turkish troops, supported by aircraft and tanks.

This Turkish force advanced down the international highway through Zakho on two axes – one through the Haftan region (north-east of Zakho), and the other into the Hakurk valley. The object was to trap ARGK guerrillas in a pincer grip between Turkish troops and hostile PUK Pesh Mergas. Throughout November, Turkish forces pushed slowly forward, occupying about 100 square miles of Iraqi terrain and causing ARGK guerrillas to scatter and withdraw deeper into trackless mountains. The main body of the Turkish force withdrew in early December, claiming to have killed at least '2000 PKK insurgents'; but leaving a contingent behind. When interviewed later, the Turkish Chief of Staff, General Dogan Gures, said he would not rule out the establishment of a 'Turkish security zone' in the Iraqi mountains (*Middle East*).

The KNA protested to both the USA and Britain that Turkish tanks were over-running their 'safe havens', but both countries remained silent: Turkey was still a vital ally, and in the USA a presidential election campaign was in full swing. Both Iran and Syria protested to the Ankara government about this military incursion, anxious to forestall what could develop into a Turkish 'protectorate' over northern Iraq, but received the bland answer that its internal PKK insurgency must be crushed at all costs. Ozal mentioned the Allies' reliance on the 'right of intervention' in the Gulf War, although its legality was far from precise, and doubt existed as to whether it would extend to Turkey. Both the Iranian and the Syrian government were anxious that the PKK insurgency should not spread into their own countries, and so they too remained silent. An aura of inertia and uncertainty hovered over the whole Kurdish region, as all waited to see whether President Bush would be re-elected or not.

EMBARGO DIFFICULTIES

In Arbil, the KNA struggled hard to survive and become an effective administration, but it was severely handicapped by the Iraqi economic embargo. During November and December spates of explosions and fire-bombing occurred on UN aid trucks moving into KNA-controlled territory, which caused the UN to halt its operations on more than one occasion. The suspected culprit remained the Iraqi Mukhabarat. However, despite the difficulties the UN continued to supply emergency aid to the Kurds. Allied pressure forced Saddam Hussein to allow the UN to recruit more local guards for its convoys, although problems still arose over individual permits. Trucks continued to be searched thoroughly at checkpoints. The acute shortage of fuel in Kurdistan soon caused valleys and hillsides to be stripped bare of trees.

The KNA approved a resolution that the Allies should extend their 'no fly zone' southwards down to the 33rd Parallel to embrace both Kirkuk and Suliemaniyeh – an extra area containing over half a million Kurds and still under Baghdad control – so that Kurdish refugees could return from the safe havens to their original homes. On 24 December 1992 the Turkish Grand National Assembly approved, but not without opposition, an extension of the Allies' request to continue using the Incirlik and Pirincilik air bases to enable aircraft monitoring the 'no fly zone' to ensure that the Kurds in it were fairly safe from Saddam's Hussein's vengeance for another six months.

13 The Turkish Problem

The Gulf War and its immediate aftermath, the Kurdish exodus from Iraq, certainly brought the Kurdish struggle to prominent international attention, something that had never really happened previously as this issue had had a low priority on the international crisis list, that is if it ever had one at all. Various Kurdish insurrections since the First World War had merited little more than 'footnote' status in international councils. The world was vaguely aware that there was some sort of Kurdish insurrection in Turkey, but interest in this respect tended to centre on human rights issues, which were constantly fed to news desks by Amnesty International and similar monitoring bodies.

Most Western governments had little time for Turkey, which was privately regarded as a non-European, debtor country, and not quite an equal in the society of developed Western democratic nations. The Turkish invasion of Cyprus in 1974 still rankled and the issue was kept alive by Greece. During the Cold War Turkey had been an unwelcome but necessary partner in NATO, but since the collapse of communism in Russia its usefulness had been limited. Western governments remained polite and correct, as it had once again proved useful in the Gulf War. Correct international relations were maintained, but Turkey's full and open acceptance as a brother European state was another matter. For some time the Kurdish insurrection in Turkey was tacitly ignored in Western circles, while Kurdish protest groups and demonstrations were tolerated. Amnesty International drew attention to atrocities committed in Turkey, and its heavy-handed security measures invoked Western disapproval, as did the Ankara government's refusal to recognise its Kurdish problem.

During the period 1991–3 the PKK further extended its dominance over other Kurdish insurrectionary groups in Turkey, becoming virtually the mainspring and mainstay of the Kurdish insurgency. It moved part of the main body of its ARGK guerrilla army into that country, increased its attacks on military targets and Korucu village guards, indulged in urban

206

terrorism, imposed itself on the Kurdish rural community and kidnapped foreigners to gain Western media recognition.

As it gathered strength the ARGK took over the insurgency in most parts of the south-eastern provinces, roughly jostling aside the armed militias of other resistance groups. As it became militarily dominant other competing militias stood back, became inactive, fragmented or were dissolved, leaving much of the field clear for the ARGK.

The thoughts and words of Abdullah Ocalan, the leader-founder, had been unquestioningly accepted by devoted PKK members and his organisation seemed to be free of dissenting factions, with their tendency to break away and form splinter parties, as had so often been the curse of some struggling resistance groups. At times his views had been openly contradicted, but nothing of this nature could be substantiated. 'Apo' had the reputation of being a strict and hard disciplinarian.

It was something of a surprise when the first hint that all might not be well in the ranks of the PKK was given by Ocelan himself, at a press conference in March 1991, when he admitted that he was facing a challenge from a faction within the PKK that wanted him to lower his sights and work for autonomy within Turkey. Ocalan had been periodically meeting and talking with Jalal Talabani of the PUK and Masoud Barzani of the KDP, both established and experienced Iraqi Kurdish resistance leaders, who had been trying to persuade him that his dream of a Pan-Kurdish independent republic – encompassing Kurdish terrain in Turkey, Iran, Iraq, Syria and also perhaps the former USSR – was unrealistic and unattainable.

They pointed out that the Kurds in both Iran and Iraq had accepted the principle of autonomy, that none of these nations would willingly relinquish any part of their terrain for such an altruistic ideal, nor would they support any Kurdish group seeking such a solution. None of these countries, which were more or less contiguous, really liked each other, but none was prepared to go to war with another for a Kurdish ideal. Majorities in their populations were mainly of Turkish or Arab stock, both of which looked down on the Kurds. None of these governments were prepared to do the Kurds any favours, although each was still prepared to manipulate them to their own individual national advantage.

Talabani said he had urged 'Apo' to cease the armed struggle, and offered to mediate between the PKK and the Turkish governments, but Ocalan remained stubborn. Talabani seemed to have a foot in several different camps, but then so did Barzani, whose KDP had long received support – since the days of his father, Mullah Mustafa Barzani, the renowned Kurdish leader – in the form of cash and ammunition in small amounts at a time from the Turkish government. The Syrian-dominated Lebanese Bekaa Valley was a convenient meeting place for Kurdish resistance leaders, and indeed of many other terrorist leaders too. The USA refused to delete the name of Syria from its list of countries supporting terrorism, despite that country entering the Allied coalition during the Gulf War.

The PKK had been receiving covert support from the Baghdad government for some time, but a comparatively new patron was the fundamentalist government in Iran, which was in ideological competition with Turkey and delighted in trying to destabilise it. Some evidence of this came to light in October 1991, when the *Cape Maleas*, a cargo ship flying the Greek-Cypriot flag, arrived from Varna in Bulgaria to anchor in the Bosphorus. When searched by police it was found to be carrying mortars and grenade launchers, which were not mentioned in the ship's manifest and were suspected of being destined for the PKK. Both arms and ship were impounded.

The Iranian government spoke up, claiming the arms were for the Iranian army, and the case dragged on through the Turkish courts. This hiccup did not prevent a Turkey–Iran cross-border security agreement being signed on 31 October; any contradiction of principles simply being shrugged off. Such agreements were not taken too seriously as there were so many hidden agendas and so much double-dealing. The only people they fooled were naïve Western statesmen, who thought they had been made in good faith and expected them to be honoured and implemented in full.

TURKISH GOVERNMENT POLICY

In the general election in Turkey in October 1991, no political party gained an overall majority, so eventually another coalition government was formed, headed by Sulieman Demirel, leader of the True Path Party (DYP), with 178 seats out of 450, and the SHP, with 88 seats.

Within Turkey there was growing awareness, and concern over the Kurdish insurrection and the way it was being handled. Already a number of Kurds had gained seats in the Grand National Assembly, but as Turks, not as Kurds, and they had strictly to toe the nationalist line by not mentioning the Kurdish cause. If they overstepped this mark they were reprimanded. In the Grand National Assembly a Kurd was still a non-person, and this was not to be forgotten. Hikmet Cetin, a Kurd, was appointed Foreign Minister, but as a Turk, not as a Kurd.

The Kurds struggled to gain constitutional recognition on a party political basis, but faced heavy odds. A loophole in the constitution had allowed the formation of the (Kurdish) People's Labour Party (HEP, Halkin Emek Partis) to champion Kurdish rights, but it was not able to get its act together in time for the October 1991 general election so it temporarily aligned itself with the Social Democratic Popularists (SHP), which allowed 22 of its 88 seats to be nominally held by HEP deputies. When the Grand National Assembly reopened, some HEP Kurdish Deputies (in an SHP guise) objected to the wording 'indivisibility of the great Turkish nation' in the oath of allegiance.

In late February 1992 a document, published by 49 SHP deputies, some but not all of whom were Kurds, was circulated calling for a cease-fire in the Kurdish region, for the lifting of the state of emergency, and for bringing those responsible for torture and killings to justice. Demirel's initial policy programme had been to extend a timid hand of friendship to the Kurds, by declaring his wish to recognise Kurdish cultural rights and provide extra investment for the underdeveloped southeastern provinces, but at the same time he insisted that strong measures should continued to be taken against the PKK. He also said that allegations of human rights abuses would be investigated. By March 1992 Demirel was admitting that he had been unable to implement any of these promises, and on the 30th of that month most of the HEP deputies, sitting in the guise of SHP ones, resigned.

A new Kurdish political party – 'OZDEP' (Freedom and Democracy Party) – was formed on 25 June 1992 by some 25 deputies, led by Mahmut Alinak, who had resigned from the

SHP and hoped to attract former HEP deputies. On 3 July more restrictions were removed from certain political parties, which had been proscribed. In September 21 deputies resigned from the SHP to form the 'Integration Party', which merged with the Republicans' People's Party (CHP). This loss of SHP deputies reduced the Demirel coalition's majority in the Grand National Assembly, but it was still able to govern.

There was a surge of ARGK activity in the south-eastern provinces in March and April, but meanwhile the question arose of whether to allow Kurds to celebrate Nowruz (New Year) on 21 March in the usual traditional manner. As Nowruz celebrations in previous years had been comparatively quiet, permission was given. Nowruz 1992 proved to be a very violent one indeed, with open clashes between the army and demonstrators in many towns and villages, it being alleged that some of them arose from the heavy-handed manner in which soldiers conducted searches for arms. There was no love lost between soldiers and ARGK guerrillas. At Cizre, for example, there was an open battle on the streets, in which ARGK members engaged in fire-fights with troops. It was a bloody Nowruz, in which up to 90 people were killed and many injured.

ARGK ACTIVITIES

April was a hectic month, during which the Turkish army, with air support, made at least three cross-border raids against the large group of ARGK guerrillas sheltering in the mountains in the Durji and Hakurk valleys, about ten miles inside the Iraqi border. In mid-April, in one action in Mardin province the army claimed to have killed '33 PKK bandits' and arrested over 200.

Turkish intelligence estimated that the ARGK had about 10 000 trained and armed guerrillas, of whom 7000 were outside Turkey, either in the Bekaa Valley or in northern Iraq. About this time the ARGK claimed it had a commando force of some 400 armed women guerillas in the mountains of northern Iraq. Western journalists were encouraged to visit and photograph them, largely to influence Western opinion and to offset Western dislike of the inequality of women in Muslim societies.

There had been a sprinkling of women activists in the ARGK

since its early days, but its claim that they lived and fought equally side by side with their male colleagues can be discounted, although there were some exceptions. Women were employed mainly on propaganda, intelligence, liaison and educational tasks. The PKK claimed that women accounted for up to 30 per cent of its strength. Certainly they were active in Western Europe, but there is less evidence of them fighting in the field inside Turkey. Their fate if captured would probably have been most unpleasant. Traditionally Kurdish women supported their menfolk when attacked, and on many occasions had taken up arms in tight corners. That was within a family or tribal setting. Recruiting women as soldiers did not generally go down well in masculine Kurdish society, but women armed and draped with bandoliers of ammunition made good propaganda pictures for the Western media.

Simple deduction was that there must have been at least 3000 ARGK guerrillas operating inside Turkey, with more infiltrating daily, the object being to create and hold no-go areas, and then develop them into 'liberated' ones. The ARGK guerrillas were in a very aggressive mood and were giving as good as they got against the army commandos hunting them down. Army attacks often caused hostile Kurdish demonstrations in Diyarbakir and other cities. The EC condemned the 'scale and severity of the actions of the Turkish army' (*Daily Telegraph*). Turkey had applied for EC membership in 1987, but was still waiting.

Prime Minister Demirel stated that between January 1992 and 10 May, 'a total of 272 "terrorists" had been killed, 39 injured, and almost 4000 captured', and that in the same period there had been '267 deaths among soldiers, police and civilians' (government release). This indicated that the army was once again making mass arrests, as well as shooting its way forwards, regardless of the presence of civilians. Army operations against ARGK guerrillas continued, and at the end of June Izmet Sezgin, Minister of the Interior, stated in the Grand National Assembly that during the previous seven months, '6796 members of the PKK had been captured alive', being confirmation of a 'mass arrests' policy. He also said that another 2000 Korucu village guards would be recruited, but here he had a problem – just how to attract them. The deadly ARGK campaign against village guards, and the unfortunate fate of any who fell into ARGK clutches, was a deterrent to Korucu recruitment.

TURKEY AND SYRIA

Alarmed at the growing size of the ARGK in the field, in April Sezgin visited President Assad in Damascus to try to persuade him either to hand over Ocelan, or eject him from Syria, and to close down the ARGK camps in the Bekaa Valley. The GAP issue was too large an obstacle between Turkey and Syria to allow any such agreement to be concluded. It suited Assad to tweak the Turkish tail with impunity for the time being, but pleasantries were observed. Protocols to mutual frontier security agreements had been signed before, but none had been implemented. One such was to undertake to intervene against any illegal activity that threatened the stability of the other; another was to strengthen the security fence along the mutual border; a third was to exchange information likely to lead to the capture of criminals and deserters. Fine words and sentiments, sufficient to maintain the thin veneer of mutual friendship, but not serious enough to entrap either into doing anything positive.

In June 1992 the Grand National Assembly approved an extension of the Allied 'Operation Provide Comfort' facilities, but that Allied aircraft could only use the Incirlik airbase until the end of the year. The USA announced it would withdraw its troops ('Operation Poised Hammer') from Silop by the end of 1993.

THE SIRNAK BATTLE

In their effort to create no-go areas, ARGK guerrillas often settled on small Kurdish towns, forcing the inhabitants to hide and succour them, until by intimidation they caused the small resident security forces to withdraw or were strong enough to challenge them in battle. An example occurred in the Kurdish town of Sirnak, near the Iraqi frontier, where the ARGK had firmly settled. There had been street fighting in this town between ARGK elements and the army during the bloody

Nowruz celebrations. Clashes began again on 18 August and lasted until the 20th. There were two versions of what happened. The army insisted that about 1500 guerrillas had attacked their barracks and buildings, whereupon the fire-fight began. On the 25th, in a media interview, Abdullah Ocalan claimed that government troops had mounted provocative attacks on the ARGK.

During the fighting at least half the notional 20 000 population of Sirnak fled to outlying villages, and many houses were destroyed as the army searched for arms and rooted out ARGK personnel. Witnesses later said that troops had set fire to shops, and that anti-tank gun fire had been directed at houses occupied by guerrillas. The army said that five soldiers and 15 civilians had been killed, but this was considered a blatant understatement. Local sources put the casualty total at over 500 – perhaps a blatant overstatement. Many more were arrested and taken away by the army.

The army immediately declared a curfew on Sirnak, where the ARGK had bitten off far more than it could chew. Journalists were barred from the town for several days, while the Turkish media called for an investigation into the behaviour of the army. The National Security Council met to consider the Sirnak incident, and issued a bland official statement that in future military measures against terrorism would go hand-in-hand with increased funding for regional development. No blame was attached to the army as such: it was all the bandits' fault. Prime Minister Demirel urged the people of Sirnak to return to their homes. Later (12th September), President Ozal, speaking to Kurds at Uludere near Sirnak, said that 'many problems could be solved if 500 000 Kurds left the area and resettled in other parts of Turkey'. This was an insight into his secret agenda.

Fierce clashes between the army and the ARGK became more frequent, as each wanted to test its strength against the other whenever conditions were favourable. In early September, when 500 guerrillas attacked a border post near Semdinli, the army immediately launched an offensive operation against the culprits in the adjacent Cudi Mountain area, some 30 miles from the Iranian border inside Turkey. In the subsequent clash the army said that '43 guerrillas and six soldiers were killed. Many were also captured' (*The Times*).

On the 29th of that month, one of the bloodiest clashes of the eight-year war occurred in the same area, in which the army claimed to have killed 75 guerrillas, but also admitted to losing 29 soldiers. Again little was said about those 'captured'. The army was looking for a fight, and the ARGK, instead of continuing its tactics of avoidance when faced with overwhelming military forces, was beginning to fight back, and in the process was taking hard knocks.

INTERNAL TERRORISM

The PKK was indulging in urban terrorism as well as that systematically designed to intimidate rural areas, but this seemed to be more spasmodic. One such incident, which took place on 25 December 1991, was the fire-bombing of a major department store in Istanbul, which happened during a spasm of rioting by Kurdish students in a protest to coincide with the funerals of ARGK members killed by troops in the southeastern provinces the previous day. Eleven people died in this fire, the store being owned by the brother of the regional governor of Diyarbakir. In February 1992 an explosion at the Istanbul Chamber of Commerce killed one person and injured 16, for which the PKK was blamed.

In an incident in September 1992 the PKK claimed responsibility for setting fire to a ferry, damaging a bridge in Istanbul, and exploding a bomb at the Istanbul office of the British Consul General. The following month, also in Istanbul, explosions occurred at seven banks, the PKK again claiming responsibility.

Security forces were accused of illegal, covert counter activities, and in particular the finger of suspicion pointed at them regarding a series of murders of journalists said to be sympathetic to the Kurdish cause. Eleven journalists were killed in 1992, five of whom worked on the pro-Kurdish *Ozgur Gundem*.

KIDNAPPING

Kidnapping foreigners for ransom, or to bring their cause to the notice of Western media, had been an occasional but not consistent policy of the various Kurdish resistance groups over the years, although abducting enemies or local personalities for vengeance, exchange or insurance purposes was a very different matter. Kidnappings were an embarrassment to governments, as invariably they were unable to resolve them satisfactorily. As a consequence, in Turkey censorship clouded many of them. In August 1991 five foreigners (three Americans, a Briton and an Australian) were abducted by the PKK from a bus as it neared the village of Elmali in Bingol province. They were eventually released, having been held for a while to heighten the PKK's profile overseas.

As more ARGK guerrillas moved into the south-eastern part of Turkey, they took to ambushing buses in order to disrupt a service upon which the local populace relied for cross-country travel, and to terrorise them. For example, in October 1992 guerrillas ambushed a bus near Solham, killing 19 passengers and injuring six. In December, in the resort of Antalya in southern Turkey, PKK activists ambushed a bus, killing three members of the security forces and injuring 25 civilians. The latter case was a reprisal for the murder of two HEP members a few days previously. Trains were also periodic targets, for example in June 1992 guerrillas killed an Iranian boy passenger and injured six other Iranians. This case caused some international complications. In another incident in October, guerrillas derailed a military train, killing two people and injuring 47 troops.

PKK OVERSEAS ACTIVITIES

At the same time in Western Europe, the PKK propaganda section was issuing material for its cause and organising protest demonstrations in major cities, most of which were peaceful. National authorities remained tolerant, having no objection to the Turkish government being shown in such a bad light. Gradually violence began to accompany the demonstrations. For example, during the Nowruz of 1992 Kurdish protest demonstrations were held outside Turkish embassies and consulates in Bonn, Geneva, The Hague, London, Oslo, Stockholm and other major cities in Western Europe. Some involved violence, which began to embarrass the countries concerned.

In January 1993 about 700 Kurds in Brussels went on a

hunger strike to 'publicise the tragedy of our people's situation in Turkey, and to make Western public opinion aware of the approaching genocide'. These hunger strikers were joined by members of the shadowy Kurdish Assembly-in-Exile (*The Times*).

THE OCTOBER 1992 OFFENSIVE

In October 1992 the army resumed offensive operations against the ARGK in the south-eastern provinces and for example, when the army was confronted in the village of Cevizdali (in Bitlis province) it used liberal fire power to bulldoze its way forward. Fifty-five people were killed, mostly villagers. That month General Dogan Gures, the Turkish Chief of Staff, stated that in a two-week operation 'over 2000 guerrillas' had been killed, boasting that he would intensify his operations in Kurdish provinces. He claimed that army offensives were weakening the ARGK. He was certainly hitting it very hard, and was reducing its strength by large-scale 'captures' and 'mass arrests', as well as inflicting heavy casualties.

THE PKK VERSUS HEZBOLLAH: 1992

Another enemy appeared on the scene to endanger the PKK (which was by no means the only major terrorist group in Turkey in open conflict with the government) – the Islamic Hezbollah, which was suspected of being subsidised by the Tehran government. The objective of the Hezbollah was to establish by force a fundamentalist regime in Turkey, similar to that in Iran. It came into violent conflict with the PKK, whose ultimate objectives differed diametrically. Clashes between them during 1992 resulted in over 150 deaths.

The Turkish authorities adopted a somewhat cynical attitude towards this feuding, until they began to realise how powerful the Hezbollah was becoming. In mid-September, Izmet Sezgin visited Tehran to see if he could persuade the Iranian government to cease supporting the Hezbollah. Previously, in January 1992, Sezgin had for the first time accused Iran, along with Iraq and Syria, of being responsible for encouraging separatism in Turkey. The Iranian government demanded that evidence of this allegation be produced. It had also become obvious to the Ankara government that Iran had changed its attitude towards the ARGK and was now providing it with sanctuary, aid and training facilities. Sezgin tried to persuade the Iranians to reverse this decision, and to cooperate.

Iran showed interest, but its price was the handing over of exiled Iranian opposition groups sheltering in Turkey. Neither would agree. Overtly, the Turkish and Iranian governments came to a mutual border security agreement, and another for mutual cooperation in drug prevention, which Sezgin signed. Iran was taking strong measures against drug traffickers, executing many of them. The situation became somewhat paradoxical as a large proportion of the PKK's income was derived from the very drug trafficking that Iran was striving to destroy.

In the past the PKK had made temporary liaisons or agreements with both left-wing and right-wing Turkish opposition groups to suit its own purposes, but never with the resurgent Iranian-supported Hezbollah, to which it was violently opposed. In some areas Hezbollah and PKK activists began to keep their distance from each other, although in 1993 the bloody clashes between them continued until March, when both agreed to a cease-fire, the excuse being the approach of Ramadan.

THE PKK CEASEFIRE OFFER

Suddenly, on 17 March 1993 Abdullah Ocalan announced a unilateral cease-fire with the Turkish government, initially to run from 20 March to 15 April, during which negotiations would be held for a political solution. He dropped his former demands for a separate Kurdish state and recognition of the PKK as a political force. The offer had been conveyed to the Turkish government by Talabani. This PKK decision was not unanimous and there was dissension within the PKK leadership over it.

Ocelan's offer received a mixed reception in Ankara. It was so unexpected. The previous day about 30 bombs had exploded in Istanbul and four other major cities, for which the PKK had claimed responsibility. Izmet Sezgin said the government would not negotiate with the PKK, and warned that it must first surrender formally, but did not reject the offer out of hand. The armed forces were very much against accepting a PKK cease-fire as they felt they were breaking the back of the insurgency with the terrific losses they had inflicted on the ARGK in the field in recent months, and that the final blow should be struck while the guerrillas were dazed and reeling under the strain. About to launch a spring campaign, the army was champing at the bit in a triumphant, aggressive mood. There was a pause while the government waited to see how the Kurds behaved during their annual Nowruz celebrations. It passed peacefully, so the planned military offensive was postponed, the formal excuse being that it would begin after Ramadan.

After further negotiations conducted by Talabani, the government announced an investment programme for the southeastern provinces of $18 billion over the ensuing five years in order to create 176 000 new local jobs each year and revive the economy of the Kurdish regions, ostensibly with the aim of curbing immigration into the main cities and other parts of Turkey in search of work. On 16 April Ocelan declared an indefinite extension of the cease-fire. Suspicion and hesitation on the part of the government remained, and Prime Minister Demirel murmured, 'The sovereignty of the Turkish Republic cannot be negotiated in this way'. He seemed to have missed the point: Ocelan was now asking for autonomy, not independence.

THE DEATH OF PRESIDENT OZAL

On 17 April 1993 President Ozal died of a heart attack, aged 66, and on 16 May was succeeded for a seven-year term by Sulieman Demirel, leader of the True Path Party (DYP) and Ozal's long-time political rival. Demirel had been Prime Minister since November 1991. This was actually his seventh term of office, and on two occasions his government had been ousted by military force. Demirel had been the first Turkish Prime Minister to visit Syria for some years, but during his January 1993 visit he had been unsuccessful in persuading President Assad to change his attitude towards the PKK.

Ozal, President since 1989, a great but controversial Turkish leader, had been responsible for converting the sluggish moribund Turkish economy into an open, free market that was forging new contacts with the West. Ozal had sought to increase the authority of his office, which at times caused friction, and was believed to have favoured a presidential style of government on the American pattern.

During the Kuwait crisis in 1990 he had opted to stand on the Allied side, expecting territorial rewards after the defeat of Saddam Hussein. In this he had been thwarted as Saddam had remained in power, even though in a somewhat beleaguered position. Ozal had also been disappointed by the ungrateful Allies, who had no intention of rearranging international frontiers for Turkey's benefit.

Ozal had been forced to go along with the Allies' plan for safe havens to protect Iraqi Kurds against Saddam's vengeance, something that ran very much against his grain. He had little time for his own Kurds, refusing to accept them as a minority, let alone foreign Kurds, although in the manner of governments in the region he had been quick to exploit them for his own purposes. The existence of the Iraqi Kurdish Autonomous Region, protected by the Allies, whose aircraft and troops operated from Turkish soil, had given hope and encouragement to Ocelan but had been an embarrassment and a worry to Ozal. Conversely, after his death Ocelan commented that Ozal might have been the one Turkish leader with whom he could have made a deal.

Later (on 12 November 1993) the daily newspaper *Hurriyet* published a purported letter from President Ozal to (then) Prime Minister Demirel, advocating the wholesale transfer of Kurdish populations from mountain villages in the south-eastern provinces in order to undermine the logistic support system of the PKK. In tactical jargon, to remove the water from the fish.

THE BINGOL AMBUSH: MAY 1993

On 23 May the Turkish National Security Council approved a partial amnesty for PKK guerrillas. The following day ARGK activists mounted an ambush in Bingol province, killing 33 unarmed soldiers and five civilians. Controversy remains over whether Ocalan authorised this attack, or whether it was a maverick action by a discontented faction that wanted to wreck the cease-fire negotiations. It certainly did that. The National Security Council immediately rescinded its decision and the army – which had never observed the cease-fire, merely modified its intensity – launched a punitive campaign.

On 8 June Ocalan – realising that his tentative peace effort had been sabotaged, and suspecting that the Turkish government did not really want the cessation of hostilities in this 'dirty war', especially as the army had continued its activities in the field – declared all-out war against the Turkish government. The opportunity to start negotiations for a peaceful solution of the Kurdish problem had been deliberately blown away by ARGK elements in favour of pursuing the armed struggle to the bitter end.

On the 8th the army stated that since 24 May it had killed over 300 guerrillas. Clashes between troops and ARGK guerrillas escalated throughout the month. The army later claimed that another 100 guerrillas had been killed during July. Mini-battles, massacres and mass arrests followed, with both sides ignoring human rights conventions. For example, on 5 July the ARGK was blamed for the massacre of 32 people in the village of Erzincan, and on the 19th it was reported that 75 people, including security forces, guerrillas and civilians, had died in a gunfight, both in Bitlis province.

PRIME MINISTER TANSU CILLER

On 13 June 1993 Tansu Ciller, the government's junior economic minister, was elected leader of the DYP in place of Demirel, and the following day became the first woman prime minister in Turkish history. A distinguished academic, she had been educated partly in the USA, spoke perfect English and had been Demirel's economic advisor before being elected to the Grand National Assembly in 1990, becoming a member of the government team in November 1991. She was also an exponent of free market policies. These were remarkable achievements for a woman in a Muslim, male-dominated society. Moreover she had persuaded her husband to adopt her family name, a most unusual and unconventional procedure in Turkey.

Prime Minister Ciller decided to adopt a conciliatory tone towards the Kurdish problem, in the hope that Ocalan might respond to a less aggressive stance. On 22 July she convened a cabinet meeting in the Kurdish town of Hakkari to unveil a $220 million development plan for the provinces of Hakkari and Sirnak. She warned that while she would not allow the country to be split, she promised to treat the problems 'of the silent majority ([of Kurds]) with a mother's love'. This did not amuse the generals, who thought they were doing rather well in the field and restlessly chafed at what they thought was to be a curb on their exploitative activities.

TERRORISM AND KIDNAPPING

The 'dirty war', although going well from a hard Turkish military point of view, was causing anxiety in Western circles, which wanted to distance themselves from it, and from Turkey if need be. In June, just before Ciller became Prime Minister, Warren Christopher, the US Secretary of State, visited Hikmet Cetin, the Turkish Foreign Minister, in Ankara and expressed his disapproval in no uncertain terms. He accused the Turkish government of 'waging a campaign against terrorists, based on motivated killings, abductions, illegal detentions, killings and torture' (US State Department human rights report), and said he would link further US aid to improvement in the Turkish human rights record.

Ocalan again resorted to kidnapping tactics, and early in July the ARGK seized six tourists in Turkey (four French, one British and one Australian), offering to release them safely if army operations were halted. This was rejected, but the tourists were safely released amid some publicity the following month. A few days later three more foreign tourists were kidnapped.

In Western Europe, on 24 June the National Liberation Front of Kurdistan (ERNK), the PKK's front organisation, launched attacks on Turkish diplomatic missions and business premises in some 18 Western cities, in which one person was killed and six demonstrators were injured.

The one death occurred outside the Turkish embassy in Berne, and the Swiss authorities asked the Turkish government to lift diplomatic immunity from four Turkish employees suspected of causing it, so they could be tried in a Swiss court. The Turkish government refused and immediately became enmeshed in a diplomatic tussle with Switzerland. Recalling its own ambassador, Turkey expelled the Swiss ambassador and two Swiss diplomats. To show their wide international reach, on 28 June protesting Kurds briefly occupied UN offices in Sydney, Australia. In Ankara the following day, the Turkish government extended the state of emergency measures.

Next Ocalan decided to hit out against the Turkish tourist trade, which the previous year had netted Turkey some $4 billion in hard currency. On 17 August 1993 the ERNK warned Western tourists to keep away from Turkey, as they could become targets of attacks. On the 20th six foreign tourists were injured in a bomb explosion in the Aegean coastal resort of Kusadasi; the following day an Italian and three Swiss tourists were kidnapped; and on the 25th six German tourists were injured in a grenade attack in Istanbul. (Previously, on 28 June, four explosions in Antalya, a Mediterranean resort, had injured 26 people, including 12 foreign tourists, but the PKK had denied responsibility and it was thought that the explosions may have been the work of Hezbollah.)

Kidnapped foreigners were usually released, often with publicity, in the following weeks, but this sometimes occurred quietly, which tended to indicate that considerable sums of money had been extracted, usually from the commercial firms that employed them. For example seven employees of an American oil company who were working in Turkey were kidnapped in August, and later ransomed. Similar incidents followed and tourism to Turkey declined. The Turkish Tourist Board had mounted a advertising campaign the previous year to try to woo Western tourists away from traditional tourist spots in Italy, Greece and elsewhere in the East Mediterranean, seemingly with some success.

On the ground, during the hot summer months of August and September, the government side scaled down the level of the conflict. This was partly due to climatic conditions, but largely to the softer military policy Prime Minister Tansu Ciller was adopting towards the ARGK. She seemed to be trying to tempt Ocalan to the negotiating table. In the field there was no let-up by the ARGK which, for example, on 4 August ambushed mini-buses near Bitlis, killing 20 civilians and injuring ten. Although the military was largely reactive at this stage, allegations were made that its counterinsurgency agents were involved in abduction and murder. Several journalists covering events in the Kurdish regions disappeared, although it was thought that Hezbollah was responsible for some of these incidents. During the last week in September the death toll in the violent unrelenting struggle in south-eastern Turkey exceeded 120.

In September Prime Minister Ciller visited Germany to try to urge the government to end its tolerant policy towards the PKK, which was said to have over 400 000 supporters in that country. She was also concerned about lack of full citizens' rights for Turks in Germany.

KURDISH POLITICAL PARTIES

In May 1993 the Democratic Party (DEP) had been formed to encompass several Kurdish elements, including the HEP and the PKK. The only political party to espouse the Kurdish cause, it had 17 deputies in the Grand National Assembly, becoming a successor to the HEP, which was banned in June. In July Mehmet Sincar, a Kurdish deputy, was shot dead in Batman town. The government blamed Hezbollah, but the PKK blamed the government. Sincar was said to have been the 54th member of a recognised Kurdish political party to be assassinated so far (*New York Times*). On 16 September Yasar Kaya, leader of the DEP, was arrested on charges of 'conducting separatist propaganda'.

The founding congress of the DEP was eventually held in Ankara on 12 December 1993, when Hatip Dicle was elected leader. The outgoing leader, Yasar Kaya, had been sentenced to imprisonment in November, although he was released from prison to attend the congress. That month a military court imprisoned the editor of the daily *Ozgur Gundem* for four years, and banned his paper from publication for two months. *Ozgur Gundem* was owned by Kaya.

'HUMAN SHIELDS'

During October 1993 the army admitted that the ARGK had strengthened its position in the south-eastern provinces, hinting that this was the inevitable result of Ciller's restraint on military operations. The ARGK was creeping back into Turkey once again in strength from the Bekaa Valley. The American Mobil Oil Company announced it was suspending operations in south-eastern Turkey, claiming it had been subjected to PKK extortion demands.

On the 15th the PKK announced a ban on all newspapers and periodicals in its areas. It also banned Turkish and foreign journalists, alleging they had colluded with the government on the coverage of the insurgency. Several national periodicals and news agencies closed down their regional offices in Diyarbakir. On the 24th the PKK added politicians to its ban, to prevent them from campaigning and speaking directly to Kurds, as Kurds were being accused of implication in the murder of the SHP regional leader. This meant that the south-eastern provinces had become a virtual political no-go area as far as the Ankara government was concerned.

During October the ARGK concentrated on attacking the Korucu village guards in order to demoralise them, making several attacks in which civilian casualties were incurred. It admitted that on the 21st, in an attack on a village in Siirt province, it had killed at least '22 women and children', alleging the village guards had been using them as 'human shields'. Other incidents of human shield tactics came to light, the army and the ARGK each accusing the other of implication. It had become a very dirty war indeed.

CILLER CHANGES POLICY

In mid-October Prime Minister Ciller visited Washington, her intention being to press President Clinton into lifting oil and economic sanctions against Iraq, and to allow the trans-Turkey oil pipeline to reopen, or at least release the oil lying in it – Turkey was missing the annual $20 million in transit fees. She was unsuccessful, and received an unwelcome lecture on Turkey's bad human rights record for her pains.

Ciller was also accused of making a statement in which she seemed to indicate a preference for a 'Basque-type' model involving a degree of autonomy for the Kurdish areas. She quickly denied she favoured such a solution, but came under pressure from President Demirel to take a harder line against the Kurdish insurgents.

At the DYP Convention in November Ciller faced strong opposition from the political and military leadership within her own party over her moderate policy towards the Kurds, being convinced that the military option was the only sure one to be pursued. Current platitudes peddled by the government for Western consumption that Turks and Kurds mingled and lived together peacefully, and that neither had any time for Kurdish separatist propaganda, were wearing thin, to say the least. Only a very small percentage of the some 12 million Kurds in Turkey wanted separatism, but Kurds wherever they were now came to be tarred with the same insurgent brush, and all Kurds, no matter how Turkish or how integrated they had become, were regarded warily by Turks.

The government secretly feared that the swell of Kurdish insurrection, supported covertly by adjacent countries, would gain in momentum and develop into open civil war, in which nations unfriendly to Turkey might try to meddle. Senior government and military leaders wanted to crush the Kurdish insurrection, regarding it as a bomb waiting to explode, before the Turkish nation became hopelessly divided.

Tansu Ciller evaded a head-on clash with her party opposition, which she would have been unlikely to win. Her personal position was insecure. She was prestige-conscious, and fully aware she was treading through an all-male Muslim minefield. She wanted to remain in her top job, to pursue her ambitions, but knew that a false step could be politically fatal. She also knew she would have much less leverage and attract less publicity as a backbencher, so she abruptly changed policies. The military got its way, and the hard line against the ARGK was resumed. On the 20th she was re-elected leader of the DYP by a large majority.

That month Ciller announced a cutback in the multi-billion dollar economic development plan for the south-eastern provinces. Work on major construction projects ceased abruptly, the ostensible reason being that contractors had complained they were being forced to pay protection money to the PKK. She also announced the creation of a 10 000-strong, specially-equipped commando force, trained in antiguerilla tactics, recruited from regular soldiers and not including conscripts.

Fifteen members of the PKK were sentenced to death at the end of a lengthy mass trial (the death penalty had still not been used since 1983).

The Prime Minister also did her best to win support from adjacent governments, which were secretly – in some cases not so secretly – supporting the PKK. In November her new Interior Minister, Nahit Mentese, in a speech warned Armenia, Iran, Iraq and Syria not to allow their territory to be used as bases for PKK guerrillas. Two hollow security agreements were concluded with Iran, and attempts were made to persuade the weak Lebanese government to assert its authority in the Bekaa Valley.

FIRE-BOMBING IN WESTERN EUROPE

In Western Europe, on 4 November the PKK opened a new phase of its struggle by launching a fire-bombing campaign, involving attacks on Turkish diplomatic and commercial premises in major cities. Five such attacks were carried out in London. In one at Wiesbaden, one person died. This caused sharp reactions from Western governments, and their security forces were mustered against the perpetrators. The attitude of tolerance changed lest this was the harbinger of an insurgent terrorist organisation moving its armed struggle to a neutral European venue.

It was not until the 18th that, in dawn raids across France, police rounded up 110 suspects and the French government banned the Kurdish Committee and other PKK front organisations. On the 26th Germany announced similar measures against PKK groups, but other Western European countries seemed reluctant to clamp down too heavily on them, probably with Turkey's bad human rights record in mind.

14 A Turning Point: 1994

In January 1994 Prime Minister Ciller said '1994 must be an important turning point in the struggle against terrorism' (*Milliyet*). The Turkish government certainly began the year with determination, as its armed forces launched attacks against ARGK strongholds in south-eastern Turkey, and also cross-border ones into northern Iraq, where a large number of ARGK guerrillas had both sanctuary and bases. Zala remained the main base, and according to Turkish sources it housed 1600 guerrillas, including the much-photographed 400 women fighters.

On the 28th Turkey conducted a massive air raid on Zala camp, involving over 50 combat aircraft. Unverifiable claims were made of casualties inflicted, but ARGK guerrillas remained in the vicinity. The Tehran government complained that Turkish aircraft had hit some Iranian border villages, killing nine people and injuring a score. The Turkish government apologised and Iran accepted its proposal for a joint investigation, but on 6 February Turkey recommenced its spasmodic bombing of Zala camp and other ARGK targets inside Iraq. The attitude of the Iranian government towards the PKK was changing as it was becoming too powerful for Tehran's liking.

SYRIA

Ciller also admitted in January, at a press conference in Ankara, that Turkish armed forces had entered Syrian territory during the recent series of 'anti-terrorist operations'. This was the first such admission. On 18 January President Assad of Syria met President Clinton in Geneva. The latter warned Assad not to support the PKK, and probably issued economic threats.

Two days later the Turkish media reported that the Syrian government had ordered Ocalan to leave Damascus and close down his PKK camps in the Bekaa Valley. Like other prominent terrorist leaders, Ocalan had a degree of mobility along mysterious underground conduits to move selectively from country to country, and on occasions had been known to

227

address gatherings at his 'front' organisations in Western European cities. Syria was alarmed by the Turkish cross-border raids and the USA's warning, and tried to restrict ARGK raids into Turkey in case they provoked further armed reprisals.

International concern was aroused by PKK involvement in drug trafficking, it being alleged that the PKK controlled a section of the Asian–Caucasian–European land route. The Turkish commissioner in charge of antinarcotic activities stated on 5 January that narcotic smuggling from Turkey into Western Europe was dominated by the PKK, and that in 1993 Kurds had been involved in 70 per cent of the cases where heroin had been seized on its way from Turkey to Western Europe. It was becoming obvious where the bulk of the PKK's wealth originated.

The foreign ministers of Turkey, Iran and Syria met on 5 February in Istanbul to review the 'Iraqi Kurdistan' situation, and all three reiterated their commitment to Iraq's territorial integrity. They urged Iraq to lift its embargoes against the Kurds (and Shias). All three were unhappy about the existence of the UN-protected Kurdish Autonomous Region, as it made their own Kurds envious.

Iran, denying the allegation made by the Director of the US CIA that Iran was supporting terrorist movements abroad, had just (on 5 January) passed the death sentence on a German national, Helmut Szimkus, who had been arrested in 1988 and accused of passing information to Iraq. The Iranian government hoped to be able exchange the German for one Iranian and four pro-Iranian Lebanese, who were being held in Germany on the charge of murdering four KDPI senior officials in Berlin in September 1992. Their trial had been complicated by allegations that Germany had been collaborating with Iraq on intelligence matters for at least two years. Protests had been made to Germany by the USA and the UK. Iran wanted its agents back. Soon exchanges were quietly effected.

ISLAMIC GAINS IN TURKEY

The Turkish Constitutional Court closed down the OZDEP (Freedom and Democracy Party) on 14 February, and in the first days of March six Kurdish deputies were deprived of their immunity, having refused to openly condemn the PKK. Ciller boasted she had 'removed the PKK from the Grand National Assembly'. In mid-March, anticipating a rowdy and unruly Nowruz celebration, the government deployed another 50 000 troops into the south-eastern provinces, bringing the total up to the 150 000 mark (official figures, which contrasted with media and PKK ones).

On the 27th local elections were held in Turkey, and the resurgent Fundamentalist Welfare Party (RP, or Rafah Partisi), made unexpected and surprising gains, especially in Ankara and Istanbul, where they obtained local political control. The RP was said to have benefited from the fact that the DEP refused to take part in these elections as a protest against the recent bombing of DEP premises in Ankara.

THE KURDISH AUTONOMOUS REGION

Meanwhile all was not well in the Kurdish Autonomous Region (KAR), where since December 1993 the PUK and the Iranian-supported Islamic League of Kurdistan (ILK) had been in violent confrontation with each other over territory and influence. Early in January representatives from the Iran-based SCIRI and Dawa organisations arrived in Arbil. They brought about a cease-fire on 17 February – signed in Sala-huddin, the HQ of the INC – but only after some 100 people had been killed. The PUK and the KDP were not getting on too well either, but at this stage they were keeping their powder dry.

The January 1994 anniversary of the Allied attacks on Iraqi forces in Kuwait and Iraq proper was a non-event in the Western world. Most Western statesmen wanted to forget the Gulf War and its aftermath, as embarrassing questions were being asked about the need and cost of maintaining Allied troops in the region, and of keeping so many Allied warplanes tied up with monitoring the Kurdish 'no fly zone' (and also the Shia one) imposed in August 1992.

Overtly, Saddam Hussein had been on his best behaviour towards the Kurds, at least since Clinton had assumed office as president in January 1993, in the hope that he would soon be able to persuade the UN to lift the economic and oil embargoes against him, and that the USA would wind down 'Operation Poised Hammer'. Saddam knew that Russia, Turkey, France and China were pressing for a relaxation of the embargoes, and that only the USA and Britain were still adamantly against the move.

Within the KAR, journalists and local Kurds employed by the UN were at risk from occasional terrorist attacks. For example nine UN guards were wounded in ambush on 27 March; two more were wounded on 2 April and the following day a German journalist was killed. Local gossip alleged that the Iraqi Mukhabarat was instigating these attacks in order to destabilise UN aid distribution and the administration of the safe havens, and that cash rewards were given for such exploits.

In mid-March the UN, mainly influenced by the USA, refused to lift the sanctions against Iraq, relying on UN Resolution 688, which called for the Iraqi regime to end its repression of the civilian population. Later the Iraqi Vice President, Taha Ramadan, declared: 'Soon our beloved north will shortly return to the motherland' (*Middle East*). The Kurds regarded this as a very serious threat. A British Foreign Office statement said 'We will remain vigilant in our resolve to maintain the safe haven. It would be extremely foolish for Saddam Hussein to try anything', which somehow failed to hearten the KAR authorities.

On 14 April a UN helicopter, a US Blackhawk (Sikorsky S-7), was mistaken for a Russian Hind (Mi-24, used by Iraq), and was shot down over Akra by UN(US) warplanes monitoring the 'no fly zone'. Twenty-two senior UN Allied military personnel and four Kurdish leaders were killed. The helicopter was taking the newly appointed UN commander of the area, together with Turkish, British and French senior representatives from the Zakho UN HQ, to a meeting at Salahuddin. US internal military disciplinary action was taken, but this 'friendly fire' incident again raised the question of the need and cost of 'Operation Poised Hammer'. KAR authorities apprehensively claimed that Saddam Hussein already had over 200 000 troops in readiness to cross the 36th Parallel as soon as 'Operation Poised Hammer' was wound up.

THE PUK VERSUS THE KDP AGAIN

On 1 May fighting suddenly flared up again in the KAR, this time between the PUK and the KDP, traditional enemies who had seemed to be behaving responsibly since the formation of the KAR. Talabani, who had been in Damascus when the fighting broke out, was unable to return to his HQ in Arbil by land as his path was blocked by Barzani's warriors. Eventually he was flown back to his HQ in a Turkish helicopter, after he had promised he would stop fighting the KDP and break off all contact with the PKK. This was another Talabani promise of convenience, not meant to be taken too seriously, and interfactional combat continued.

TURKEY VERSUS THE USA

Meanwhile the Turkish armed forces had been hammering hard against the ARGK, which was suffering reverses, taking casualties and had mostly been driven out from Turkish terrain into sanctuary areas just inside Iraq. Moreover, army 'scorched earth' tactics were clearing a wedge of frontier terrain, driving out Kurdish inhabitants. The PKK propaganda section claimed that 800 000 Kurds had been involved in these clearances, that over 1000 villages had been destroyed and that thousands were fleeing into Iraq. This was confirmed to some extent as UN safe haven camps, which had been in the process of closing down, had to reopen again – this time to accept Turkish Kurdish refugees instead of Iraqi ones.

On 31 May the USA, increasingly concerned about allegations of Turkey's lack of respect for human rights in its campaign against the PKK and the ARGK, and also exasperated at the lack of progress on the Turkish Cyprus issue, threatened that future American economic aid to Turkey would be conditional on an improvement in these issues. Prime Minister Ciller sharply replied that if this occurred she would withdraw all American facilities in Turkey, and might also reject US aid outright. Loss of the use of the Incirlik and Pirincilik bases would neutralise American influence in the region, and as the British and French would hardly go it alone without the USA this could mean the effective end of the 'no fly zone' for Iraqi aircraft over the KAR. Economic aid to foreign countries was America's main, and in many cases only, means of influence, without which it went naked into council chambers.

THE PKK APPEALS FOR A DIALOGUE

On 19 April Yani Kilmaz, the PKK's representative for Western Europe, appealed to the Turkish government for a dialogue, emphasising that he was not making this offer from a position of weakness as for the first time the Kurds had 30 000 armed people. That figure may or may not have been accurate, but it was obvious that the ARGK was not doing at all well in its battle against the Turkish army. There was no response from Ankara. The army knew it was doing well and did not intend to stop, thinking it had got the ARGK on the run.

THE PKK'S CAMPAIGN AGAINST TOURISTS IN TURKEY

Having failed in 1993 to evoke any favourable response from foreign governments in support of its objectives through public demonstrations against Turkish diplomatic and commercial buildings in Western Europe, and as its November fire-bombing campaign had caused France and Germany to proscribe its front organisations, Ocalan decided that the PKK would act to sabotage the booming Turkish tourist industry. This attracted some six million visitors in 1993 (Turkish Tourist Board figures), netting over $4 billion for the very weak Turkish economy. Turkey was well set to entice Western tourists away from other traditional East Mediterranean resorts, including those of Greece, its traditional enemy.

One of the first PKK incidents in this respect was on 3 April, when a bomb explosion in the Grand Bazaar in Istanbul killed two foreign tourists and injured several others. The PKK was openly blamed by the police. This was followed on 26 May by the seizure of 17 PKK members, who had travelled from Greece to the Turkish port of Izmir in three small boats, in which were found quantities of explosives and detonator devices. They claimed that in Greece they had been trained in sabotage techniques, but allegations that Greece was running training courses for PKK terrorists were flatly denied.

A further terrorist incident occurred on 2 June in the resort of Fethiye, when an explosion injured six foreign tourists, three of whom were British. On the 22nd in Marmiris another explosion injured 24, of whom eight were British, one of these later died. In both cases small bombs had been placed in litter bins on the beaches. Police began to patrol beaches and holiday resorts in an attempt to deter terrorists and detect any devices planted by them, while the Turkish authorities vainly told foreigner visitors there was no need to worry. Tourist bookings gradually dropped. A bizarre incident on the 29th, when a shepherd boy, aged 13, shot dead a British tourist, added to the uncertainty, although in this case there was no terrorist involvement.

THE PROSPECTS

Finally, what of the future of the Kurds? It is doubtful whether the 1920 dream of an independent pan-Kurdish state, including a seat in the United Nations forum, will materialise unless violent political eruptions in the region cause international boundaries to be redrawn. Even then the prospect is remote, as although Kurds share an age-old culture, language and customs, so far the Kurds and their political leaders have shown little inclination or aptitude to unite amongst themselves.

The lesser option, that of autonomy to one degree or another, is a much more viable one, and in principle at least has been accepted in Iraq and tacitly in Iran at one time or another.

In Iraq Saddam Hussein, who is waiting to move into the KAR as soon as Western defence of the region is withdrawn, can be expected to extract vengeance, causing a further exodus of refugees and halting the prospect of autonomy for some time. As probably half of the more than 3.5 million Kurds in Iraq are detribalised already, and for economic reasons alone this proportion will steadily increase, the scope for armed resistance in the mountains will be reduced. Recognition of Kurdish ethnic status has already been achieved, so this may be a first step to wards eventual autonomy.

The government of Iran, a country of many ethnic groups, is at the moment strongly opposed to Kurdish autonomy. Its 6.5 million Kurds are suffocated by military manpower, and their resistance parties are leaderless because of assassination operations. Unlike in Iraq, the Kurds in Iran have remained in their homeland and have not intermixed to any extent on a national level. A change of government in Tehran could be to the advantage of the Iranian Kurds, so some future form of autonomy should not be ruled out.

In Syria, resident Kurds, who probably number about 800 000, have ethnic status, but because of their small numbers and scattered locations they are unlikely to obtain autonomy. They are conscripted into the armed forces, and so are being processed into national integration in a country of several ethnic and tribal groups of peoples.

In Armenia, now an independent country, the some 300 000 Kurds have been given temporary ethnic status by the government for political expediency and opportunistic reasons. Armenians and Kurds are traditional enemies, and Armenia is in confrontation with Azerbaijan, another traditional foe. The fate of the Kurds in Armenia is doubtful and uncertain.

Turkey, which has at least 12 million Kurds, a large proportion of whom are still resident in their homeland areas, refuses to recognise them as Kurds and has been fighting a bloody war to force integration on them. The Kurdish spirit of resistance is strong, and the Turkish government is unlikely to obtain a military victory. Eventually the Kurds in Turkey may achieve autonomy, but much blood may be spilt before the Ankara government comes to terms with this fact.

It is most likely that in the interim the governments of Turkey, Iran, Iraq, Syria and Armenia will continue to repress the insurgent tendencies of their own Kurds, while at the same time manipulating others' Kurdish minorities for their own devious ends, which they have all been doing for years. The Kurds will reciprocate in kind, as they too have been doing for years.

The Kurdish diaspora, which is increasing due to both political and economic reasons, especially in Western countries, will keep the Kurdish culture alive and the Kurdish ethnic flag flying abroad for a generation or two, generally finding tolerance, although this could be dissipated by terrorist activity. Western sympathy is ephemeral, and nowadays much conditioned by the television satellite truck. If only Kurds could make friends, learn how to keep them, and become more tolerant of each other.

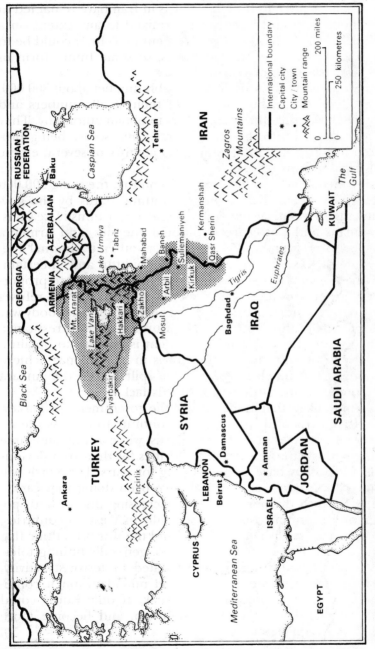

1. Traditional Kurdistan

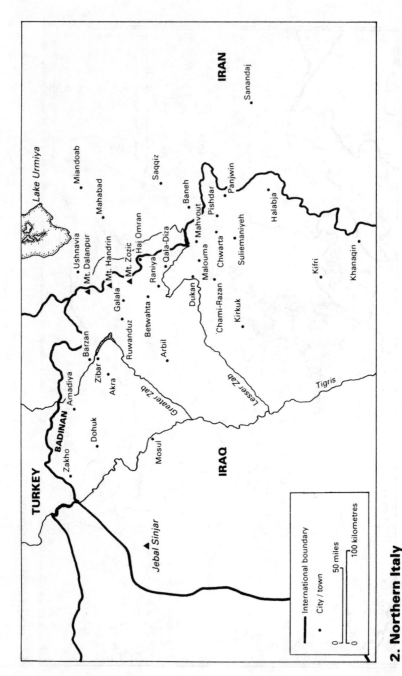

2. Northern Italy

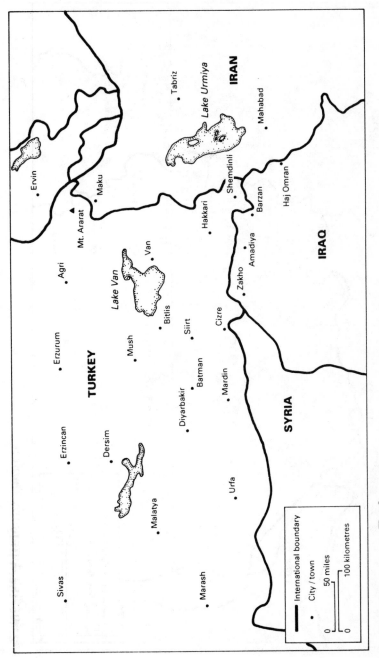

3. South-eastern Turkey

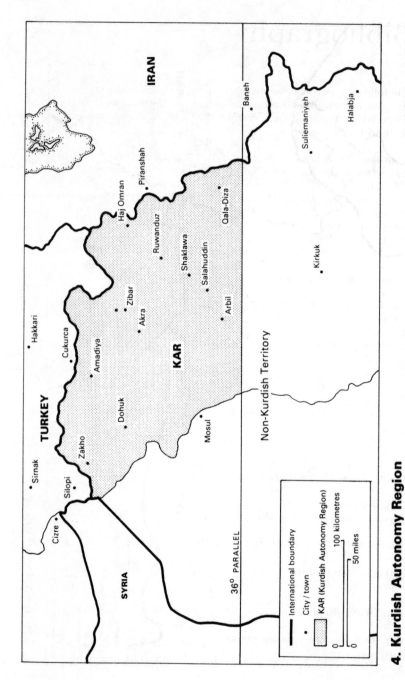

4. Kurdish Autonomy Region

Bibliography

The following works are among the many I have read with profit and pleasure, and I would like to record my thanks to the authors, editors or compilers. Where material has been used in this book, due acknowledgement is made within the text.

Adamson, David (1964) *The Kurdish War* (London: Allen & Unwin).
Arfa, Hassan (1966) *The Kurds* (London: Oxford University Press).
Bois, Thomas (1965) *The Kurds* (Beirut: Khayats).
Bulloch, John and Harvey Morris (1993) *No Friends but the Mountains* (London: Penguin).
Chaliand, Gerard (1993) *People without a Country* (London: Zed Press).
Dann, Uriel (1969) *Iraq Under Kassem* (New York: Praeger).
Eagleton, William (1963) *The Kurdish Republic of 1946* (London: Oxford University Press).
Ghassemlou, Abdul Rahman (1965) *Kurdistan and the Kurds* (London: Collets).
Guest, John S. (1989) *The Yezidis* (London: KPI).
Kinnane, Derk (1964) *The Kurds and Kurdistan* (London: Oxford University Press).
Kurdish Library, *Kurdish Life* (periodical – New York, USA).
Kutschera, Chris (1979) *Le mouvement national kurde* (Paris: Edition Harmattan).
McDowall, David (1985) *The Kurds*, Minority Rights Group, Report No. 23 (London: Minority Rights Group).
Mauries, René (1967) *Le Kurdistan ou le Mort* (Paris: Robert Laffont).
Schmidt, Dana Adama (1964) *Journey among Brave Men* (Boston: Little, Brown).

The following periodicals, news agencies and so on were also consulted.

UK: *Guardian, Daily Telegraph, Middle East Economic Digest, Observer*, Reuters, *Sunday Telegraph, The Sunday Times, The Middle East, The Times.*

USA: *International Herald Tribune, Kurdish Life, Kurdish News and Comment, Newsday, New York Times, Washington Post, USA Today, Time.*

France: Agence France-Presse, *Le Monde.*

Turkey (extracts in translation): Anatolian News Agency, *Gunaydin, Hurriyet, Milliyet, Ozgur Gundem.*

Iran: Islamic Republican News Agency, *Kayan, Tehran Times.*

Iraq: *Baghdad Times*, Iraqi News Agency, Radio Baghdad, Voice of Iraqi Kurdistan.

Index

241